Green Building & Remodeling

FOR

DUMMIES®

by Eric Corey Freed

BICENTENNIAL

1807

WILEY

2007

BICENTENNIAL

Wiley Publishing, Inc.

Green Building & Remodeling For Dummies®

Published by
Wiley Publishing, Inc.
111 River St.
Hoboken, NJ 07030-5774
www.wiley.com

Copyright © 2008 by Wiley Publishing, Inc., Indianapolis, Indiana

Published simultaneously in Canada

For general information on our other products and services, please contact our Customer Care Department within the U.S. at 800-762-2974, outside the U.S. at 317-572-3993, or fax 317-572-4002.

For technical support, please visit www.wiley.com/techsupport.

Wiley also publishes its books in a variety of electronic formats. Some content that appears in print may not be available in electronic books.

Library of Congress Control Number: 2007939643

ISBN: 978-0-470-17559-0

Manufactured in the United States of America

This book is printed on recycled paper.

10 9 8 7 6 5 4 3

WILEY

About the Author

Eric Corey Freed is an architect, lecturer, and writer based in San Francisco, California, with 15 years of experience in green building. He is a practitioner in the tradition of organic architecture, first developed by Frank Lloyd Wright.

Eric is founder and principal of organicARCHITECT, part architecture firm, part think tank. In addition to designing award-winning green buildings, the firm publishes its research and produces the annual organicAWARDS (www.organicawards.com) to recognize designs that are both innovative and environmentally responsible.

During Eric's early years working in his hometown of Philadelphia and in New York City, noted architect and critic Philip Johnson cited Eric as "one of the real brains of his generation." After several years in Santa Fe, New Mexico, working with natural building materials, he moved to San Francisco in 1997 to join the heart of the green building movement.

In 2002, he was Founding Chair of Architecture for the San Francisco Design Museum, the exhibits of which were featured in *Metropolis, ARTNews,* and *Newsweek.* In 2005, *San Francisco* magazine named Eric the city's "Best Green Architect."

Eric teaches in the Sustainable Design program he co-developed at the Academy of Art University and the University of California, Berkeley. He is on the boards of Architects, Designers & Planners for Social Responsibility (ADPSR), Natural World Museum, Green Home Guide, and West Coast Green, as well as the advisory boards of nearly a dozen other organizations.

A much sought-after lecturer, Eric speaks extensively around the United States, giving nearly 50 talks a year, and consults directly to large companies seeking to transition into sustainability.

His monthly column, *Ask the Green Architect,* is published by GreenerBuildings and syndicated to dozens of other publications. He is a regular columnist for *LUXE Magazine* and his work has been featured in *Dwell, Natural Home, Newsweek,* and *Town & Country,* among others.

Eric loves talking with people about design and the environment. For more information on his work and activities, visit www.organicarchitect.com or contact Eric directly at info@organicarchitect.com.

Dedication

This book is dedicated to my beautiful wife, Laurie. If you wish to "be the change you wish to see in the world" it helps to have someone with whom to share your vision. I strive to make the world a better place for her.

This book is also dedicated to my dad, my first mentor.

Author's Acknowledgments

A hundred times every day I remind myself that my inner and
outer life depend on the labors of other men, living and dead,
and that I must exert myself in order to give in the same measure
as I have received and am still receiving.

—Albert Einstein

As a teacher and mentor, I am fortunate to meet hundreds of students a year. Their questions, enthusiasm, and energy inspire me each day.

I am privileged to work with some of the most fun and passionate people who contributed their research and ideas to this book: Joey Becker, Lamia Bensouda, Sara Buck, Hannah Hunt, Elisa Kim, Tanya Lee, Amie Lewis, Liz Maquire, Emily Naud, Emily Privot, Jessica Resmini, David Waldorf, Marita Wallhagen, and Drew Wentzel.

Building Green (www.buildinggreen.com) is a daily and invaluable resource, and I drew heavily on their insight and expertise.

The following people must be thanked by name, (and you can just assume they know what they did to deserve mention): Nick Aster, Chris Bartle, Nicole Cassani, Howard Chambers, James DeKoven, Gabrielle Fladd, Gil Friend, Stacey Frost, Jennifer Gadiel, Matt Golden, Christi Graham, Jeff Hamaoui, Ryan Hamilton, Zem Joaquin, David Johnston, Miriam Karell, Hunter Lovins, Joe Lstiburek, Willem Maas, Tyler Manchuck, Joel Makower, William McDonough, Laura Rodormer, Michael Sammet, Amy Sagalkin, Richard Silver, Mark Singer, Arthur Young, Dennis Yanez, and Jerry Yudelson.

I would particularly like to thank my editor, Elizabeth Kuball, for being such a strict taskmaster and keeping me on schedule through a strategy of fear and intimidation. The staff at Wiley Publishing, Inc., is incredibly impressive and I am appreciative of their dedication.

This book could not have been possible without my clients, the generous patrons providing the canvas on which I paint.

Publisher's Acknowledgments

We're proud of this book; please send us your comments through our Dummies online registration form located at www.dummies.com/register/.

Some of the people who helped bring this book to market include the following:

Acquisitions, Editorial, and Media Development

Project Editor: Elizabeth Kuball

Acquisitions Editor: Mike Baker

Copy Editor: Elizabeth Kuball

Technical Editor: David M. Handman

Editorial Manager: Michelle Hacker

Consumer Editorial Supervisor and Reprint Editor: Carmen Krikorian

Editorial Assistants: Erin Calligan Mooney, Joe Niesen, Leeann Harney, and David Lutton

Cover Photos:

Cartoons: Rich Tennant
(www.the5thwave.com)

Composition Services

Project Coordinator: Lynsey Osborn

Layout and Graphics: Carl Byers, Shane Johnson, Barbara Moore, Laura Pence, Christine Williams

Proofreaders: Laura L. Bowman, Cynthia Fields, Jessica Kramer

Indexer: Potomac Indexing, LLC

Special Help: Reuben W. Davis, Melissa K. Jester

Publishing and Editorial for Consumer Dummies

Diane Graves Steele, Vice President and Publisher, Consumer Dummies

Joyce Pepple, Acquisitions Director, Consumer Dummies

Kristin A. Cocks, Product Development Director, Consumer Dummies

Michael Spring, Vice President and Publisher, Travel

Kelly Regan, Editorial Director, Travel

Publishing for Technology Dummies

Andy Cummings, Vice President and Publisher, Dummies Technology/General User

Composition Services

Gerry Fahey, Vice President of Production Services

Debbie Stailey, Director of Composition Services

Contents at a Glance

Table of Contents

Introduction

*O*ur grandchildren will look back at this time in history, this push toward a sustainable world, as the moment of the greatest opportunity, excitement, and challenge in human history. As you read this book, you won't be able to help but get caught up in this feeling. You've heard about green building, maybe even read books and magazines about various homes with a green focus. Now is the time to plan *your* green dream home and discover the art of building in a responsible manner.

As you learn more about green building, you may start to have feelings of guilt. After all, the act of building is disruptive. Building a home, even a green home, uses materials, resources, and energy, and it produces waste. This is inevitable. And there is no perfect green material — all materials will have *some* impact on our planet. But don't beat yourself up about what you can't control; instead, focus your energy on what you *can* control.

For thousands of years, human beings built their homes out of natural materials, using the sun to heat and cool, and harvesting the rainwater for other uses. We can learn from our past to understand how to build our future. In fact, in the future, I believe that all buildings will be green buildings.

Whether your green dream home is a simple remodel, or a multi-million-dollar mansion, *Green Building & Remodeling For Dummies* is for you. Instead of making you feel guilty about the environment, this book guides you step by step toward selecting the finishes, systems, and structure to make your dream a reality.

About This Book

Building or remodeling a home is a stressful, expensive, and exhilarating experience. Countless details and decisions go into design and construction. This book is not a comprehensive guide to building or remodeling your home. Several other *For Dummies* books are far better at covering those topics in greater detail. But if your interest is in *green* building and remodeling, and examining the issues, costs, and considerations surrounding it, this book provides all the answers you need — a wonderful, easy-to-use reference you can take with you anywhere.

Although dozens of books have been written about green building, most are targeted at professionals already interested in green building, while others assume that readers have some experience with it. Part of the reason I chose to write this book was to create this missing piece — a book targeted at normal people wanting to green their homes, but not having any idea where to start.

I divide this book into five parts, each targeting a different area of understanding in building a green home. Each chapter is broken down into specific topics, each exploring the various issues and questions that will arise in looking at your own home. For example:

- The various people you'll need on your team, from architects to financing people
- How to develop a set of priorities for the materials you choose, including wading through the endless choices available
- How certain construction methods influence your design
- Comprehensive advice on how to budget these features into your home, and ways to save money in the process

The wonderful design of the *For Dummies* series is that *you* decide how to read it. You can start to read from any point in the text, getting just to the information you need. The table of contents in the front and the index in the back help you find exactly the information you want.

Conventions Used in This Book

I use the following conventions throughout the text to make everything consistent and easy to understand:

- All Web addresses appear in `monofont`.
- New terms appear in *italics* and are closely followed by an easy-to-understand definition. Everything is in plain English to make it accessible.
- **Bold** text indicates keywords in bulleted lists or highlights the action parts of numbered steps.

When this book was printed, some Web addresses may have needed to break across two lines of text. If that happened, rest assured that I haven't put in any extra characters (such as hyphens) to indicate the break. So, when using one of these Web addresses, just type in exactly what you see in this book, pretending as though the line break doesn't exist.

What You're Not to Read

This book was carefully written so you can easily find and understand everything you need to know about green building and remodeling. I know you're busy and don't have time to read every single word, so I've designed this book so you can identify the stuff to skip over. Unless you're trapped in a remote mountain cabin, please feel free to skip the following:

- ✔ **Text in sidebars:** Those shaded boxes that appear from time to time in the book are called sidebars. These include fun, extra asides in case you're looking for more detail. But they're nothing essential or required to make your home green.

- ✔ **Anything with a Technical Stuff icon:** This information is interesting, but a little nerdy, so if you skip it, it's not the end of the world.

- ✔ **The tiny text on the copyright page:** Do you really care about the publisher's address? I don't either. Skip it unless you want to test your eyesight.

Foolish Assumptions

Throughout the writing of this book, I had only you (the gentle reader) in mind. Don't be alarmed, but here's what I assumed:

- ✔ You've already heard about green building, and you are interested in it enough to buy this book.

- ✔ You're not a hippie, but you probably recycle.

- ✔ You don't want to live in a mud hut.

- ✔ You either own, or are thinking about buying, a hybrid car.

- ✔ You want to improve your home through remodeling, adding on, or building something new.

- ✔ You're not a lottery winner, and you have real concerns about cost and budget. You need and want to make well-informed decisions regarding the budget and the long-term costs of operating your home.

- ✔ You're willing to be realistic and accept certain realities about cost, availability, and the environment.

- ✔ You're aware of the environmental issues facing our planet. You know that global warming, air and water pollution, and an energy crisis are all real problems that need to be addressed.

- ✔ You don't want to feel guilty about your own impact on the environment — you'd rather do something positive to better it.

How This Book Is Organized

This book is divided into five parts. Feel free to jump to any part you want! The following sections explain what you'll find and where it will be.

Part I: The Need for Green

This section begins by defining what makes a building green. In order to understand green building, you first need to understand the huge impact buildings have on our planet; Chapter 2 covers this, as well as identifying the hidden opportunities in any building. Because you probably already live in a house, Chapter 3 discusses remodeling issues and ways to add value to your existing home. Before you start a construction project, you'll need to put a team together, and Chapter 4 explains how to find good professionals.

Part II: Paying Attention to Material Matters

This section is the core lesson in materials. Beginning with exploring the entire life of materials in Chapter 5, you see how to analyze any material or product for its green qualities. Chapter 6 explores an innovative way to create new sustainable materials and talks about how to choose between the various choices out there. In Chapter 7, I get into the details of a green house, from the walls to the floors and everything in between.

Part III: Green Building Methods

This part focuses on construction methods. I cover framing in Chapter 8, natural building in Chapter 9, and manufactured systems in Chapter 10. Don't worry, though: I evaluate the pros and cons of each system I introduce, allowing you to make the decision about what's right for your own home.

Part IV: Green Building Systems and Site Planning

This part offers a detailed look at the wonderful world of the sustainable systems that go into a building. Chapter 11 begins with the variety of energy systems available. After this come the heating and cooling systems that keep you and your family comfortable, explored in Chapter 12. The last type of systems, water systems, are discussed in Chapter 13. And Chapter 14 covers the landscape and orientation of the building, where you'll see there is more to landscape than just grass.

Part V: The Part of Tens

Because green building is so misunderstood, Chapter 15 gives you ten of the most common misconceptions people have regarding green building. Chapter 16 explains the things you should do for every green building project. You may start drooling when you read Chapter 17 and the ten green materials you can't live without. Finally, plan your weekend projects with Chapter 18's list of ten things you should do right now in your own home.

Appendix

The appendix is a helpful reference guide. From sources to find green materials, respected green certification, and detailed information on the LEED Green Building Rating System, the appendix covers information you'll want to have handy.

Icons Used in This Book

To make this book easy to read and simple to use, I include these helpful icons to help you find the key ideas and information:

Discover ways to protect the health of you and your family wherever you find this icon.

This icon highlights information that's so important you'll want to remember it later.

Although this information may be fascinating, it's not critical to your understanding of the subject. Unless you're feeling like an overachiever, feel free to skip it.

Using expert advice and real-world experience, these tidbits save you time and money — and preserve your sanity!

Avoid costly mistakes by following the sage advice next to this icon.

Where to Go from Here

Everything in this book is organized as an independent topic, so you can jump to just that section and understand it completely. If you already understand the reasons why you should build green, but you don't understand green materials, jump ahead to Chapter 5 to find out about analyzing materials. Unsure what solar panels really do? Flip to Chapter 11 to explore all the energy systems. Even if you're just looking for quick tips on what you can do in your current home right now, turn to Chapter 18 for a complete list.

If it all sounds interesting and you're not sure where to begin, you'll enjoy Part I. It gives you a firm foundation in understanding the issues around green building and remodeling. From there, skip around to the areas that interest you.

Finally, give yourself a pat on the back for doing your part to save our environment. Small steps you can take in your own building or remodeling project can reap major rewards for you, your family, and the planet.

Part I

The Need for Green

"We're gonna be late with the play room. The fellas started horsin' around on break and now they're into Act II of *Peer Gynt*. And you know, you just don't rush Ibsen."

In this part . . .

I begin this part by defining what makes a green building. In order to understand how green building and remodeling works, you need to understand the huge impact buildings have on our planet; Chapter 2 covers this subject, as well as identifying the hidden opportunities in any building. Chapter 3 discusses remodeling issues and ways to add value to your home. Finally, before you start a construction project, you need to put a team together; Chapter 4 explains how to find good professionals for your team.

Chapter 1

Going Green

*T*he way people construct their buildings is about to change radically. It *has* to. The majority of modern-day buildings waste energy, water, and resources beyond comprehension. It's not our fault, really. Most architects and builders are completely unaware of the impact buildings have on people's health and the environment.

Green building is a way of looking at buildings that allows people to be more responsible with energy and natural resources. Going green is usually the most logical and economical choice, whether you're building or remodeling your home. In the near future, all buildings will be green buildings, whether by preference or regulation — it's inevitable.

Because green building is a mystery to most people, various rumors, misconceptions, and misperceptions swirl around it. You've probably heard a range of odd and funny comments about green building. In this chapter, I dispel these myths and explore why your new home or remodel should incorporate the green building techniques outlined in this book. In addition, I cover the steps to building a green home, including how to select a proper building site. I conclude the chapter with a discussion on costs and the new mindset you'll need in building your green dream home.

The first green buildings

When do you think the first green building was built? Odds are, you're picturing something built in the past 50 years or so. What if I told you that the first truly green buildings were the stone dwellings of the Anasazi Indians from A.D. 1?

The Anasazi were a rich culture of farming people who lived in the Four Corners region of the United States (where Colorado, New Mexico, Arizona, and Utah meet) up until 1300, when drought forced them to migrate. The best examples of their buildings appeared around 700 and consisted of apartment-house-style villages. These villages, built at the tops of mesas, included multiple-room dwellings of beautiful stone masonry.

Why are the pueblos of the Anasazi considered to be green buildings?

- Understanding the sun and heating, the Anasazi oriented their dwellings to the light. These were textbook passive solar buildings featuring natural ventilation.

- Rainwater was captured and irrigated because water is a valuable resource.

- The Anasazi buildings predated electricity but were heated and cooled without heat or air-conditioning.

- Natural stone, mud, and wood were the only materials used.

- The buildings of the Anasazi were completely nontoxic and healthy.

- Centered around a village concept, the Anasazi buildings fostered interaction and a sense of community.

Many of the so-called "innovative" green features we marvel at today are actually ancient methods of building. Fresh air, passive solar orientation, passive cooling, and many other concepts have been in use for thousands of years.

For a more modern example of green building, you just need to look to the global energy crisis of the 1970s for some pioneering efforts in energy conservation. Arguably, the pioneering Willis Faber and Dumas Headquarters by architect Norman Foster could be considered the first modern green building. Built in 1977, the building features a grass roof, a naturally sunlit atrium, and mirrored windows used to reduce solar gain.

Why is this building considered to be a green one?

- The building is located in the center of the town of Ipswich, centrally located for ease of access.

- The building features a landscaped roof garden.

- The glass curtain wall is tinted to counter solar gain and is suspended from a continuous clamping strip. The building's design exhibits a pioneering use of low energy consumption.

- An irregular shape of black glass creates a striking and natural form.

- The building is designed to encourage social contact. These social ideas shaped the arrangement of the plan.

Understanding Why Green Matters

Green building is the healthy, common-sense choice for a better life. In traditional construction, the quality of the indoor environment is often far more polluted than the outdoor one, because of the building materials we use, our inadequate lighting, and a variety of other variables.

Green buildings are sited, designed, constructed, and operated to enhance the well-being of their occupants, and to minimize negative impacts on the community and natural environment. Buildings consume 40 percent of the world's total energy, 25 percent of its wood harvest, and 16 percent of its water. Compared to traditional construction, a green-built home takes some of this pressure off the environment.

You're losing money on every green feature you *don't* include. Any time you build a new home or remodel an existing one, you have the opportunity to save money in the *operational* costs of your home. After all, you'll spend a great deal more money on the operation, maintenance, and utilities in your home than you ever spent on the initial construction costs.

A green building:

✔ Provides a healthier and more comfortable environment

✔ Incorporates energy- and water-efficient technologies

✔ Reduces construction and demolition waste

✔ Brings higher resale value

✔ Includes renewable energy technologies

✔ Improves indoor air quality and occupant satisfaction

✔ Is easier to maintain and built to last

All these factors can save you money in both the construction and operation of your home — and they're all good reasons to go green with your building or remodeling project.

Looking at Cost in a New Way

The common perception is that a green building costs more than a traditionally built one. The fact is, with a clear construction budget, there is no reason you can't build a green building for the same price as, or less than, a traditional building. In the following sections, I break down the three major types of expense in every building project, and let you know where green building fits in.

Initial costs

The *initial cost* is the actual cost of the material or product — what you pay once to buy the material or product and install it in your home.

If you compare similar materials (a traditional one, and a green one), the costs often end up being the same. For example, a bamboo floor is installed exactly the same way as a traditional wood floor. The material costs are now the same, and the use of bamboo doesn't result in the clear-cutting of a forest. So bamboo is a better environmental choice, and it doesn't cost you any more at the outset than another type of wood floor would.

Although some green materials do cost more than their traditional counterparts, there are also many more green products whose costs are far *below* the standard. Advances in recycling, new materials, and better designs have allowed for a new generation of environmentally friendly products that are less costly to produce. Of course, green materials also have a very important long-term benefit of not destroying the planet's resources.

The trouble arises when you try to compare apples to oranges. For example, if you're comparing a building with solar panels to a traditional building without solar panels, of course the traditional building costs less. But this comparison focuses solely on the upfront cost of building and fails to take into account how the building with solar panels will *immediately* begin producing energy and eliminate your monthly electricity bill. The lifecycle cost of the solar building will be much less. This monthly benefit, called a *return on your investment,* pays for any additional upfront costs of purchasing the solar panels, in most cases within five to ten years.

Lifecycle costs

Lifecycle costs are the costs of a product or material over the product or material's entire life — not at the moment of purchase and installation.

Green products and systems pay for themselves at least ten times over the life of the building. This is true even if the features cost more at the outset (see the preceding section).

Homes are built to last for at least a century. In that time, the cost of heating, cooling, and maintenance will be far greater than the cost of construction. Turn your attention to these costs to discover the savings — they can be enormous.

For the items that may increase your initial costs during construction, be sure to calculate the return on investment — the period of time it takes to realize the savings for items such as solar panels or added insulation.

Maintenance costs

Many people overlook *maintenance costs,* the costs associated with maintaining the house. Seen as the *cost of owning a home,* these maintenance costs are often high. Some homeowners are unprepared for these expenses, so they ignore problems until serious damage occurs.

Green building encourages the use of durable and unfinished materials to save on the costs and effort of maintaining your home. From the expense of painting and staining, to the effort of changing light bulbs, you can save a lot by going green.

It Is Easy Being Green: Steps to a Green Building

Although every home project will be unique and different, the steps to planning a green building are similar. The following list shows what you need to consider in the early planning phases for a typical green building:

1. **Decide whether you want to remodel or add on to your existing home, or build a new home (see Chapter 3).**

2. **Plan your financing; consider a green mortgage program (see Chapter 4).**

3. **Choose a site — preferably in a dense area, with lots of sunlight (see Chapter 14).**

4. **Research the planning code requirements for height limits, setbacks, and allowable size (see Chapter 4).**

5. **Ask about priority permitting for a green building (see Chapter 4).**

6. **Have a survey prepared by a civil engineer (see Chapter 4).**

7. **Diagram the site for sunlight, wind, views, and features (see Chapter 14).**

8. **Research grants and incentives for green builders (see the appendix).**

9. **Interview and hire an architect (see Chapter 4).**

10. **Create the preliminary design (see Parts II, III, and IV).**

11. Talk to your neighbors about your project before you begin (see Chapter 4).

12. Orient rooms based on the location of the sun (see Chapter 14).

13. Set priorities for the materials you use, giving preference to healthy, natural, and low-toxic finishes (see Chapters 5 and 6).

14. Consider exposing the structure to reduce your use of materials (see Chapter 7).

15. Dimension the building to match the unit of construction — 16 inches, 24 inches, and so on (see Chapter 8).

16. Provide space for thicker walls to allow for more insulation (see Chapters 8, 9, and 10).

17. Choose a structural system based on local resources and know-how (see Chapters 8, 9, and 10).

18. Design the roof to allow for solar panels (see Chapter 11).

19. Design to allow for passive solar heating and cooling (see Chapter 12).

20. Allow space for water-recycling systems, such as graywater and water catchment (see Chapter 13).

21. Design the shape of the roof to accommodate rainwater catchment (see Chapter 13).

22. Design the roof to allow for a green roof (see Chapter 13).

23. Interview and select a contractor (see Chapter 4).

24. Obtain all required permits and approvals (see Chapter 4).

25. Prepare a plan for construction waste management (see Chapter 3).

Location, Location, Location: Choosing a Site for Your New Green Home

Although most homes sit on their lots arbitrarily facing the street, a green building turns toward the sun and wind to use these natural features to your advantage (see Chapter 14). Consider the following when shopping for a site for your new green home:

✔ **Encourage in-fill development.** An *in-fill development* is a project built on an existing building site, usually between other buildings. Building on an in-fill site is better than destroying a pristine natural lot.

✔ **Minimize dependence on your car.** Locate your new home close to public transportation or bicycle paths, or within walking distance of shops and basic services. Include a home office in your design to reduce commuting; you'll reduce your stress and save on fuel costs.

✔ **Locate buildings to minimize environmental impact.** Design the home to preserve open space and wildlife habitats. Avoid sensitive areas such as natural wetlands. Try to keep as many of the existing trees as possible.

Designing Your Way to a Better Green Home

The more time you spend in the initial planning phase, the more time and money you'll save during construction. Consider the following issues at the beginning of the design process:

✔ **Go for a smaller home instead of a large one.** Many people have a tendency to build the largest home they can afford, only to find the large home a waste of space and expensive to heat and cool. Consider doing more with less and making the house not so big. Create multipurpose spaces — such as a home office that doubles as a guest room; they're much better uses of space.

✔ **To save on construction costs, consider building more floors instead of a sprawling one-story home.** Going up is usually cheaper than spreading out. A multistory home also reduces the impact on the landscape.

✔ **Make the structure adaptable to other uses, and choose materials and components that can be reused or recycled.** Avoid putting anything painted outside; it will have to be repainted every three to five years. Use unfinished, natural materials instead. (Refer to Chapter 5.)

✔ **Consider an addition to your existing home instead of building new.** Remodeling your home is a form of recycling. Before assuming you need to build something new, consider putting an addition on your home instead. Take the money you save and put it into more important things, like solar panels. (See Chapter 3 for a full discussion on remodeling versus building new.)

✔ **Work with green professionals.** Building or remodeling a green home is much easier when you work with sympathetic professionals. Choose people already familiar with green building practices. From green financing to green contractors, everyone on your team can find ways to protect the environment and save you money at the same time. (Chapter 4 outlines all the people you'll need on your team and tells you how to find them.)

✔ **Make it easy to recycle.** Early on, make provisions for storing recyclables. For example, install recycling bins in the kitchen, with an undersink bucket with a lid for compostable food waste. If you have it, you'll use it.

✔ **Choose healthy and low-toxic materials.** At the beginning of your design, commit to using only healthy materials in your new home. (Chapters 5 and 6 help you find these materials.)

✔ **Select recycled and sustainably harvested products.** In the early parts of design, you probably already have ideas for finishes. (For example, you may already know what kind of floor you want in your living room.) Chapter 7 helps you select recycled and sustainably harvested materials. Order samples early so you're ready to choose the right one.

✔ **Minimize waste and speed up installation by designing around standard sizes.** For example, design your bathroom to fit the tiles you're planning to install.

✔ **If you're building out of wood, consider using optimum value engineering techniques.** You'll use up to 55 percent less wood. (Chapter 8 explains the benefits of this practice.)

✔ **Design for alternative construction techniques.** Don't just assume you'll build your new house out of wood. Several alternative construction methods may be better choices. (Turn to Chapter 9 for an explanation of natural building methods; Chapter 10 includes discussion of manufactured building methods.)

✔ **Design an energy-efficient building.** Making an efficient building is the easiest thing you can do to save energy. Use high levels of insulation, high-performance windows, and tight construction. (Refer to Chapter 11 for more on all these options.)

✔ **Design buildings to use renewable energy.** Consider solar water heating and photovoltaics, or design the roof for future solar panel installation. (See Chapter 11 for more information.)

✔ **Let the sun shine in.** *Daylighting* (using natural sunlight to light a room) is an easy way to bring warmth into your home while reducing energy use. (Find ideas in Chapter 11.)

✔ **Use the sun to heat and cool the building.** Passive solar heating, daylighting, and natural cooling can be incorporated cost-effectively into most buildings. (I explore these in Chapter 11.)

✔ **Consider a graywater system.** You can save the soapy water that has been used for bathing, dishwashing, or clothes washing and reuse it later for flushing toilets or irrigating the garden. (You can read about the benefits in Chapter 13.)

✔ **Use the rainwater.** Clean water falls on your roof every time it rains. Collect this water and use it to flush your toilets or water your lawn. (I describe these systems in Chapter 13.)

✔ **Design water-efficient, low-maintenance landscaping.** Lawns require a great deal of maintenance, pesticides, and mowing. Avoid this high impact with native and natural landscaping. (Chapter 14 provides alternatives.)

✔ **Avoid potential health hazards, including radon, mold, and pesticides.** The issues of mold and radon are important concerns. Protect your home by designing to reduce their risk. Design insect-resistant detailing to reduce the use of pesticides. (See Chapter 14 for more information on all these topics.)

Following the Rules

You may assume that building codes would favor green materials, given their tendency toward less-toxic materials. In reality, building codes have little to say about the finishes or fixtures in a building. Generally, codes exist to protect the health, safety, and welfare of the inhabitants.

Bottom line: You should be able to use green finish materials as freely as traditional building materials. On the other hand, the walls, floors, or beams in a building impact the occupants' health, safety, and welfare, so they do fall into the purview of the local building code.

Ancient alternative materials such as straw bale or adobe are still not accepted by many building departments. Cost-saving measures such as the use of finger-jointed wood studs are also frowned upon by the local building inspectors. You'll have to check with your local building department before planning any construction project with these nontraditional methods.

Any wood intended for structural use must be inspected and grade stamped prior to use, or it will not comply with the building code. Ask the supplier for grade stamps — some suppliers provide this service for a reasonable fee. (*Note:* This rule does not apply to finish and nonstructural wood.)

Always check with your local jurisdiction before using any unusual materials.

A number of local governments have discovered the value in getting people to build green buildings. In addition to being a healthier way to build, green buildings reduce the strain on the local infrastructure. Cash-strapped governments can save considerable amounts of money simply by getting their residents to reduce their energy, water, and waste. Whether you live in these areas or not, visit the Web sites of the following agencies to download their free and incredibly useful green building guidelines and checklists:

✔ **Alameda County (California) Waste Management Authority (ACWMA; `www.stopwaste.org`):** ACWMA has been a pioneer in green building. Its free guides are so well done that the City of San Francisco adopted them for its own use.

✔ **Chicago Department of the Environment (`www.cityofchicago.org/environment`):** Chicago has been striving to become the greenest city in the United States through visionary programs promoting green roofs and energy efficiency. Its green building checklists are a valuable tool.

✔ **City of Seattle Green Building Program (`www.seattle.gov/dpd/GreenBuilding`):** Seattle is a visionary city in terms of promoting green building. Although its guides are written specifically for the unique climate of Washington, they're beautifully done and incredibly informative, no matter where you live.

✔ **Scottsdale (Arizona) Green Building Program (`www.scottsdaleaz.gov/greenbuilding`):** It comes as no surprise to find green building being discussed in the hot, dry climate of Arizona. The benefits of green building are even greater there. The drawings and checklists provided by the Scottsdale Green Building Program are a wonderful resource.

✔ **RecycleWorks, San Mateo County, California (`www.recycleworks.org`):** Located just south of San Francisco, San Mateo County is one of the most populated regions in the Bay Area. Its RecycleWorks program offers innovative programs and checklists to help people build green homes.

Picturing the Perfect Green Room

If you're starting on a journey, you need to know where you're going. In the following sections, I cover four common rooms (kitchen, bathroom, bedroom, and nursery) and show you how you can create the ideal green room — and home. The information shown in these diagrams is covered throughout the book, but here you can see an overview of what the perfect green room should look like — think of this section as a green road map.

The perfect green kitchen

On first glance, Figure 1-1 illustrates what looks like a typical kitchen, but a closer look reveals all the green opportunities that were capitalized on — opportunities you can capitalize on in your own kitchen.

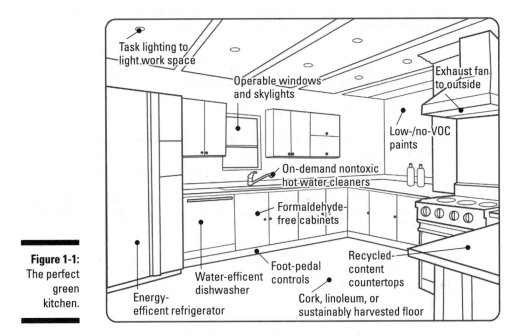

Task lighting to light work space

Operable windows and skylights

Exhaust fan to outside

Low-/no-VOC paints

On-demand nontoxic hot water cleaners

Formaldehyde-free cabinets

Recycled-content countertops

Foot-pedal controls

Water-efficent dishwasher

Energy-efficent refrigerator

Cork, linoleum, or sustainably harvested floor

Figure 1-1: The perfect green kitchen.

Courtesy of GreenHomeGuide.com.

Fresh air is important throughout your home, but especially in the kitchen. Windows and skylights are the most energy-efficient way to vent cooking vapors from your kitchen. Vent your Energy Star–rated exhaust fan directly to the outside to remove smoke, gas, and odors (see Chapter 11).

Natural sunlight is free and offers the best quality of light you can find (see Chapters 11 and 13). Place the work and food preparation areas near windows and skylights so you won't need to use electric lighting, saving energy and money.

While you're cutting down on your lights, switch your bulbs to energy-saving compact fluorescent bulbs (see Chapter 11). Advancements in the bulbs now provide better color and light quality.

The appliances in your kitchen consume most of your home's energy. Replace old appliances with new, Energy Star–rated appliances (see Chapter 11). The money saved could pay for your new appliances in less than a year.

If your plumbing fixtures were installed before 1992, replace them with new low-flow fixtures (see Chapter 13). You'll get the same pressure with much less water use. Fun options such as foot-pedal controls will reduce the amount of water you use in a simple way (see Chapter 13).

The perfect green bathroom

Figure 1-2 shows the ideal green bathroom.

Instead of vinyl flooring, buy natural linoleum (see Chapter 7). Made from sawdust and linseed oil, it's the healthy choice. Natural linoleum comes in a large selection of colors, and you can cut it into any pattern you desire.

Avoid cabinets using formaldehyde-based particle board. Select alternative materials such as bamboo, FSC-certified wood, and wheat straw panels (see Chapter 7).

Select a green countertop, such as recycled glass, salvaged stone, or paper resin materials (see Chapter 7). Wall tiles are available from recycled glass and ceramic sources (see Chapter 7).

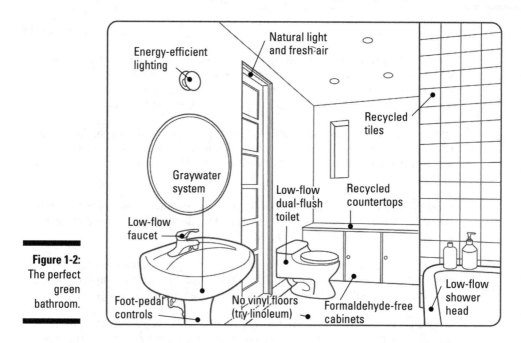

Figure 1-2:
The perfect green bathroom.

Courtesy of GreenHomeGuide.com.

Without sufficient ventilation, the toxic substances in conventional caulking can have serious health impacts. Safer, green alternatives are now available (see Chapter 7).

Paint the walls with low- or zero-VOC paints (see Chapter 7). Open the window to allow fresh air into the bathroom.

Older toilets use as many as 5 gallons per flush. Replace old toilets with a dual-flush model (see Chapter 13). Consider a composting (waterless) toilet as the greenest choice (see Chapter 13).

Purchase nontoxic cleaning products, soaps, and lotions (see the "Green cleaning alternatives" sidebar in this chapter). Not only are they safer for you and your family, but they stop chemicals from washing down the drain and polluting the water supply.

The perfect green bedroom

Figure 1-3 shows the opportunities for greening your bedroom.

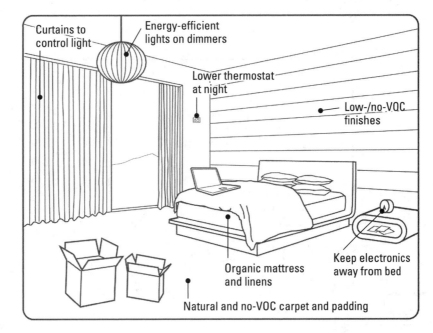

Figure 1-3: The perfect green bedroom.

Courtesy of GreenHomeGuide.com.

For many people, their bedroom doubles as a TV room, office, and reading room. Avoid sleeping problems by using your bedroom only for sleeping. Design the room specifically for that purpose with black-out curtains and operable windows for fresh air.

Insulate all the walls of the bedroom with formaldehyde-free insulation to block unwanted noise from disturbing you (see Chapters 11 and 12). Turn the thermostat down and use an extra blanket instead. A timed, programmable thermostat can warm up your room before you wake up (see Chapter 12).

Select a mattress and linens made of natural materials. You can find an incredible selection at stores like Gaiam (www.gaiam.com). Select nonvinyl carpeting (see Chapter 7) and low- or zero-VOC paints (see Chapters 3 and 7). Removing VOCs will help you sleep better.

Keep your electric clock away from your head. The electromagnetic field is known to disturb dream patterns.

The perfect green nursery

In Figure 1-4 you see how to make the perfect green nursery for your new-born baby.

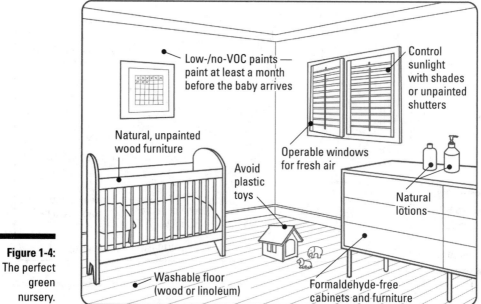

Low-/no-VOC paints — paint at least a month before the baby arrives

Control sunlight with shades or unpainted shutters

Natural, unpainted wood furniture

Operable windows for fresh air

Avoid plastic toys

Natural lotions

Figure 1-4: The perfect green nursery.

Washable floor (wood or linoleum)

Formaldehyde-free cabinets and furniture

Green cleaning alternatives

Cleaning is often considered a healthy thing to do. After all, it feels kind of good and self-satisfying to remove all the inevitable dust, food crumbs, fallen hairs, and other gross remnants of daily life.

Ironically, people typically clean their homes with chemically intensive and potentially toxic cleaning materials. Did you ever wonder why you have to wear gloves (and sometimes even masks) to clean? The chemicals used to clean are adding to the already overloaded toxic soup in most indoor spaces.

The American Association of Poison Control Centers (www.aapcc.org) ranks household cleaners as the leading source for acute human exposure to toxic substances. In addition, these caustic cleaners, pesky pesticides, raucous removers, and other potent products with their toxic ingredients also damage our environment through their production, use, and disposal.

Fortunately, a number of commercially available healthy alternatives exist:

✔ **Ecover** (www.ecover.com): Established in 1980, Ecover is one of the global leaders in healthy cleaning products. Not only are the products healthier, but the company is incredibly dedicated to sustainable business. Their solar-powered factory features green building features such as passive solar and water-efficient methods.

✔ **Seventh Generation** (www.seventh-generation.com): Named in deference to the Iroquois Great Law of Peace, "in our every deliberation we must consider the impact of our decisions on the next seven generations," Seventh Generation offers a full line of household cleaning products, including paper and baby products. Its Web site is an incredible resource for information on healthy living.

✔ **Mrs. Meyers** (www.mrsmeyers.com): With their striking graphics and packaging, Meyers's products are made with natural essential oils and are all biodegradable and phosphate-free.

✔ **Method Home** (www.methodhome.com): With their sensuous, almost sexual, bottles designed by Karim Rashid, Method Home has targeted its market quite differently. Selling on design and style, rather than simply on health, these gorgeous bottles are filled with all-natural ingredients.

Instead of purchasing new products, your kitchen offers a wide array of ingredients for naturally cleaning your home and office. Save some money and make batches of your own household cleaners. Eco-cleaning is easier than you may think. Most everything you need is already in your pantry. Basic products will tackle most of your cleaning and disinfecting needs, plus it will make your home smell fresh without the need for harsh perfumes or chemicals. Here are the basics you need:

✔ **White vinegar:** A natural disinfectant and stain remover, white vinegar also reduces mineral and lime deposits. Vinegar is a perfect substitute for ammonia-based cleaners. You can use white wine vinegar, but white distilled vinegar is cheaper. Don't use malt vinegar — unless you want your house to smell like a bar after a long night.

✔ **Baking soda (also called bicarbonate of soda or sodium bicarbonate):** Baking soda is the miracle cleaner. When mixed with water, it forms a paste that cuts through grease and dirt on almost any surface. In powder form, the abrasive texture can scrub out problem stains. Often vinegar and baking soda are mixed together for maximum cleaning strength.

(continued)

(continued)

- **Lemons:** The citric acid in lemon juice makes it perfect for bleaching, disinfecting, deodorizing, or cutting grease.

- **Olive oil:** Olive oil is a wonderful alternative to furniture polish. Don't worry about using the extra-virgin type — the most basic, cheapest olive oil will do.

For general cleaning, try damp dusting; it ensures that dust isn't scattered around. For best results, soak your duster in two parts water, two parts vinegar, and two drops of lemon oil. Then wring out and store in a covered glass jar until you need it.

Remember: Manufacturers can make almost any claim they want about their products. Buzz words like *biodegradable, all-natural, nontoxic, hypoallergenic,* and *fragrance-free* technically don't have to mean anything. Building health expert Debra Lynn Dadd (www.dld123.com) writes, "In general, it is best to avoid using products that say 'Danger,' 'Poison,' or 'Warning,' on the label." Dadd continues, "I do all of my cleaning with a squirt bottle of 50-50 distilled white vinegar and water, liquid soap, and baking soda."

A newborn baby has not yet developed resistance to chemicals. Because babies can spend up to 18 hours a day in their nurseries, the finishes you select are even more important for their health.

Try to create a nontoxic nursery using zero-VOC paints (see Chapter 7). Pregnant women should avoid painting altogether — have someone else do it. Paint at least one month before the baby is due, and open the window to flush the room with fresh air.

A space heater will help the paint cure faster.

Avoid wall-to-wall carpeting, because it traps dust mites and allergens (see Chapter 7). A natural linoleum floor is the best choice, but wood works just as well (see Chapter 7). And be sure to clean the floor well.

In order to block and control the sunlight, use wooden shutters. Leave them unpainted, or use zero-VOC paints or stains (see Chapter 7). Aluminum miniblinds work just as well as wood and don't require paint.

Select naturally finished wood furniture with pure, organic cotton and wool linens (see Chapters 7 and 18). Avoid plastic toys; most are made in China and can contain traces of lead and other potent toxins. Cloth and wood toys are a better choice.

Clean your green nursery with natural or nontoxic cleaning products. You can find some homemade cleaners on the Cheat Sheet in the front of the book, and nontoxic cleaners in the "Green cleaning alternatives" sidebar in this chapter.

Chapter 2

Green Building in an Organically Grown Nutshell

*U*nless you've been living under a rock, you've no doubt heard about the environmental crisis facing the planet. From global warming and air and water pollution, to the destruction of the rain forest and oil spills, the bad news about the planet is everywhere.

It's not just in Al Gore's movie, either: Mainstream media powerhouses (including the *New York Times, The Economist,* and *Oprah*) have dedicated considerable coverage to sustainability issues. The rise of people's interest in green is not the overnight sensation it may appear.

After more than 30 years as an architectural subculture, sustainability has finally penetrated all areas of building. After all, the building industry traditionally has the largest environmental impact of any industry. Combine this impact with the crippling rise in oil and electricity costs (some 40 percent in the last decade), and you can easily understand this interest. Homeowners can no longer afford to ignore the environmental impact of their own homes, both economically and globally.

In this chapter, I tell you what green building is and why it's necessary.

Playing the Name Game

Green, eco, sustainable, ecological. . . . You hear these terms used more frequently, but what do they mean? These words are used to define the same thing and are often interchangeable. In recent years, the term *green* seems to be the most popular among journalists (and it's the term I've chosen to use as part of the title of this book).

In the early part of my career, in the late 1980s, when people heard the term *green buildings,* they would often ask, "Do they come in any other color?" Today, this confusion has changed, as issues of sustainability are becoming more important to the general public.

Uncovering the meaning of sustainability

Back in 1954, R. Buckminster Fuller, the famous architect and theorist, defined *sustainability* as:

> the conscious design of our total environment, in order to help make the Earth's *finite resources* meet the needs of *all of humanity* without disrupting the ecological processes of the planet.

Notice that Fuller said "finite," not "infinite," when talking about natural resources. Many people believe that the Earth can provide an endless supply of wood, oil, or stone — after all, the planet is huge, right? But if you stop to think about it, assuming that natural resources are infinite just doesn't make sense.

Fuller also said that we have to meet the needs of "all" of humanity — not just rich people, and not just Americans. This is the same man who figured out how to house, clothe, and feed everyone on the planet. He didn't keep it secret either; he published it in one of his 28 books. At the time, he was dismissed as an eccentric and dreamer; only now, over 50 years later, are people starting to understand Fuller's genius.

In 1994, the United Nations (UN) came up with their own definition of *sustainability:* "meeting the needs of the present, without sacrificing the needs of our future." People everywhere have been consuming as if there's no tomorrow, and with little regard for the barren world that our children and grandchildren will inherit.

The concept of sustainability is also based on the ancient Great Law of the Native American Iroquois people, which states, "In every deliberation, we must consider the impact on the seventh generation. . . ." Each decision they made was based on the effect it would have seven generations into the future. This philosophy ensured their survival.

Because our resources are so finite, we need to adopt a similar approach — whether you go with Fuller's definition, the UN's definition, or the philosophy of the Iroquois.

Getting back to your roots

The prefix *eco–* comes from the Ancient Greek word *oikos,* which loosely translates to "house." In the case of environmentalism, the house being referred to is the Big House, the planet Earth, and it's the only house we have. The suffix *–nomy* means "management" and the suffix *–logy* means "knowledge." So, the term *economy* literally means "house management" and *ecology* literally means "house knowledge."

The funny thing is, people often assume that you need to sacrifice economy in order to achieve ecology. But as you can see, the two terms are interrelated. After all, nature has a perfectly balanced economy. When a tree sprouts in the spring, you don't look at it and ask, "Gosh, how many leaves does it take?!" The number of leaves depends upon the sun, the water, and the soil.

If you change your thinking about economy and ecology, and think of the two terms as part of the same concept of the Earth as our home, you can begin to understand sustainability.

Green Building: An Idea Whose Time Has Come

In the last hundred years, the environmental devastation from our way of life has been enormous. Due to the human industrial revolution, we have lost 50 percent of our wetlands, 50 percent of our forests, and 70 percent of our marine fisheries. These natural systems balance our life support system by cleaning our water, producing our air, and providing our food. This impact is severe, and it's getting worse.

As the global population soars to a projected 10 billion people by 2050, the resources of the planet will not be able to support all our needs. If we continue to consume at the current rate, you will see drastic changes in your lifetime. The way you get your food and water, as well as how you travel, will change as these resources become scarcer.

A brief history of the environmental movement, through 1970

1832 Artist George Catlin proposes a "nation's park" after visiting the West and observing Native American tribal cultures.

1836 Ralph Waldo Emerson's essay "Nature" is published, articulating his belief that God's work is visible through nature.

1847 George Perkins Marsh delivers a speech to the Rutland County Agricultural Society, calling farmers' attention to the effect of human activity on the land. Many of the ideas expressed in the speech would become the philosophical foundation for the conservation movement.

1848 Women's Rights Convention, Seneca Falls, New York. The early conservation movement had roots in the intense intellectual ferment of this period, which also spurred action for women's suffrage and abolitionism.

1849 The U.S. Department of the Interior is established.

1851 Henry David Thoreau, writer, poet, and transcendentalist, delivers a lecture to the Concord Lyceum, in which he says, "In Wilderness is the Preservation of the World."

1854 Thoreau publishes *Walden,* an autobiographical account of his experiment in solitary living, which gave him the freedom to adapt his living to the natural world around him.

1858 Mt. Vernon Ladies Association acquires 200 acres of George Washington's estate, one of the first acts of private historic preservation in the United States. Frederick Law Olmstead and Calvert Vaux win the competition for the landscaping of Central Park in New York City, called Greensward.

1863 Central Park in New York City is completed. The park is a milestone in the development of the American parks movement.

1864 Yosemite becomes a California state park by an Act of Congress. George Perkins Marsh's *Man and Nature* is published.

1866 German biologist Ernst Haeckel firsts coins the term *ecology*.

1872 Inspired by William Henry Jackson's photographs and Thomas Moran's paintings, Congress sets aside Yellowstone as the nation's — and the world's — first national park. Tree-Planting Day is first observed in Nebraska. Soon known as Arbor Day, this tradition is widely observed across the United States, particularly in schools.

1873 *Forest and Stream* magazine (currently known as *Field & Stream*) is founded; it will become the premiere sportsmen's publication and a forum for conservation advocacy.

1875 The American Forestry Association is founded. Congress passes an act prohibiting the unauthorized cutting of trees on government property.

1876 John Muir publishes *God's First Temples: How Shall We Preserve Our Forests?*

1885	New York state creates large forest preserves in the Adirondack and Catskill mountains, and opens Niagara Falls State Reservation, the first state park in the eastern United States.
1887	Theodore Roosevelt helps found the Boone and Crockett Club for wealthy big game hunters and conservation.
1890	Congress passes legislation that establishes Sequoia National Park and, less than a week later, Yosemite and General Grant national parks, in California.
1890s	Influenced by ideas and practices introduced from Germany, the forestry movement in the United States begins to promote scientific and "efficient" forest management.
1891	Congress passes the Forest Reserve Act, granting the president the power to establish forest reserves. President Benjamin Harrison sets aside land in Wyoming to form the nation's first forest reserve. In 1907, forest reserves are renamed "national forests."
1892	John Muir founds the Sierra Club, dedicated to preserving wilderness.
1894	Yellowstone National Park is established. Congress passes an act prohibiting hunting in Yellowstone Park. The legislation establishes the idea that national parks should not be used for hunting.
1897	Congress enacts the Forest Management Act, which designates forest reserves as national resources for timber harvesting, grazing, and mining. Gifford Pinchot is appointed chief of the Division of Forestry in the Department of Agriculture, the precursor to the U.S. Forest Service.
1899	Congress passes a bill establishing Mount Rainier National Park in Washington.
1908	Under the auspices of the Antiquities Act, Pinchot signs the Grand Canyon National Monument into being on January 11, 1908. Pinchot would create 18 in all, among them Montezuma Castle, Arizona; Gila Cliff Dwelling, New Mexico; Devil's Tower, Wyoming, properly known as Bear's Lodge by native Americans; and Muir Woods, in Marin County, California.
1907	John Muir begins campaigning to save Hetch Hetchy Valley, a part of Yosemite National Park, from the clutches of San Francisco political power.
1911	Ellen H. Richards, chemist, publishes *Conservation by Sanitation: Air and Water Supply; Disposal of Waste,* a work particularly concerned with water pollution and its effect on human health, and one of the first works concerned with "human conservation," the impact of environmental factors (especially in urban areas) on human health and well-being.
1918	The Save the Redwoods League is formed.
1935	Bob Marshall co-founds the Wilder-ness Society.
1960	Ceila Hunter founds Alaska's first statewide environmental organization, the Alaska Conservation Society.
1962	Rachel Carson publishes *Silent Spring,* a story of the detrimental effects of pesticides on the environment. The book is widely credited with launching the modern environmental movement we know today.
1970	20 million people celebrate the first Earth Day on April 22.

Although the effect to the natural environment has been destructive, it's only part of the full story. After all, you're probably thinking, "This is terrible news, but what does it have to do with building or remodeling my home?" Well, quite a bit, actually. Many people think that the automobile is to blame for the majority of the damage to the environment. Although dependence on cars does have a negative effect, the biggest impact on the environment, the greatest source for pollution, and the leading demand for the consumption of resources are buildings.

Buildings consume 40 percent of the world's energy and materials. If you factor building construction into that, the number jumps to 48 percent. Building use represents 70 percent of total human consumption (that includes everything: energy, water, and materials combined). A whopping 17 percent of all manufactured wood and 25 percent of all the water supply go into the operation of buildings. Nearly half (45 percent) of carbon emissions, the pollution causing global warming, comes from buildings. Cars are only responsible for a third of all emissions.

Once only of interest to hard-core environmentalists, the rise in energy prices, dependence on fossil fuels, and growing concerns over the damage done to the planet has boosted green building into the spotlight of mainstream interest. Today, those in the business of designing and constructing buildings are faced with the new challenge of environmental responsibility. The rise in energy costs, shortage of building materials, and growing consumer demands are driving this market to seek out better and more efficient ways to construct buildings. In addition, new legislation, stricter building codes, and rising health-care costs are forcing builders to build green — whether they want to or not.

Research has shown that, although an overwhelming majority of designers feel a responsibility to offer green building solutions, only a fraction of them do so. They blame this discrepancy on a "lack of information."

More important than any statistic, however, is the good feeling you have when you know you've done what's right for both your family and your community. Promoting continued health, financial savings, and social responsibility, green building is the construction standard for the future — and the smart solution for today.

More than any other industry, buildings are responsible for most of the damage done to the environment. Anyone building or remodeling a home is in a position to effect great change on the planet. So far, most of it has been negative — but you can change that by making better choices.

Envisioning the Total Green Building

So what does the perfect green building look like?

✔ The building is oriented to the sun, using the winter sun to warm the rooms and blocking the heat from the summer sun.

✔ The rain falling on the roof is stored for later use to flush the toilets.

✔ The soapy water from the building's sinks is saved and used to water the yard.

✔ All the materials used in the building are healthy, and none has that new-paint or new-carpet smell.

✔ The building produces more energy than it uses.

✔ The roof is covered with plants to filter the rainwater, clean the air, and insulate the building.

✔ All the walls are made from natural materials that don't require cutting down an entire forest or release nasty chemicals into the air.

✔ The building checks the weather report to decide (on its own) whether the lawn watering system should be activated.

All these ideas are just some of the many examples of what constitutes the ideal green building. Most of this may sound like science fiction to you, but believe it or not, all these ideas are available *today*.

In the future, the term *green building* will, I hope, be redundant. Using the term *green building* would be like saying, "structurally sound building" or even "code-compliant building." In the future, *all* buildings will be green buildings.

Some innovations to our buildings could include

✔ **Carpet:** Carpeting will be made of healthy materials. Instead of rubbing toxins into your skin, it will feed vitamins into your children as they crawl across the carpet surface. It will be dirt repellant to reduce the need for vacuuming.

✔ **Energy:** Energy-producing solar panels will integrate seamlessly into the building the same way windows and doors do. They will rotate to follow the sun throughout the day.

✔ **Flooring:** Bio-based finish materials will heal when damaged and thicken like a callus where they get worn.

✔ **Roofs:** Roofing materials will be able to darken in cold temperatures to absorb heat, or lighten in warm temperatures to reflect heat.

Such ideas are not impossible. In fact, as energy, water, and material use issues become more critical, such innovations will be *necessary*.

Looking at the Pros and Cons of Green Building

Like most new ideas, green building offers both advantages and disadvantages. Be sure to consider these opportunities when getting into any green building project.

Connecting to nature

I did a house for a lovely retired couple, Marvin and Gloria. One of the many questions I ask during my intensive interview process is, "If, heaven forbid, there were a fire in the house and you could only grab one thing on your way out the door, what would it be?"

Both Marvin and Gloria unflinchingly agreed on a vase they pulled from a dusty corner. So I asked them to tell me about the vase.

"Oh, our kids gave us this vase for our 35th wedding anniversary and it's such a wonderful memory of such a happy time. We can replace jewelry and books, but not this vase."

So I thought about it and wondered why such a treasure would be in a dusty corner. They had asked for a built-in cabinet in their living room, and I thought we could design this cabinet around this vase. I would put a narrow spotlight on it and size the area perfectly. When guests come into their home, they would see this vase and know it has importance. I knew that guests would even ask about it and engage with their hosts.

Well, Marvin and Gloria loved the idea. But that wasn't enough for me. I like to tie everything back to nature.

The built in cabinet was on the north wall. Because, as an architect, I know where the sun is every minute of every day, I suggested that we put a window on the south wall and position it such that at noon on their anniversary, the sun would come through the window and light up the vase.

There are no wires, no tricks, just an old-fashioned understanding of the systems around us. This play of light is genetically programmed into the house — and I love that.

This one example exemplifies my goal for each project. I look for a spark of inspiration for the entire design. When this happens, I connect this to nature. It requires extra thought and care, but it's worth it.

The pros

Obviously, a green building helps protect the planet's natural resources. But green buildings offer numerous benefits beyond simply saving the planet.

Perhaps the best endorsement for green building is how you can't afford to *not* employ green principles. You're losing money on every green feature you ignore. People build their homes to last for 50 to 100 years or more. Imagine all the money spent during the life of the building, and you can start to get a sense of the real cost of buildings.

In short, a green building has the potential to

✔ Provide a healthier and more comfortable environment

✔ Improve long-term economic performance

✔ Incorporate energy- and water-efficient technologies

✔ Reduce construction and demolition waste

✔ Bring higher resale value and building valuations

✔ Use renewable energy to lower the cost of electricity

✔ Improve indoor air quality and occupant satisfaction

✔ Be easier to maintain and built to last

All these benefits will save you money. Still not convinced? Consider the following benefits of green buildings.

A green building costs less than traditional buildings over the life of the building

Lifecycle cost is the cost of a building throughout the entire life of that building.

An upfront investment of just 2 percent in green building design, on average, results in lifecycle savings of 20 percent of the total construction costs — more than ten times the initial investment!

For example, people often ask how much solar panels will cost. I always tell them that solar panels are free. Why? Because, although solar panels will cost you about $25,000 upfront, after five to ten years, they pay for themselves.

If you're comparing the cost of building a home with solar panels to the cost of a building a home without solar panels, of course, the traditional building appears to cost less. But this focuses solely on the upfront cost of building, not on the total cost over the life of the building. The building with solar panels produces energy and lowers your monthly electricity bill as soon as it's installed. Therefore, the lifecycle cost of the solar building will be much less. This monthly benefit, called a *return on your investment,* pays for any additional upfront cost involved in purchasing the solar panels. Most people see a return within five to ten years.

Green buildings are healthier than traditional buildings

In 1990, asthma was the seventh leading chronic illness in children. Today it is number one. The direct cause of asthma is poor indoor air quality.

Americans spend 80 percent to 90 percent of their time indoors, typically with little fresh air. And we fill our buildings with toxic materials. We cover the walls in paints filled with chemicals, seal our floors with more chemicals, and seal the joints of our openings with even more chemicals. We're polluting our indoors as much as the outdoors. And some of the people who are at greatest risk from all this pollution are our children. Children don't have the same resistance to toxins as adults do; their immune systems aren't fully developed.

Autism rates have skyrocketed in the past decade. The U.S. Centers for Disease Control and Prevention now estimates 1 in 150 children suffer from autism. Since 1990, there has been a tenfold increase in the incidence of autism. Scientists are citing mercury poisoning as the leading cause of this alarming rise. This mercury is dumped into our air and our water from the burning of coal. More than three-quarters of the electricity in the United States is produced from the burning of coal, pumping some 63 million tons of mercury into the atmosphere each year.

Mercury has been linked to numerous other health problems, including endocrine disruption and cardiovascular disease. It only takes 1/70th of a tea-spoon of mercury to contaminate a 20-acre body of water and make all fish within it toxic to humans. (This is about the amount of mercury in a typical medical thermometer.)

Green buildings improve the indoor air quality with natural and healthy mate-rials. In addition, they promote the use of alternative sources of energy to replace the burning of coal, such as clean solar and wind power.

Green buildings perform better than traditional buildings

Painting your home is a large expense and one you might even try to put off until absolutely necessary. Anytime you paint an exterior material, you have to repaint it every three to five years. If you choose a material with an inte-grated color, like colored stucco, you can save thousands on these painting costs. Such simple performance choices as these lower your maintenance costs, saving you money and protecting the environment at the same time.

Green buildings provide an excellent return on your investment

Even with a five- to ten-year payback, many people still find the upfront costs of solar panels to be prohibitive. But there are other, simple measures that can pay for themselves much more quickly. Just doubling the amount of insulation pays for itself in a matter of months or even weeks.

According to the U.S. Department of the Interior, the amount of energy lost due to uninsulated homes is equal to the amount of fuel delivered through the Alaskan pipeline. That is the equivalent of 2 million barrels of oil per day wasted. This is more oil than the United States imports from Saudi Arabia. In other words, if we simply insulated our existing buildings, we could completely remove the need for Saudi Arabian oil imports.

Simple measures, such as switching to compact fluorescent bulbs, will save you $30 per bulb. They use a tenth of the energy of incandescent bulbs and last four times as long.

Even renters can save about 50¢ per square foot each year through strategies that cut energy use by 30 percent. This can represent a savings of $5,000 or more over five-years in a 2,000-square-foot home.

The best place to start looking for savings is in energy efficiency. If every home in the United States used an Energy Star refrigerator, the United States could close ten aging power plants. The second best place to save money is in energy reduction. Replacing your burned out light bulbs with compact fluorescent bulbs would prevent enough pollution to equal removing a million cars from the road. And natural light easily replaces the need for lights in the first place.

The energy savings alone in a green building could pay for green improvements several times over with a return on investment within one to seven years.

A $4 investment (per square foot) in building green nets a $62 benefit (per square foot) over 20 years:

- ✔ Estimated health and productivity benefits: $46
- ✔ Operations and maintenance: $8.50
- ✔ Energy savings: $5.80
- ✔ Emissions savings: $1.20
- ✔ Water savings: $0.50

You can take advantage of tax incentives and rebates when you build green

All 50 states in the U.S. now offer hundreds of rebates, incentives, and programs to promote green building practices. On the federal, state, and local levels, these programs are designed to save you money. From rebates for solar panels, to incentives for purchasing Energy Star appliances, money is available for you to do the right thing for the planet. (See the appendix for more information and where to find the rebates in your area.)

Green buildings are beautiful

The recent popularity in green building has brought with it innovative advances in materials. Some of the most unusual, beautiful, and interesting new materials have been green ones.

The cons

Green building is not without its disadvantages. In the following sections, I fill you in.

Debunking a common misconception

The chief complaint most people have with green building is cost. Despite the numerous studies and data showing otherwise, most people still assume a green building costs more.

This is not true — but it's a common misconception promoted by ignorant architects and contractors who are afraid of building in a different way. Good architects and contractors know how to save their clients money. The client sets the budget, and a project should come in at or below that budget. With a clear direction of budget, there is no reason you can't build a green building for the same price as, or less than, a traditional building.

When you compare similar materials, the costs end up being the same. For instance, a renewable bamboo floor installs the exact same way as a traditional wood floor. The material costs are now the same, and use of the bamboo does not result in the clear-cutting of a forest.

Although some green materials do cost more than their traditional counterparts, many more green materials cost far less than the standard. Advances in recycling, new materials, and better designs have allowed for a new generation of environmentally friendly products that are less costly to produce. Of course, green materials also have a very important long-term benefit of not destroying the planet's resources.

Some building professionals are resistant to going green

The construction industry represents 20 percent of the U.S. economy, comprising $1.27 trillion of the gross domestic product (GDP). With such large amounts of money and influence, the construction industry is inherently risk adverse. The industry has been building in relatively the same fashion for the last hundred years.

This fear of the unknown is perhaps the biggest hurdle to implementing green building ideas. As the ideas become more commonplace, these fears will subside. Until then, you'll undoubtedly meet people — including architects, contractors, and developers — scared by the idea of trying a different brand of paint, even though it's healthier.

Green buildings can introduce new problems

Some of the advantages I mention earlier in this chapter also introduce new issues to the building. Thinking through these issues at the beginning will help mitigate them. A good designer knows how to control, diffuse, and use light to create a healthy and comfortable indoor environment. Consider:

- Adding natural daylight brings in more light and more glare. You'll need to control the light with shades or overhangs.

- Adding a green roof adds weight, and you may need to beef up the strength of your roof to support this weight.

- Certain green finishes may need to be special-ordered and may have longer delivery times. Plan ahead for these potential delays.

- Orienting your home to the sun may mean turning the house in a different direction from that of the neighboring homes. Your neighbors may complain.

- Water-saving features, such as dual-flush toilets, require guests to pay attention to how they flush the toilet.

- Using natural ventilation to cool your home will not be as precise as air-conditioning. It may take some time before you acclimate to not having the temperature set to the exact temperature you like.

Chapter 3

Remodeling with a Green Eye

- -

In This Chapter

▶ Deciding whether to remodel an existing home or build something new

▶ Understanding the environmental benefits of remodeling

▶ Concentrating on the areas that add the most value to your home

▶ Finding design opportunities in your existing home

▶ Knowing how to survive the remodel

- -

*I*f you're thinking about remodeling your home, you're not alone. Last year Americans spent $173 billion on remodeling projects. If you're hoping to make better use of space, add storage, or simply update finishes, a remodel can transform your home.

Given the amount of wood, concrete, and steel needed to create a new home, remodeling your existing home instead of building something new is one of the greenest things you can do. The average new home uses 13,127 square feet of lumber; that's about the size of three basketball courts — and a lot of wood — that you can save by remodeling your home instead.

If your house is architecturally sound and if it has the potential to meet your needs, a well-planned renovation project can transform an ordinary house into your green dream home. If your home is more than 20 years old, chances are, it's missing important features such as insulation, energy-efficient windows, and water-saving fixtures. A green remodel is your opportunity to fix these shortcomings, saving you money on your monthly utility bills.

In this chapter, I explore remodeling with an eye toward all things green. I show you how to turn those little annoyances into design opportunities.

Deciding Whether to Remodel

Remodeling has the potential to transform your home into something that you wouldn't even recognize when complete. Most people aren't aware of the possibilities open to them. A good architect or interior designer can help you uncover this potential.

To decide if a remodel will work in solving your house issues, look at your current home. Do you suffer from any of the following?

- ✔ **Clutter:** You may think you need a bigger home to hide that clutter around your home. What you really need is smarter storage, not more space to fill with more clutter.

- ✔ **Noise:** People often complain that their old house has "thin walls" and they can hear noise from the other rooms. Adding insulation to these walls will help make the house quieter.

- ✔ **Limited use:** If your dining room is too small to allow you to entertain, you may think you need a new home. An addition can convert your dining room into enough space for the perfect dinner party.

- ✔ **Darkness:** Even the darkest room in your home can probably be brightened with a good remodel. New windows, skylights, or nice lighting can brighten your existing home.

- ✔ **Problems with temperature (too hot or too cold):** You might think of your house as always uncomfortable: too hot or too cold. Adding insulation and a new heating system can greatly improve the comfort of your existing home.

If your main complaints focus on your personal comfort, a green remodel can easily turn your messy, dark, or drafty house into the perfect place to entertain friends.

In the following sections, I outline some of the benefits of remodeling and give you some questions to ask yourself in order to decide whether remodeling is right for you.

Recognizing the benefits of remodeling

Remodeling your existing home instead of building something new offers several benefits for both cost savings and environmental advantages. Consider these benefits:

- ✔ Remodeling greatly reduces the amount of raw materials you would use if you built a new home from scratch.

✔ Remodeling involves less work than building, and less work means less construction cost.

✔ The money you save in the initial construction costs (over what you would've spent on a new home) can be put toward nicer finishes and appliances.

✔ Upgrading your appliances to energy-efficient models will lower your monthly utility bills.

✔ Choosing green finishes that are low in toxins or are toxin free makes your home healthier for your family.

✔ Green buildings may fetch a higher resale price than their nongreen counterparts.

Asking yourself some questions

If you're not sure whether to remodel or build a new home, ask yourself some questions:

✔ Are my rooms drafty?

✔ Is my home uncomfortable?

✔ Do I need more storage?

✔ Were my appliances purchased before 1990?

✔ Do I have high utility bills?

✔ Does my home contain lead paint?

✔ Do I have mold issues?

✔ Is there any minor dry rot in the wood in the home?

✔ Is my roof old and in need of replacing?

✔ Do I have ample space but find myself sick of the appearance?

✔ Do I have continual maintenance issues with my home?

Each of these questions addresses an issue of comfort — and the good news is that each of them can be remedied. If you answered yes to any of these questions, a well-planned remodeling project can correct these issues.

Now ask yourself the following questions:

✔ Does my home need major structural upgrades before any work can begin?

✔ Does my home contain asbestos (in the shingles, insulation, or tiles, for example)?

✔ Does my lot not allow room for expansion?

✔ Is my home already overbuilt compared to the other homes in the neighborhood?

✔ Am I planning on moving in less than five years?

Each of these questions addresses a structural or planning issue. These issues require more cost and effort. If you answered yes to any of these questions, the problems with your home may be too costly to fix, and a remodel may not help.

Of course, if you're planning on selling your home in the near future, a basic remodel may help it sell faster. If you see deficiencies in your home, potential buyers will, too.

Planning Your Remodel

When you've decided that you're ready to remodel, you may be tempted to dive right in and run out to your local home improvement center. But before you begin, you need a plan. Part of remodeling is working with existing walls, ceiling heights, and window locations. Plus, you need to consider other factors, such as your budget, the resale value of your home, and the return on your investment that you're likely to get when you sell.

For most people, planning isn't much fun. But if you don't plan, you'll pay for it with added costs — both in time and money.

If you plan on doing any of the work yourself, make a schedule and stick to it. Half-completed remodeling projects are surprisingly easy to walk away from and never finish. Divide each task into smaller weekend projects. If you can finish each part over a single weekend, you'll be more likely to get it all done.

Considering all things financial

A key part of planning your remodel is considering the cost of the upgrades and if and when you'll get your money back in terms of a higher resale value. In this section, I fill you in on all these details.

Thinking about resale value

Looking at other homes in your neighborhood will help you determine where to focus your remodeling efforts. Look at surrounding property values and comparable homes in the area. If the other homes in the area offer large master suites with walk-in closets, but your master bedroom doesn't offer much in the way of closet space, you may want to consider including a master suite in your remodeling project.

Drive around the neighborhood, talk with your neighbors, and consult a real estate agent to assess what's appropriate for your specific neighborhood.

Older homes can pose a challenge when you're remodeling, but they also have an inherent charm that's missing from most new houses. When you choose to recycle your existing home, you want to make sure that you don't lose the allure and character of your house. Those are the traits that will appeal to a buyer down the road.

Knowing where to get the most bang for your buck

You can spend a fortune remodeling a home, but not every improvement you make will reap rewards when it comes time to sell. You need to know which areas to focus on to get the most for your money.

On average, any money you spend on a remodel should increase the value of your home by one and a half times that amount. So if you spend $10,000 on a remodel, your home should increase in value by $15,000. But adding certain rooms adds more value than others. Here are three rooms where you can get the most bang for your buck:

- **Bedrooms:** Adding bedrooms to your home is a great way to increase your home's value. A legal bedroom is any room with light, access to fresh air, and a closet.

- **Kitchen:** Upgrading an old, outdated kitchen is the best investment you can make in your home. Although the kitchen is the most expensive room in a home to build, the payback in increased value is enormous.

- **Bathrooms:** Although you don't want too many bathrooms, having well-located bathrooms adds to the value of your home. A half bath (with just a toilet and sink) is less expensive than a full bathroom (with a toilet, sink, and shower or bathtub), but it carries the same value.

Most older homes have several areas you may have overlooked that offer potential use. You may be able to capture valuable space in the following places:

- **Attic:** If your attic is tall enough to stand in, consider adding a staircase from the floor below it and finishing the space to make a new room. Dormers are an inexpensive way to add ceiling height and windows to an existing roof. Rooms up that high may also offer a great view.

- **Basement:** Clear out those old boxes and take advantage of the space in your basement. If you have a high ceiling (or at least a ceiling of standard height — say, 8 feet), finish the space and create the perfect play room for the kids, a spare bedroom, or a movie room for the family. If you have to excavate the floor to get more ceiling height, the costs won't be worth the added value.

Figuring out how long your payback should be

When it comes to remodeling, the length of the payback refers to how long it takes for you to see a return on your investment. For example, if you pay to install solar panels on your roof, how long will it take you to make up the cost of that investment and start reaping the benefits of your lower energy bills?

In general, for upgrades to the energy efficiency of your home, expect a payback of less than five years.

Eyeing green remodeling projects

If you don't know where to start with your remodeling and you need some suggestions, consider some of the following green projects (see Figure 3-1):

- **Remove moldy carpet.** Exposure to carpet mold is one of the leading causes of respiratory problems. Keeping your carpets clean and dry will prevent the growth of mold. Moldy carpets should be removed and the source of the water leaks fixed.

- **Install dual-flush toilets.** In the average home, the toilet accounts for approximately 30 percent of household water. High-efficiency toilets use at least 20 percent less water than standard toilets. Dual-flush water-saving toilets save you money (about 20 percent on your monthly water bills) and reduce sewer loads, not to mention conserving water.

- **Install efficient windows.** Windows are thermal holes. An average home may lose 30 percent of its heat or air-conditioning energy through its windows. Energy-efficient windows save money on heating and air-conditioning each and every month.

- **Install energy-efficient appliances.** The typical household spends $1,400 per year on energy bills. And in this typical home, appliances account for about 20 percent of your energy bills. You can save a lot of money — including more than $400 per year on heating bills — with high-efficiency appliances such as Energy Star appliances.

- **Insulate your water heater.** Most people tend to overlook the expense of heating water for their daily needs. But 25 percent of every dollar you spend on energy goes to heat your water. Insulated water heaters are more efficient. Using an insulated water heater, you can save $156 on water heating over the life span of the water heater, which is generally four years.

- **Install a low-flow showerhead.** Inexpensive and easy to install, low-flow showerheads and faucet aerators can reduce your home water consumption and your energy cost as much as 50 percent, without sacrificing water pressure. You could save $100 per year on water and energy costs.

✔ **Install natural insulation in your walls and attic.** Natural insulation in walls, such as Thermafleece (www.secondnatureuk.com) and Warmcel 100 (www.excelfibre.com/building/products3.html), are highly effective and have an exceptionally low impact on the environment. By reducing heating demand, both insulations will significantly reduce household carbon-dioxide emissions.

✔ **Use nontoxic cleaning methods.** Today's modern home is loaded with toxic and polluting substances. The effects of these substances range from long-term health concerns for the family, to environmental pollution caused in manufacturing and disposal. Alternative, nontoxic cleaning methods are much healthier and environmentally responsible. These methods include baking soda, borax, white vinegar, isopropyl alcohol, and trisodium phosphate.

✔ **Nontoxic paints:** Indoor paints and finishes are among the leading causes of harmful indoor gases. Recently developed low-VOC and zero-VOC paints are durable, cost-effective, and much less harmful to people and the environment.

VOC stands for *volatile organic compound.* VOCs are the harmful chemicals in paint and the source of that new-paint smell.

✔ **Install a programmable thermostat with a timer.** To maximize your energy savings without sacrificing comfort, you can install an automatic setback or programmable thermostat. If you forget to turn down the heat before you leave for work in the morning, a programmable thermostat will adjust the temperature setting for you. You can save 5 percent to 15 percent per year on energy bills by using a programmable thermostat with a timer.

✔ **Test your home for radon.** Radon is a naturally occurring gas that comes from the decay of uranium found in nearly all soils. Long-term exposure to elevated levels of radon increases your risk of lung cancer. Testing for radon is easy, inexpensive, and should only take a few minutes through low-cost, do-it-yourself radon test kits, which are available in hardware stores and other retail outlets.

✔ **Insulate your roof.** Roof insulation reduces the amount of heat that flows from a house through the roof to the cold outside air. By reducing this heat loss, roof insulation reduces the amount of energy needed to heat the house in the winter. You can save 13 percent per year on your heating bills by insulating your roof.

✔ **Install solar panels.** The average solar heating system pays for itself in four to seven years. Not only can installing solar panels save you money by reducing or eliminating your electric bill, but it will also generate pollution-free and maintenance-free electricity. You can save $500 per year on energy bills by installing solar panels on your roof.

✔ **Switch to a solar water heater.** A solar water heater is an environmentally sustainable home energy system that doesn't produce harmful greenhouse gases. You can save 50 percent to 85 percent per year on your energy bills by using a solar water heater.

✔ **Install sun tunnels.** These mini skylights are easy to install through an existing attic. Because they use flexible tubes to carry the light through your attic, you can place them almost anywhere and bring light to a previously dark corner, thereby saving money on your electric bill.

✔ **Put in a whole-house fan.** You may see up to a 30 percent savings on air-conditioning costs with a powered attic fan. Depending on the weather where you live, you may even be able to use a whole-house fan in place of an air-conditioning system, to bring in cooler outside air and protect against mold or mildew caused by attic humidity.

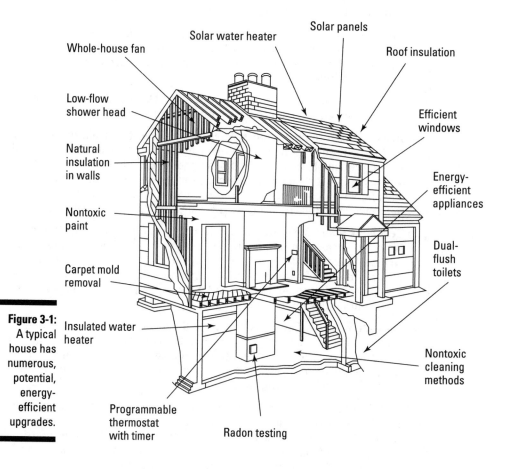

Figure 3-1:
A typical house has numerous, potential, energy-efficient upgrades.

Solar water heater
Solar panels
Whole-house fan
Roof insulation
Low-flow shower head
Efficient windows
Natural insulation in walls
Energy-efficient appliances
Nontoxic paint
Dual-flush toilets
Carpet mold removal
Insulated water heater
Nontoxic cleaning methods
Programmable thermostat with timer
Radon testing

The top two: Kitchens and bathrooms

When it comes to caring for your home, you've probably updated your furniture or painted the walls on your own. These changes are relatively easy. Installing cabinets, appliances, or plumbing is usually beyond the ability — or the interest — of the typical homeowner. For this reason, bathrooms and kitchens are the most common renovation projects people request. And bathrooms and kitchens are also the two places in your home where you can reap the greatest reward when it comes time to sell your house.

Bathrooms

You're in your bathroom every day, several times a day, which makes it one of the most scrutinized rooms in a house. You may focus on those ugly pink tiles from the 1980s, but appearance isn't all that matters when it comes to a green bathroom remodel: You can make some significant changes that won't affect appearance at all, but will save energy and money while helping the environment.

A bathroom remodeling checklist

Finish materials (see Chapter 7):

❑ Use low-/no-VOC paint.

❑ Use low-/no-VOC adhesives.

❑ Use low-/no-VOC sealers.

❑ Use formaldehyde-free cabinetry.

❑ Use FSC-certified wood.

❑ Use finger-jointed trim, where small pieces of wood are joined together to form a long length of trim.

❑ Replace vinyl with rapidly renewable flooring, like cork or linoleum.

❑ Use recycled-content glass or ceramic tiles.

Framing (see Chapter 8):

❑ Salvage materials from demolition.

❑ Use engineered lumber.

❑ Use FSC-certified wood for framing.

Energy systems (see Chapter 11):

❑ Install compact fluorescent light bulbs.

❑ Install dimmers and occupancy sensors.

❑ Install cellulose, recycled-content, or formaldehyde-free insulation.

❑ Caulk around windows.

❑ Replace windows with new energy-efficient windows.

Water systems (see Chapter 13):

❑ Install insulation wrap around your water heater.

❑ Convert to a tankless water heater.

❑ Insulate hot- and cold-water pipes.

❑ Add flow reducers to all faucets and showerheads.

❑ Replace toilets with dual-flush or low-flow models.

❑ Add a water filter to your sink.

In Figure 3-2, you can see a typical bathroom and the green features to include in every bathroom remodel:

- **Water filter:** Filter the water coming out of the tap with an inexpensive filter. It will improve the taste of the water and eliminate the need to buy bottled water.

- **Compact fluorescent bulbs:** Save money and energy with compact fluorescent bulbs. Look for color-corrected bulbs to light areas where you put on makeup.

- **Double-paned low-E window:** *Low-emissivity* (or low-e) windows use energy-efficient, insulated glass. Keep your heat from leaking out of your home with energy-efficient windows.

- **Flow reducers:** You can reduce the amount of water you use without losing water pressure by installing a simple flow reducer.

- **Formaldehyde-free MDF substrate:** Most cabinetry is made from plywood with toxic glues. Skip the formaldehyde.

- **FSC-certified wood:** Buy cabinets using sustainably harvested wood stamped by the Forest Stewardship Council (FSC).

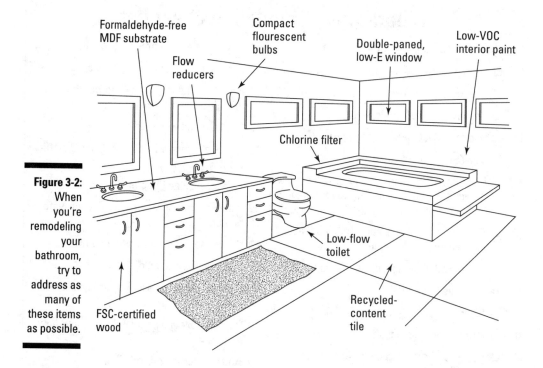

Figure 3-2: When you're remodeling your bathroom, try to address as many of these items as possible.

✔ **Low-flow toilet:** You can save thousands of gallons of fresh water a year by choosing a low-flow toilet. They look and cost the same as their traditional counterparts, too.

✔ **Low-VOC interior paint:** Paint the walls with a low or no-VOC paint to create a healthier room.

✔ **Recycled-content tile:** Dozens of manufacturers offer beautiful tiles made from recycled glass, stone, or ceramics.

Kitchens

Your kitchen is the heart of your home. Unfortunately, older homes have small, utilitarian kitchens not designed for socializing. In Figure 3-3, you can see a typical kitchen and the green features to include in your kitchen remodel:

✔ **Built-in recycling center:** Set aside space for recycling and composting bins to encourage their use.

✔ **Compact fluorescent light bulbs:** Energy-saving light bulbs save energy and money. Light the work surfaces with directional lights.

A checklist for remodeling your kitchen

Finish materials (see Chapter 7):

❏ Use low-/no-VOC paint.

❏ Use low-/no-VOC adhesives.

❏ Use low-/no-VOC sealers.

❏ Use formaldehyde-free cabinetry.

❏ Use FSC-certified wood.

❏ Use finger-jointed trim, where small pieces of wood are joined together to form a long length of trim.

❏ Replace vinyl with rapidly renewable flooring, like cork or linoleum.

❏ Use recycled-content glass or ceramic tiles.

❏ Vent range hood to outside.

Framing (see Chapter 8):

❏ Salvage materials from demolition.

❏ Use engineered lumber.

❏ Use FSC-certified wood for framing.

Energy systems (see Chapter 11):

❏ Install compact fluorescent light bulbs.

❏ Install dimmers and occupancy sensors.

❏ Install cellulose, recycled-content, or formaldehyde-free insulation.

❏ Replace appliances built before 1990 with Energy Star models.

❏ Insulate around the refrigerator. Move the refrigerator away from the sun and oven.

❏ Replace windows with new energy-efficient windows.

Water systems (see Chapter 13):

❏ Insulate hot- and cold-water pipes.

❏ Add flow reducers to all faucets.

❏ Add a water filter to the sink or whole house.

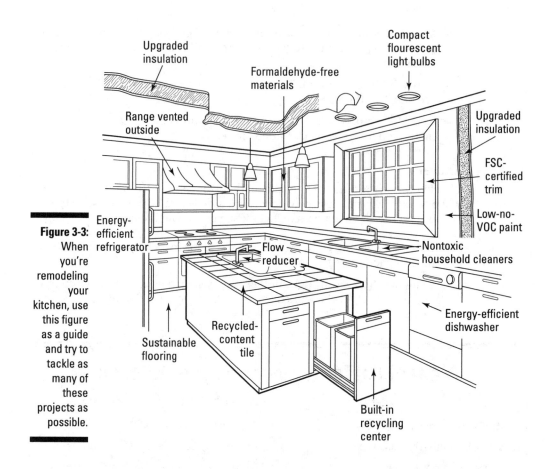

Upgraded insulation

Formaldehyde-free materials

Compact flourescent light bulbs

Range vented outside

Upgraded insulation

FSC-certified trim

Low-no-VOC paint

Energy-efficient refrigerator

Flow reducer

Nontoxic household cleaners

Sustainable flooring

Recycled-content tile

Energy-efficient dishwasher

Built-in recycling center

Figure 3-3: When you're remodeling your kitchen, use this figure as a guide and try to tackle as many of these projects as possible.

✔ **Energy Star dishwasher and refrigerator:** These two appliances consume more energy than any other. Find the most energy-efficient models available.

✔ **Flow reducer:** Save water without sacrificing water pressure with an inexpensive flow reducer.

✔ **Formaldehyde-free materials:** Most cabinetry is made with cheap plywood held together with formaldehyde. Select formaldehyde-free wood instead.

✔ **FSC-certified trim:** Choose sustainably harvested wood that is stamped from the Forest Stewardship Council (FSC).

✔ **Low-VOC interior paint:** Stay healthy with low- or no-VOC paints.

✔ **Range vented outside:** Carry the cooking fumes outside to keep the air fresh.

- ✔ **Recycled-content tile:** Gorgeous choices in tile are available with recycled metals, glass, and ceramics.

- ✔ **Sustainable flooring:** Cork and linoleum are durable and comfortable flooring choices for your kitchen.

- ✔ **Upgraded insulation:** While remodeling your kitchen, insulate the existing walls.

Because most of the energy in the home is consumed in the kitchen, these energy-saving suggestions will significantly reduce your monthly utility bills.

Surviving Your Remodel

Renovating your home is a stressful process. From the cost to the dust to the interruption, remodeling will turn your daily life upside-down. Seeing your family home get torn apart adds to the regular construction stress. Keeping the end result in mind will help you survive these traumatic times. In the following sections, I give you some tips on how to survive your remodel.

Living in the house during construction

Whether due to cost concerns or curiosity, you may want to live in your house during your remodel. If you're doing minor work, this isn't an issue, but if you're doing an extensive remodel, it can be like living in a war zone.

Talk to your contractor about whether it'll be okay for you to live in the home during construction. If you decide to stay in the house, keep in mind the following suggestions:

- ✔ **Make sure that your contractor alerts you in advance of any interruptions to the power or water.** If you know that the power or water will be turned off, you can plan to take showers or power down your computer beforehand.

- ✔ **Plan a long vacation to coincide with the more disruptive construction work.** You may need a vacation during the remodel just to relax!

- ✔ **Create a backup plan for cooking and showering for those times when things don't go as planned.** Knowing what to do ahead of time will alleviate most of your construction stress.

The majority of the stress people feel from construction comes from having unrealistic expectations. Expect to have dust in your clothes, no access to your stuff, and early mornings when you're awakened by all the noise. If you expect the construction process to be tough, you won't be surprised by it. Set your expectations ahead of time — and you'll find yourself delighted by the result.

Health risks: Handling surprises as they come

When construction begins and the demolition opens up the walls, finding some surprises is common. Be aware of the potential health risks described in the following sections.

Put some extra money in your budget to pay for these unexpected problems as they arise. Your homeowner's insurance may cover some of the expense of cleanup.

Asbestos

Asbestos was commonly used in insulation, tiles, and siding from the 1940s through the 1970s. It's dangerous if it's broken and fibers are released into the air. Don't sand or break up any material you suspect may contain asbestos.

Exposure to asbestos dust is dangerous! Check with your local building department for more information on asbestos abatement. You may need a licensed abatement contractor.

Mold

When moisture gets into a wall and is not given a chance to dry, mold can form. Even unseen mold can create respiratory illness and other sicknesses. Fix the source of the leak and remove the moldy and damp materials completely.

Lead paint

If your home was built before 1978, you could find some layers of lead paint below the current paint. Originally used as a pigment in paint, lead was found to be hazardous, because it flakes off and turns into dust, which can be inhaled.

Exposure to lead paint flakes or dust is dangerous! Your local building department can provide you with more information on removing lead from your home.

Vinyl

Polyvinyl chloride (PVC), or vinyl, is one of the most common synthetic materials. Approximately 75 percent of all PVC manufactured is used in construction materials. It creeps into all sorts of unlikely building products. PVC is the worst plastic from an environmental health perspective, posing great environmental and health hazards in its manufacture and disposal.

Chances are, you've got vinyl in your home. As you remodel, take out the vinyl and recycle it. Your local waste company can tell you how and where to recycle vinyl.

Chapter 4

Working with Building Professionals

*B*uilding or remodeling your home can cost you time, stress, and several thousands of dollars. Such a significant investment requires the right professionals to help you keep "home sweet home" from turning into the "money pit."

In this chapter, I fill you in on all the people you may need during this process, give you some things to consider when choosing them, and help you know what to expect after you have them onboard.

Identifying the People You Need on Your Team

For any home building or remodeling project — whether it's green or not — you need a team of people to help you accomplish your goal. The people on your team will need special expertise to ensure a successful project. The perfect person to help you is often someone who has worked on similar-size projects before, with a comparable budget and scope of work.

Choose someone knowledgeable, with a good reputation and a passion for green building issues. Don't be afraid to ask questions and take the time to research before choosing someone.

This is *your* house. You owe it to yourself to find people you like working with.

Real estate agents

When you're building or buying a new home, a real estate agent is often the first person you encounter in the process. Beyond simply collecting her commission after selling you a home or a piece of land, a real estate agent is an expert at handling contract negotiations and will be able to tell you about the features of the neighborhood you're considering.

Don't be afraid to use your real estate agent for her knowledge — you're paying for it! If you plan on building a new home or addition on any property, explain this to the agent. She'll be able to provide information on the local zoning and building codes and let you know what's possible (and what's not). Real estate agents are also great referral sources for finding mortgage brokers, architects, and contractors, so be sure to ask for your agent's help with that as well.

The Certified EcoBroker program (www.ecobroker.com) offers a way for agents to distinguish themselves and attract green-minded buyers. Agents who have gone through the certification program will be able to offer you a valuable insight into choosing an energy-efficient home as well as rebates available for green buildings. To date, nearly 750 agents have been certified in 31 states. Ask your agent if she's a Certified EcoBroker, or go to www.ecobroker.com to search for a Certified EcoBroker in your area.

Mortgage brokers

Perhaps the biggest financial burden you'll ever face is your mortgage. But unless you're a rock star or a hotel heiress, a mortgage will be the only way you can build your green dream home.

Love thy neighbor

Construction brings incessant noise, parking traffic, and unsightly scaffolding. Your neighbors have to suffer along with you, and can make your daily lives miserable. One poorly timed complaint to your local building department can halt your construction project faster than you can say "cup of sugar." Be a good neighbor and review your plans with them before starting any construction. Instead of telling them what you're already planning, ask your neighbors for their thoughts and concerns. Doing so will greatly reduce complaints and hard feelings.

A mortgage broker will help you find the best loan and rate for a construction loan for your new home. Before talking with a mortgage broker, do your homework and research the best rates available to you. The business section of your local newspaper will carry a list of the best available rates, or visit sites like www.bankrate.com for a listing. When you meet with your broker, ask him to match these rates. Be prepared to bring with you the paperwork to prove your income and assets. The broker will need this information in order to find you the best loan for your needs.

Keep in mind the mortgages and construction loans available to you will vary based on your income, your credit rating, and the value of the property after the project is complete.

Because the lender cares about the property value after completion, it may have some say in the size of your project. Don't be surprised if the lender asks you to reduce the size of the home, change the number of bedrooms, or consider using traditional construction methods instead of green ones. Your broker can help negotiate the terms with a wide array of lenders.

A movement of green financing options has been growing. The idea is simple: A green building has lower operating costs, enabling the homeowner to afford a larger mortgage. New mortgage programs for green buildings are now available in certain areas. Ask your broker for more information.

The Energy Efficient Mortgage (EEM) program was developed for Fannie Mae by the U.S. Department of Housing and Urban Development (HUD) to encourage people to buy greener homes. However, the maximum mortgage available is only $160,950, making this federal EEM obsolete for many homebuyers. If you live in an area with a lower cost of living, where building a home for less than $160,950 is feasible, be sure to visit www.hud.gov for more information.

For a wonderful, detailed discussion of mortgages, I recommend *Mortgages For Dummies,* 2nd Edition, by Eric Tyson, MBA, and Ray Brown (Wiley).

Architects

Whether you're remodeling your home or building a new one, a good architect is vital to a successful project. From designing the house, through finding and negotiating with a contractor, an architect is the most important part of the process.

Architects are licensed by the state to certify their training in the legal and safety issues around construction. Although the regulations vary in each state, you'll need an architect to prepare drawings for anything requiring changing a structural wall in order to get a building permit. For minor projects, such as painting, replacing windows, or upgrading appliances, permits are not required — but an architect will be able to help you with all this and more.

Bring the architect into the project as early as possible to help you evaluate locations, define project goals, and prepare initial schedules.

My story

I knew I wanted to be an architect at the age of 8, when, after showing my father drawing after drawing of buildings, he joked about it.

"What is an arkitek?" I would ask.

I took an early interest in drawing nothing but buildings, especially houses. Luckily, my father encouraged and supported this obsession.

When I was 10, I saw my first Frank Lloyd Wright building (Beth Shalom Synagogue in Philadelphia), and I realized that there was more to building than mere shelter. It was the first building I could not conceive of on my own. All the buildings around me were decorated boxes, but this was something different. I discovered that architecture could be unique, raise the human spirit, and connect to nature at the same time.

By the time I was in college, I was in contact with former Wright apprentices. By the time I graduated, I was working for them.

My interest in green building grew out of this early interest in Frank Lloyd Wright and what he called "organic architecture." With that grounding in nature, environmentalism was the next logical evolution. I didn't choose green building—it wasn't as if one day I woke up and said, "Okay, I'll build differently now." Green building is a very logical way of building, and the more I learned, the more sense it made.

People don't ask to live in a windowless, toxic gas chamber that wastes energy—but that's often what they get. Imagine a building that produces more energy than it uses, creates oxygen, supports

health, and doesn't consume our resources. Doesn't that make more sense?

Of course, you don't put toxic chemicals into your building! Of course, you orient the building to the sun! Of course, you let fresh air into the building! It would be stupid to do it any other way, right?

Our traditional methods of building raised good questions with no good answers. It was logic that brought me to the inevitable conclusion: Every building should be a green building.

My firm, organicARCHITECT, began after I moved to San Francisco in 1997 and couldn't find a mentor similar to those I had in New York and New Mexico. I knew nothing about getting clients, but I had this hope that if I spoke passionately about what I believed about architecture, clients would follow.

After the dot-com boom (and subsequent bust), strange and interesting opportunities began to emerge. Other architects were asking me to advise them on how to make their projects more environmentally friendly. I quickly realized that the sooner every architect was a green architect, and the sooner every building was a green building, the better it would be for everyone.

Today, the office of organicARCHITECT exists as a community resource, and produces a great deal in addition to designing buildings. Just as in nature, everything is connected. Using what we learn from our own designs, we teach other architects how to be green with their buildings. The research produced from this design and consulting work is then published and made available to everyone.

Find an architect you're comfortable with and who can produce a design you'll love. Friends and family are good places to start for referrals. Here are some other suggestions for ways to find a good architect:

- ✓ **Look around your neighborhood for new houses you like, and ask the homeowner who the architect was.**

- ✓ **Contact your local office of the American Institute of Architects (AIA; www.aia.org) for a referral.** Be sure to ask for architects who focus on residential projects. *Note:* The AIA will only give you names of its members, and not all architects are members of the AIA. This is a good place to start, though.

- ✓ **Use the Internet to locate green architects.** If you can't find a local green architect, don't despair. Many green architects are willing to take on projects around the country, so don't be shy about contacting an out-of-state architect to discuss your green dream home. Several wonderful green directories will help you find the perfect architect, including:

    - GreenHomeGuide: www.greenhomeguide.com

    - Green Building Blocks: www.greenbuildingblocks.com

    - Vivavi's Modern Green Living Home Directory: www.modern greenliving.com

When you compile a list of architects whose work you like, meet with each of them to get an idea of a personality fit. During your meetings, look around the office for green building books, catalogs, and magazines. Ask each architect the following questions:

- ✓ Have you worked on projects of a similar size and type to my project?

- ✓ What green building training have you had? What continuing education programs have you attended?

- ✓ Can I see some examples of green materials from your sample library? (A green architect will be able to show you products with recycled, reclaimed, and nontoxic content.)

- ✓ Can you tell me about some of the green building features of past projects in your portfolio?

- ✓ May I have the names and contact information of clients whose projects were similar to mine? (Be sure to actually follow up and talk to the references you're given.)

- ✓ Can you give me a list of standard green building measures you include on all projects? Based on what I've told you about my project so far, what green features would you think to include in the project?

During the meeting, the architect will be interviewing you as much as you are interviewing him. He'll be looking at your goals, concerns, and budget for the project. Make sure you have ideas about of each of these issues before your meeting.

For full design and construction observation services, expect to pay anywhere from 7 percent to 18 percent of the cost of construction for your architect. This fee is *on top of* the cost of construction, so plan your budget accordingly.

Hiring a design professional will quickly pay for itself in the time you'll save in reduced hassles, in an expedited permitting process, and in researching materials. A good architect will also help you avoid costly construction mistakes by monitoring the contractor's work.

Contractors

A general contractor is the person who takes the drawings from the architect and builds the home. Most licensed contractors are competent, honest, hardworking, and financially responsible. That said, given the potentially large amounts of money you'll give to your contractor, the risks are enormous. Do your homework and you can avoid the rare case of being a victim of an unscrupulous contractor.

How do you pick a stranger to build your home? When you're looking for a contractor, consider the following sources:

- ✔ **Ask friends and family for contractors who have worked on their homes.**

- ✔ **Ask your architect for referrals.** She should know several wonderful contractors that she already has a relationship with.

- ✔ **Contact the National Association of Home Builders (NAHB; www.nahb .org).** The NAHB is known as "the voice of the housing industry," and it's a great source for contractor referrals.

- ✔ **Contact the National Association of the Remodeling Industry (NARI; www.nari.org).**

- ✔ **Go to GreenHomeGuide.com, an online directory that features listings of green professionals around the country and includes reviews by past clients.**

When you've gathered names of contractors who might be a good fit for your project, meet with each one and ask them the following questions:

✔ What do you want to accomplish in doing this project?

✔ What are your concerns about the project?

✔ What do you see as the challenges of this project?

✔ Have you done similar-size projects in the past?

✔ What green building features do you include in your work?

✔ Is my construction budget realistic?

✔ I am concerned about _____. How will you handle this issue?

If a contractor you're considering shows any of these warning signs, find someone else:

✔ He doesn't return your phone call after a second attempt.

✔ He shows up late to your first meeting.

✔ His job site is messy or disorganized.

✔ He is not licensed or bonded.

✔ He doesn't carry insurance.

✔ He has no business office address. (He might say, "I work out of my truck.")

✔ He has a history of liens against his past projects. (You can check with your local assessor's office to find this information.)

✔ He has unresolved complaints against him with your local Contractors State Licensing Board (CSLB).

✔ He doesn't have any references, or the references he does offer are generic and not glowing about his work.

✔ He likes to avoid paperwork.

✔ He tries to talk you out of your green goals for the project.

✔ He tries to talk you out of something you really want.

When you're gathering bids from several contractors, all the bids should be within 20 percent of one another. If they aren't, then someone misunderstood or omitted something in the project.

Selecting the lowest bidder is not the way to go. Often, the lowest bidder is skimping on the details and cutting corners. Review the bids carefully to ensure everything you want is included. Your architect can help you with this process.

Given the surge in interest in green building, contractors are seeking ways to distinguish themselves from their competition while demonstrating their commitment to the environment. Luckily, several builder certification programs have emerged (though many are regional and only available to those in that area). Certification provides several benefits, including providing a recognized and established standard to measure green building services. Check with your local building department to see if a certified green builder program is available in your area. Also explore the builder programs listed in Table 4-1.

Table 4-1		Green Builder Programs	
Name of Program	**Area**	**Web Site**	**Description**
Austin Energy Green Building Program	Austin, Texas metro region	`www.ci.austin .tx.us/green builder`	The city of Austin has been a pioneer in green building. Its Green Building Program is open to all building professionals. To join, the basics contractor must attend the seminar, attend a minimum of two technical seminars, and submit at least one project report per year.
Build It Green	California	`www.build itgreen.org`	Build It Green (BIG) provides a Certified Green Building Professional (CGBP) certification for California building professionals. The 16-hour course teaches participants how to apply green building methods and materials in remodeling.
Build San Antonio Green	Texas	`www.builds agreen.org/ certification .htm`	Build San Antonio Green was developed by the Metropolitan Partnership for Energy and is co-administered with the Greater San Antonio Builders Association. To become a Certified Green Building Professional, contractors must attend the orientation session plus two additional technical sessions per year.

Name of Program	Area	Web Site	Description
Built Green	Colorado	`www.built green.org`	Built Green is a voluntary program to encourage green building. Using a checklist of over 200 green building features, builders choose their relevant building options. Builders must choose a minimum number of points from the checklist in order to be certified.
Energy Star–Rated Builder	United States	`www.energy star.gov`	A division of the U.S. Department of Energy, Energy Star promotes superior energy efficiency. Contractors may become certified Energy Star partners by signing a partnership agreement and agreeing to actively build new Energy Star–qualified homes according to the Energy Star guidelines.
Green Built Home	Wisconsin	`www.greenbuilt home.org`	Green Built Home (GBH) is a program of the Wisconsin Environmental Initiative. A voluntary green building initiative, GBH reviews and certifies homes that meet sustainable building and energy standards.
Nebraska Certified Green Builder	Nebraska	`http://www. neo.ne.gov/ home_const/ greenbuilt homes.htm`	The Certified Nebraska Green Built Homes program is conducted by the State of Nebraska's Energy Office, the Nebraska State Homebuilders Association, and the Nebraska Green Building Council.

Interior designers

An interior designer can often make the difference between a good project and a great project. From selecting wall finishes, rugs, and furniture to arranging these things, an interior designer can transform your home into a work of art. Many interior designers are now specializing in green building by choosing low-toxic finishes, sustainably harvested furnishings, and naturally derived fabrics.

Begin collecting magazine photos of rooms you like (and even those you dislike). These photos will help you communicate your tastes to your interior designer.

When you talk to prospective interior designers, be sure to explain your green goals and get a feel for how receptive they are. You want someone who can get behind your desire to go green with your house, and who sees this as an exciting aspect of the project, not a problem.

Landscape architects

If you have a large yard or property, a landscape architect can transform a pile of weeds into a beautiful outdoor "room." A landscape architect doesn't just select plants; she can design a trellis to shade you from the sun, as well as planter beds to form activity areas and decks perfect for watching the sunset. Think of a landscape architect as an architect for the outside. (Turn to Chapter 14 for more on the issues and opportunities for landscaping around your home.)

Mechanical engineers

You may never need a mechanical engineer for your new home. But if you're planning a large home, a mechanical engineer can design and select the heating and cooling systems. Mechanical engineers are trained in passive solar design, finding ways to heat and cool the building using only the sun.

Your architect and contractor can help you determine whether a mechanical engineer is needed and where to find one. And if you use a mechanical engineer, be sure to explain the energy-efficiency goals to your mechanical engineer so he can select the proper systems for your home.

Green building consultants

If you already have an architect and contractor you enjoy working with, but they don't have any green building experience, a green building consultant can help. This growing field now offers experienced experts who can evaluate your plans and create a list of recommendations to improve the energy efficiency and health of your home. A green consultant can source materials, provide design advice, and even perform an energy analysis to calculate how much money you can save.

Fees for green building consultants vary wildly, so be specific in your requests.

Finding Green Professionals

Several sources for finding green professionals exist. The issue isn't where to find information, but which information to trust and use.

Countless local green business programs are emerging every day. The popularity of green building is quickly growing in popularity among consumers, creating the demand for green directories. In Northern California, for example, the Association of Bay Area Governments coordinates its Certified Green Business Program (www.greenbiz.ca.gov). As of this writing, over 700 businesses across the seven Bay Area counties have passed the requirements needed to be a green business. EnviroStars (www.envirostars.com) is similar to the California program and handles the Puget Sound region in Washington. Participation in these programs is voluntary and free.

Several *non*certified directories of green businesses exist as well, and the following are worth looking into:

- **Building Concerns:** www.buildingconcerns.com
- **CoOp America Green Pages:** www.greenpages.org
- **EcoDirectory:** www.ecodirectory.com
- **Green Building Blocks:** www.greenbuildingblocks.com
- **GreenHomeGuide:** www.greenhomeguide.com
- **SustainLane:** www.sustainlane.com

Listing in the preceding sites is free or available to anyone for a nominal fee, so be sure to confirm the green credentials and qualifications of these companies for yourself.

The U.S. Green Building Council (USGBC) offers a professional accreditation for those trained in the LEED Rating System (see the next section for more on LEED). To become accredited, a building professional needs to pass the exam (which is on the LEED system, not on green building). Those who pass are awarded a LEED Accredited Professional Certificate. If you decide to get your home LEED certified, find a LEED Accredited Professional to help you prepare the paperwork needed for the certification. A complete directory of the LEED Accredited Professionals is available online at www.usgbc.org.

Getting Certified: Looking at Leadership in Energy and Environmental Design (LEED)

You're proud of your new home and want to tell the world about what you've done. Consider having your home certified to be as green as you made it.

Since its founding in 1991, the U.S. Green Building Council (USGBC; see Figure 4-1 for the organization's logo) has emerged as a recognized and respected leader among green professionals. To help the construction industry define green building, the USGBC discovered a need for a method of scoring buildings to evaluate their "greenness." Leadership in Energy and Environmental Design (LEED; see Figure 4-2 for the LEED logo) is the USGBC's Green Building Rating System, and it defines a voluntary guideline for developing high-performance, sustainable buildings.

Figure 4-1:
The U.S.
Green
Building
Council
(USGBC)
logo.

LEED has quickly become the industry standard for green building in the United States. Today, LEED buildings can be found in 24 countries and all 50 states. As of this writing, LEED has been adopted by 9 federal agencies, 20 states, and 49 U.S. city and county governments as the green standard in the construction of all municipal facilities.

There are currently over 30,000 LEED Accredited Professionals trained in this rating system and nearly 3,000 buildings on their way to certification. This represents about 8 percent to 10 percent of the U.S. new construction market, and this number is growing quickly.

Figure 4-2:
The Leadership in Energy and Environmental Design (LEED) logo.

Still in its early stages, some people have found LEED to be confusing and difficult to implement. Although LEED lists prescriptive requirements, there are no practical applications listed. A member of the construction team is left to guess how to meet the qualifications of each LEED point. The USGBC had enough foresight to understand this, and the LEED system is structured to be open ended and consensus based. The system is continually being refined, and draft versions are left open for comment and debate. In the near future, LEED will simply get better and better.

The LEED system works by dividing the building into six categories:

- ✔ Sustainable sites
- ✔ Water conservation
- ✔ Energy and atmosphere
- ✔ Materials and resources
- ✔ Indoor environmental quality
- ✔ Green design innovations

It lists opportunities for a building to earn points in each of these categories. The final number of points determines the green level of the building — Certified, Silver, Gold, or Platinum.

The benefits for getting your home LEED certified include the following:

- ✔ Having a LEED-certified home increases the value of the home.
- ✔ A LEED-certified home attracts potential buyers to your home.
- ✔ Tax breaks, expedited permitting, and other perks may be available for a LEED-certified building. (Ask your local building department for more information.)

The costs to get your home LEED certified may discourage you from making the effort. Costing anywhere from a few thousand dollars up to $10,000 or more, LEED certification is expensive. (The complicated paperwork takes a great deal of time — which is what makes it so expensive.)

The first step toward getting any building LEED certified is to register online at the USGBC Web site (www.usgbc.org). The cost for this is a simple flat fee of $450 for USGBC members ($600 for nonmembers). Your architect or engineer should handle this registration, but will charge you for the extra work involved with the paperwork.

The nature of your project will determine the version of the LEED system that you'll follow. Currently, the USGBC offers the following types:

- ✔ **LEED-NC:** New commercial construction and major renovation projects
- ✔ **LEED-CI:** Commercial interiors projects
- ✔ **LEED-CS:** Core and shell projects
- ✔ **LEED-EB:** Existing buildings
- ✔ **LEED-H:** Homes
- ✔ **LEED-ND:** Neighborhood development

Despite the cost, LEED is a great tool to use as a reference to build a green home, even if you don't get the full certification.

Numerous local green building programs exist all over the country — but LEED is the only nationally recognized one. Fees vary from program to program, but they're generally less than $100 just to cover processing costs.

After your green dream home is finished, don't keep it a secret! Invite others into your home to see the green features you've added. Local green home tours are popping up all around the country; consider including your project on such a tour. When you show other people what's possible in green building, they'll be more comfortable including these ideas in their own homes.

Part II
Paying Attention to Material Matters

The 5th Wave   By Rich Tennant

"I've never seen a home this green, Mr. Edmund.
As far as I can see, the paint's not flaking;
your house is pollinating."

In this part . . .

This part is all about materials. I begin by exploring the entire life of materials in Chapter 5; there I tell you how to analyze any material or product for its green qualities. Chapter 6 covers an innovative way to create new sustainable materials and talks about how to choose among the various choices out there. In Chapter 7, I get into the details of a green house, from the walls to the floors and everything in between.

Chapter 5

Looking at a Material's Life Cycle: From Cradle to Grave

In This Chapter

▶ Exploring the life of our materials

▶ Understanding by-products

▶ Redefining the idea of waste

▶ Questioning manufacturers about their products

▶ Testing typical materials for their greenness

*G*reen, green, green. The term has surged in popularity so much it now occupies the ranks of other one-namers like Madonna and Cher. With this greater interest comes a flood of new products, each with often vague and cryptic claims about their greenness. Even a well-intentioned manufacturer can inadvertently make an inflated environmental claim about its products. Referred to as *greenwashing*, these exaggerated assertions range from tiny overstatements to outright lies.

But how do you separate fact from fiction when it comes to the green qualities of a product or material? In this chapter, I introduce you to the life cycle of just about any product you'll use in building or remodeling your home. I give you a list of questions you can use to ask manufacturers about their products. Finally, I fill you in on some typical building materials and tell you how to look at their "greenness." After reading this chapter, you'll be able to examine the greenness of any material you want to put into your home.

Looking at Life Cycle

Everything — every material, every product — has a life cycle. A *life cycle* is the journey a material goes through during its entire life. Every material starts in some raw form, is processed, and is made into a finished product. At some point — five, ten, or dozens of years later — the material reaches the end of its life and is disposed of. (In fact, most construction materials end up in a landfill.)

If you were to map out the typical stages of the life cycle of any material — from its birth (production) to its death (disposal) — it would look something like the process shown in Figure 5-1.

A life cycle is divided into three phases:

✔ **Production:** Raw materials are extracted and processed into a finished product. This occurs before you even get to see the product in your home.

✔ **Use:** The finished product is used and needs to be operated, maintained, and repaired. The length of this stage varies from one material to the next.

✔ **Return:** At some point, the product is no longer needed or needs to be replaced. It's thrown into a landfill, recycled, or degrades back into some raw material.

In the following sections, I provide more detail on each of these phases.

Phase 1: Production

The birth of any product begins with production. In this phase of the life cycle, products are created through a variety of methods, but all go through the following stages:

1. **Whatever the final product is, some raw materials must be extracted to make that product.**

   Whether they are mined out of the earth, cut from a forest, or mixed from chemicals, these raw materials are used to produce the final product.

2. **The raw materials are extracted, grown, mined, or harvested in some way.**

   This process of extracting, growing, mining, or harvesting the raw material is known as the *supply-chain process*.

3. **The materials are manufactured into their finished form, leaving behind unused materials.**

4. **The finished product is packed up and shipped, often great distances to a regional warehouse or local store, or even directly to the consumer.**

5. **At the construction site, the product is unpacked and installed.**

   Depending upon the material, this installation may require adhesives, sealants, urethanes, or sanding. These typically contain harmful chemicals or require labor-intensive methods.

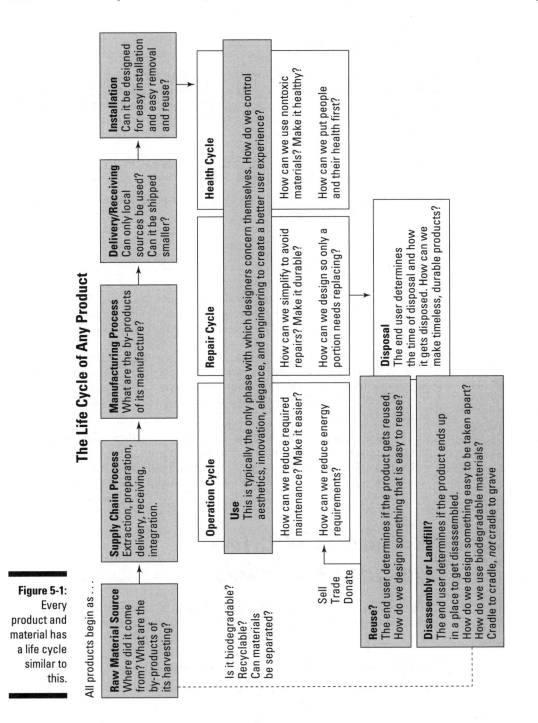

Figure 5-1:
Every product and material has a life cycle similar to this.

Phase 2: Usage

After the material is produced (see the preceding section), it's finally installed and ready for use. This is the part you're most familiar with. You know what the product looks like, you know how to use it, and you may even know how to maintain it. But even within this phase, there are some things to consider:

- **Operation cycle:** Whether the product needs electricity, batteries, oil, or pedaling, the product may need something in order to operate.
- **Repair cycle:** The product should be built to last, be durable, and be easily repaired if needed.

Phase 3: Return

At some point, maybe 5 years or 50 years from now, the material comes to the end of its useful life. Most of the time, it ends up in the landfill, where decades pass before it begins to break down. But some materials offer green benefits:

- **They are recyclable.** Most metal, glass, or plastic materials can be recycled. Because *construction waste* (the leftover materials and trash from building your home) accounts for nearly a quarter of landfill debris, 30 to 50 million tons of waste a year could potentially be saved, just by recycling.
- **They are biodegradable.** Natural, plant-based products are *biodegradable,* capable of being broken down by living things like microorganisms and bacteria. Whereas most landfill contents spread toxins into the air and water, biodegradable materials can actually feed the soil.

Understanding the Effort That Goes into Materials

In looking at materials, you need to understand the notion of *embodied energy.* Embodied energy is all the energy and effort that went into the making of a material, including all the effort from:

- **Extraction:** The material is harvested from nature.
- **Processing:** After it's harvested, the material is processed into a usable form for manufacturing.

- ✔ **Manufacturing:** The processed material is fabricated into the final product.

- ✔ **Transportation:** The finished product is shipped (often long distances) to a warehouse or store.

- ✔ **Installation:** After it arrives on the construction site, the final product must be cut, fit, and installed.

People usually overlook embodied energy when they think about green products, but it's a large portion of the overall impact of a material on the environment.

For example, the chair you're sitting on while reading this book has energy in it. Sure, it isn't plugged into the wall (unless you're sitting in one of those vibrating massage chairs!), but there *is* energy within the chair. Energy is embodied within it. Most likely someone had to farm cotton, chop down wood, forge nails, and shear sheep just to get the raw materials together.

In the beginning, there was the life cycle

Life cycle assessment (LCA) is the formal study of the environmental impact of products, processes, or services, through analysis of their production, usage, and disposal. In other words, LCA is the process of looking at where a product, process, or service came from; how people will use that product, process, or service; and what happens to the product, process, or service when people are done with it.

The concept of life cycle assessment dates back to a famous case from 1969. The Coca-Cola Company was trying to determine the better bottle: glass or plastic. Because glass is a natural material, most people expected glass would be the better environmental choice. Using a form of life cycle assessment, they determined that a plastic bottle would ultimately be the best environmental choice. Although contrary to expectations, Coca-Cola made its decision based on the following environmental considerations:

- ✔ Coca-Cola could produce plastic bottles in its own factory, reducing the need for transportation and the energy transportation would use.

- ✔ The lower weight of plastic bottles would reduce the energy needed to ship the bottles. Glass is heavier and more breakable than plastic.

- ✔ At that time, plastic was easier to recycle than glass.

As you can see, neither container is perfect. Plastic is made from petroleum (oil) and glass must be shipped long distances. This type of exploration of the life cycle of each material allows you to make a choice based on all the variables. Maybe by looking at the damage from this life cycle analysis, you can find ways to lessen the impact.

Some of these materials may have even traveled a long distance to get to the factory. All these steps involved in making the chair required energy.

After the materials were gathered up, someone had to process them into fabric and cut the wood into a structure. All these steps *also* required energy.

Finally, someone had to ship these products to the store. The store is probably located far away from the factory, so the chair had to travel by plane, truck, or train to get there. All these steps *also* required energy.

All these efforts to make your chair add up to an immense amount of energy and effort. By examining this embodied energy, the goal is to find ways to reduce it. (You can find more information on embodied energy, as well as ways to choose products for your home that have less embodied energy, in Chapter 6.)

For example, if your chair were made out of salvaged scrap wood, no new trees would have to be destroyed to extract the wood. If when the wood was being cut, the leftover scraps were saved for later reuse, it would save future materials. If all this was done by a local craftsman, your new chair would not have to be shipped long distances, saving gasoline and greenhouse gas from the exhaust. This is how embodied energy can be reduced to lessen the environmental impact of a product.

Being Clear about By-Products

When a material is manufactured and produced, by-products are created. *By-products* are all the leftover materials created from the material's life cycle, including:

- ✔ **Extraction:** Typically destroys natural resources. For example, harvesting wood often results in the total destruction of a forest.

- ✔ **Manufacturing:** Often creates pollution. For example, manufacturing steel gives off tons of greenhouse gas.

- ✔ **Processing:** Often demands large amounts of energy, which is usually provided from unsustainable fossil fuels.

- ✔ **Transportation:** Typically shipped using trucks, which consumes gasoline and spew exhaust and greenhouse gas into the air.

- ✔ **Installation:** Often requires energy and special chemical finishes, such as sealants or lacquers.

Yep, those are the same things that require energy to create the product in the first place (see the preceding section). A product not only requires energy to come into existence, but it produces by-products along the way.

When you think of by-products, you probably assume they're all bad. But that's not necessarily the case. For the most part, by-products are potentially valuable resources — we're just not smart enough to know how to deal with them yet.

 Ask product manufacturers about the by-products they create and what they do with them. Many products now contain their own scrap recycled back into the product.

Recognizing That There Is No Such Thing as Waste

Any time by-products go unused, they become waste. In fact, any time you have leftover materials that you don't know what to do with, that's waste, too. But what is waste, anyway?

Waste is a label, a term people use to describe all the unused and squandered resources. A majority of the time, these unused resources are bagged up and sent into a landfill where they take hundreds, if not thousands, of years to break down. As this garbage breaks down, it slowly leeches toxic chemicals into the soil and water. People consume the food grown from this soil and water and, eventually, these toxins end up in their bodies.

Nature does not have this concept of waste. All by-products in nature become food for something else. Consider the following examples of how nature uses resources:

- ✔ **To feed the soil:** As leaves fall from the trees each autumn, they break down into mulch and nourish the soil.
- ✔ **To fertilize the soil:** Waste from animals becomes fertilizer for the soil. Certain plants even thrive based on the presence of specific animals.
- ✔ **To clean the air:** Plants absorb the carbon dioxide you exhale and convert it back into breathable oxygen.
- ✔ **To filter the water:** Using a natural process called *bioremediation*, microorganisms feed on bacteria to clean the water.
- ✔ **To provide food:** Bees produce honey from the nectar of flowers, consuming some of it to secrete wax to build the hive of their honeycomb.

Nature provides for a continuous cycling and recycling of its elements. If this weren't the case, we'd be up to our eyeballs in waste, and our natural resources would have been depleted years ago.

Waste is the result of a poorly designed system. Nature is ultimately the best-designed system and a model for how people should look at their own processes (for more on using nature as a model for design, see Chapter 6).

When you accept waste as the result of bad design, and when you see the elegant and efficient model of nature, you realize the truth: There is no such thing as waste.

What we throw away

Americans generate anywhere from 200 to 250 million tons of solid waste each year. That translates to about 3½ to 4½ pounds of landfill per person per day. Only 20 percent to 30 percent of that waste gets recycled.

As part of the immense environmental impact of buildings, construction waste accounts for almost a quarter of what goes into a landfill. This makes buildings the largest contributor to landfills. In response, many cities are now requiring construction waste to be recycled, to keep it from ending up in the landfill.

The waste from building construction activities breaks down like this:

- **Demolition:** 50 percent
- **Renovation and remodeling:** 40 percent
- **New construction:** 10 percent

Because half of construction waste comes from demolition activities, restoring and keeping old buildings saves a great deal of the material we would otherwise throw away.

All this construction waste is made up of the following ingredients:

- **Concrete and rubble:** 40 percent to 50 percent
- **Wood:** 20 percent to 30 percent
- **Drywall:** 5 percent to 15 percent
- **Asphalt roofing:** 1 percent to 10 percent
- **Metals:** 1 percent to 5 percent
- **Bricks:** 1 percent to 5 percent
- **Plastics:** 1 percent to 5 percent

Most of this construction waste could be recycled if people paid closer attention to how they demolish their buildings. Carefully taking old buildings apart is called *deconstruction* instead of demolition. If just a quarter of the buildings demolished every year were deconstructed instead, approximately 20 million tons of debris could be diverted from landfills.

Total waste from the typical 2,000-square-foot home adds up to about 8,000 pounds of debris, taking up 50 cubic yards of space in the landfill. That's about the size of a bedroom in the house you just built.

Talking to Manufacturers about Any Material

Whenever you're choosing among various products to use in your building or remodeling project, you want to find out some key information from the products' manufacturers.

For example, say you're getting ready to buy countertops. You start by making a list of the countertops you like best. After you've identified your favorite products, find out which companies manufacture those products. For each product, write down the company's contact information alongside the name of the product and any other identifying information you can find (such as the manufacturer's product ID number). This information is often on the back of the sample you see at a showroom or store. (For more on finding materials, turn to Chapter 7.)

Not every manufacturer will have the same identifying information for every product. You just want to assemble as much identifying information as possible so that the manufacturer knows exactly which product you have a question about.

After you have your list of products and manufacturers, start by calling the first one on your list, and move through your list until you've found the answers you need from every manufacturer. Be sure to ask each manufacturer the questions in the following sections — you want to be able to compare the answers to all the questions from all the manufacturers, so you can get an accurate picture of how they stack up.

You can find many of the answers to these questions from the manufacturers themselves in the form of a material safety and data sheet (MSDS). Every manufacturer is required by law to produce an MSDS for every product it sells. The MSDS includes information about the product such as ingredients, toxicity, health effects, proper storage, disposal, and special handling procedures. The exact contents of the MSDS will vary from product to product, but they're basically the same.

You can request the MSDS directly from the manufacturer or find the MSDS online at Web sites such as MSDS Search (www.msdssearch.com) or MSDS Online (www.msdsonline.com). In addition, each sales representative should be able to provide some answers about the products he sells. If the sales rep doesn't know, ask him to find out.

Where did this material come from?

From the obvious (wood comes from trees) to the obscure (linoleum comes from linseed oil), this question explores the source of the product. When looking for green materials, try to choose from one of four possible sources:

- ✔ **Reclaimed:** Reusing materials salvaged from other uses, reclaimed materials offer old material quality no longer available. For example, the siding of an old barn can be milled into new flooring.

- ✔ **Recycled:** Unlike reclaimed materials, recycled materials are put back into the material production and reprocessed into new finishes. Sourced from various materials, recycled materials often have slight imperfections that add to the final appearance. For example, glass tiles can be made from recycled windshields.

- ✔ **Sustainable harvested:** Yielding materials without completely destroying the chance for future harvesting, sustainable-harvested materials will be around for future generations. For example, bamboo wood is actually a grass, and the root continues to grow after being harvested.

- ✔ **Rapidly renewable:** Instead of needing the 50+ years required to grow an entire forest, rapidly renewable materials grow back within five to ten years. Typically from exotic sources, these resources also offer some unique aesthetic options. For example, cork flooring comes from the bark of a cork tree; cork will grow back in less than seven years, making it "rapidly renewable."

In addition to helping preserve our resources, these materials also offer finishes that are more unusual and attractive than their traditional counterparts.

What are the by-products of its manufacturing process?

The manufacturing of any product brings with it some unwanted results. These by-products are frequently difficult to measure precisely, but they're easy to identify in a general way. Deforestation, pollution, global warming, and landfill debris are the most common by-products to look for.

Most manufacturers are not fully aware of the impact of their own products. By asking the questions in this section, you're actually helping bring green issues to the attention of the manufacturer.

Look for products where the manufacturing process is low in pollution. Make sure the manufacturer did not destroy something else to get to this material.

How is the material delivered and installed?

The average item on a grocery-store shelf travels over 1,800 miles to get there. Most of the products people use trek great distances to reach them. Choosing locally produced materials will lessen the energy used. Select local materials that traveled les than 500 miles to get to you.

The installation of the materials may require additional finishes, such as sealers on a granite countertop or urethane coatings on a wood floor. These things add to the labor (and the cost) of using this material. Pick materials that don't need these extra finishes.

How is the material maintained and operated?

From sealers and lacquers to paints and oils, many materials require continual care and maintenance. Other products require constant energy, even when they're not in use. Give preference to products that are durable and easily repaired. Does this product need continual energy by being plugged in all the time, or does it use batteries? Does it need to be painted (and then repainted)?

How healthy are the materials?

Most people in the United States spend 80 percent to 90 percent of their time indoors, so the healthy aspects of the materials used in home construction is important. From the paint on the walls, to the hidden adhesives under the rug, most people's homes are full of pollutants. Specifically choosing healthy materials will reduce these dangers.

What do you do with the materials when you're done with them?

The product manufacturer should be able to tell you how to safely dispose of their products. Most might just tell you to "throw it in the trash," but this isn't a good answer. Look for materials that are recyclable so they can be reused in the future.

The typical kitchen remodel is good for 15 years. By the time your new kitchen is ready for a facelift, you may have moved to a new home. Designing with durable, recyclable, or biodegradable materials will help ensure safe reuse, even if you aren't around. Look for the following traits in the materials you use in your home:

- **Durability:** If the product is durable, it will have a longer life and you'll use it for a longer period of time.

- **Recyclability:** If you don't mind taking special care to recycle a material, then choose something that will be recyclable. This is the best choice.

- **Biodegradability:** If you think you'll just end up throwing the product in the trash, at least choose a biodegradable material. This means the product can break down naturally and not spread toxins into the ground.

Putting Standard Materials to the Life Cycle Test

Buildings consume a whopping 40 percent of the world's materials. The construction of a typical 2,000-square-foot home uses approximately:

- 1,397 tons of concrete

- 13,127 board feet of framing lumber

- 6,212 square feet of plywood sheathing

- 2,325 square feet of exterior siding material

- 3,100 square feet of roofing material

- 3,061 square feet of insulation

- 6,144 square feet of drywall

- 2,085 square feet of flooring material (carpet, tile, or wood)

With all the materials that go into a single home, the impact on the environment is immense. In the following sections, I put some of the more traditional and common construction products to the life-cycle test.

Concrete

From the walls of the foundation to the mortar in the tile, concrete is used in nearly every construction project. You can't avoid it.

Here's a look at the life cycle of concrete:

- ✔ **Where does concrete come from?** Concrete is natural, made up of sand, Portland cement, stone, and water. *Verdict:* Good.

- ✔ **What are the by-products of making concrete?** The production of the chief ingredient — Portland cement — requires an immense amount of energy, and the by-product is greenhouse gases. *Verdict:* Bad.

- ✔ **How is concrete delivered and installed?** Concrete can be made locally or even right on the job site. *Verdict:* Good.

- ✔ **How is concrete maintained and operated?** Concrete is durable, can be left unpainted, and is virtually maintenance free. *Verdict:* Good.

- ✔ **How healthy is concrete?** Concrete is stable and does not release any harmful chemicals. *Verdict:* Good.

- ✔ **What do we do with concrete after we're done with it?** Concrete is technically recyclable and could be reused. However, reuse and recycling don't happen with concrete as often as they should. *Verdict:* Fair.

By asking these simple questions, you can see the only real issue with using concrete comes from the by-products created from Portland cement. But instead of using Portland cement, you can use fly ash. *Fly ash,* the soot by-product of coal-fired electric plants, can substitute for 15 percent to 50 percent of the Portland cement in the concrete. This saves 44 trillion Btus of energy annually in the United States, while preventing the mercury content of the fly ash from seeping into the food and water supply.

Bottom line: Fly ash concrete is the most responsible choice. After it's mixed with concrete, the mercury in the fly ash is safe and completely contained. Any concrete contractor or structural engineer can find sources of fly ash. For more information, visit www.flyash.com.

Wood

Nearly all (some 90 percent) of the homes built in the United States are framed out of wood. Plus, if you consider trim, furniture, cabinets, and doors, wood is used throughout the design of a home.

Here's how wood stands up to the life cycle test:

- ✔ **Where does wood come from?** Wood is natural and renewable, coming from various species of trees. *Verdict:* Good.

- ✔ **What are the by-products of harvesting wood?** Most wood is sourced from the clear-cutting of forests. Cutting down the forest just to get to the wood is like shoveling up the lawn to get the blades of grass. *Verdict:* Bad.

✔ **How is wood delivered and installed?** Most wood comes from the Pacific Northwest and Canada, and is shipped around the United States and Canada. Energy is required to ship and mill the wood. It is installed easily, and the most junior person on the construction site knows how to work with wood. *Verdict:* Fair.

✔ **How is wood maintained and operated?** The wood itself is durable and easily refinished, but it's traditionally covered with sealers and coatings that release harmful chemicals. *Verdict:* Fair.

✔ **How healthy is wood?** The wood itself is very healthy, because it's a natural material. However, it's often finished with chemical sealers. *Verdict:* Good.

✔ **What do we do with wood after we're done with it?** Wood can be reclaimed and milled into other uses. It can be recycled and turned into particle board. *Verdict:* Good.

The source of wood has the greatest environmental impact. Instead of using wood from destructive sources, you can get sustainably harvested wood. Certified by the Forest Stewardship Council (www.fscus.org), this wood has been certified to come from well-managed sources. Expect to pay 20 percent more for sustainably harvested wood than you would pay otherwise.

Regardless of the type of wood you use, be sure to seal it with nontoxic finishes (see Chapter 8).

Glass

You probably couldn't imagine your home without glass. The windows and doors of your home rely on glass to let in light and provide you with the views of your yard or neighborhood. Other products, such as glass tile and lighting fixtures, make glass one of the most common materials in your home.

So how does glass stack up on the life-cycle test? Read on:

✔ **Where does glass come from?** Glass is made from sand, specifically silica. It comes from a natural and abundant raw material. *Verdict:* Good.

✔ **What are the by-products of producing glass?** The formation of glass requires heat and molten tin, which requires energy and produces some greenhouse-gas emissions in the process. *Verdict:* Fair.

✔ **How is glass delivered and installed?** Unlike most other construction materials, glass is often produced locally and is available everywhere. *Verdict:* Good.

✔ **How is glass maintained and operated?** Except for protection from the occasional flying baseball, glass is durable and easily maintained. It requires only simple cleaning. *Verdict:* Good.

✔ **How healthy is glass?** Glass is completely inert and does not release any chemicals. It is also mold resistant, unlike other exterior materials like wood. *Verdict:* Good.

✔ **What do we do with glass after we're done with it?** Glass is one of the most commonly recycled materials on the planet. Americans recycle 20 percent of the glass we use. *Verdict:* Good.

Glass is already a very green material, but using recycled glass lessens its minimal impact further. Producing recycled glass requires less energy because the crushed recycled glass melts at a lower temperature. Recycled glass products are readily and easily available and often aren't even advertised as recycled. The costs are the same as new glass.

Steel

The high strength of steel makes it ideal for use in structural beams and foundations. But steel is also used in everything from cabinets, to furniture, to doorknobs. You find steel everywhere.

Here's how steel measures up on the life-cycle test:

✔ **Where does steel come from?** Structural steel is an alloy produced from iron ore. Mined out of the earth, the production of steel creates extensive environmental destruction. *Verdict:* Bad.

✔ **What are the by-products of producing steel?** The steel industry is one of the largest energy consumers in manufacturing. The intense heat required in steel production comes from the burning of coal and releases thousands of tons of greenhouse gas as a result. *Verdict:* Bad.

✔ **How is steel delivered and installed?** Steel is produced in a relatively small number of plants around the United States. Due to the weight and size of most steel elements, it requires a great deal of energy to transport. *Verdict:* Fair.

✔ **How is steel maintained and operated?** The strength and durability of steel is unsurpassed. It requires little, if no, maintenance. *Verdict:* Good.

✔ **How healthy is steel?** Steel is inert and does not release any chemicals. *Verdict:* Good.

✔ **What do we do with steel after we're done with it?** Steel is highly recyclable. Steel has risen in price in the last decade, making it one of the most valuable resources to save from the demolition pile. (In fact, many contractors have to lock up their construction sites at night to prevent the steel awaiting installation from being stolen.) *Verdict:* Good.

The embodied energy of steel creates a great deal of environmental impact (see "Understanding the Effort That Goes into Materials," earlier in this chapter). Due to the cost of the energy required to mine and produce it, most structural steel contains up to 80 percent recycled content in order to lower costs. If you're using steel in your construction project, look for the highest recycled content available.

Brick

Bricks add a rustic and human scale to a home. In the U.S. Northeast and Midwest, brick is a common finish material in buildings. Bricks also make attractive walkways and fireplaces.

Here's where brick comes out on the life-cycle test:

- ✔ **Where does brick come from?** Dating back nearly 10,000 years, brick is a ceramic material created from the firing of clay. It is a natural material and does not have the same impact as the mining or quarrying of stone. Aggressive clay mining can destroy farmland, which is why China imposed a ban on brick in 2000. *Verdict:* Fair.

- ✔ **What are the by-products of producing brick?** Due to the heat required to fire the clay, brick production demands high energy and generates some greenhouse gases. *Verdict:* Bad.

- ✔ **How is brick delivered and installed?** Bricks are designed to fit in one hand. Their relatively small, modular size makes them very resource efficient and encourages use of the entire brick. *Verdict:* Good.

- ✔ **How is brick maintained and operated?** The thermal mass of brick helps maintain the temperature of the building. The brick itself requires little maintenance. *Verdict:* Good.

- ✔ **How healthy is brick?** Brick is inert and does not release any chemicals. *Verdict:* Good.

- ✔ **What do we do with brick after we're done with it?** Although technically recyclable, most people don't pay much attention to protecting bricks during demolition. If preserved, reclaimed bricks have a certain charm. *Verdict:* Fair.

The durability, strength, and natural material of brick make it a good choice for green building. Reclaimed bricks do not require the embodied energy of new bricks.

Drywall

Drywall is one of the most common materials used in construction today. Walls are typically covered with drywall, making it one of the most common materials in a home.

Here's how drywall stacks up on the life-cycle test:

- ✔ **Where does drywall come from?** Drywall, often referred to as *gypsum board,* is the traditional wall finish for interior walls and ceilings. This rigid panel consists of an inner core of gypsum plaster, wrapped with paper. *Verdict:* Fair.

- ✔ **What are the by-products of producing drywall?** The gypsum is mined and creates some substantial environmental impact. *Verdict:* Bad.

- ✔ **How is drywall delivered and installed?** Formed into wide boards, drywall lends itself to leftover pieces created in the course of installation. (Up to 17 percent of drywall is wasted during construction.) Because it generally comes in 4-foot widths, designing (or having your architect design) rooms to be some module of 4 feet reduces waste. Drywall cannot be left unfinished; it's typically painted. Use a zero-VOC or low-VOC paint to reduce the release of chemicals. *Verdict:* Good.

- ✔ **How is drywall maintained and operated?** Drywall is easily patched and repainted. *Verdict:* Good.

- ✔ **How healthy is drywall?** Drywall is a relatively healthy material, especially when a healthy paint is used to finish it. *Verdict:* Good.

- ✔ **What do we do with drywall after we're done with it?** Drywall is easily damaged in the demolition process, making it difficult to recycle into a reusable form. Scrap pieces of drywall can be recycled if separated from the other construction waste. *Verdict:* Fair.

Given the impact of gypsum mining, using recycled-content drywall is a great idea. Several manufacturers offer recycled-content drywall paper as well.

Vinyl

Vinyl creeps into a surprising number of construction products. It can be found in everything from pipes, to floor tile, to windows. In fact, it's often hard to know when or where vinyl will show up. You have to look carefully for it!

Here's where vinyl comes out on the life-cycle test:

- ✔ **Where does vinyl come from?** Vinyl, also referred to as *polyvinyl chloride* (PVC), is a type of plastic polymer made from petroleum, and is one of the most common synthetic materials. *Verdict:* Bad.

- ✔ **What are the by-products of producing vinyl?** Often referred to as the "poison plastic," vinyl has been linked to numerous rare cancers occurring in the factory workers and in neighborhoods surrounding the production plants. *Verdict:* Bad.

- ✔ **How is vinyl delivered and installed?** So toxic it is only produced in a handful of locations, raw vinyl is shipped to thousands of manufacturers around the world to be made into everything from siding to children's toys. It has to travel vast distances, using immense amounts of energy. *Verdict:* Fair.

- ✔ **How is vinyl maintained and operated?** Vinyl is incredibly flexible and durable. It does not require additional painting or finishing. *Verdict:* Good.

- ✔ **How healthy is vinyl?** In its final state, vinyl is inert and does not release chemicals. In a fire, however, vinyl produces smoke fumes so toxic that they can kill the inhabitants in 20 minutes. The health issues surrounding the production of vinyl are severe. *Verdict:* Bad.

- ✔ **What do we do with vinyl after we're done with it?** Although technically recyclable, vinyl is so *difficult* to recycle that most recycling plants will not accept it. Even if it does manage to find its way to a recycling center, it can only be made into more vinyl. *Verdict:* Bad.

When most people think of vinyl, they probably think fondly of their old vinyl LP records. But the truth about vinyl is less romantic. PVC appears in thousands of different formulations and configurations. Approximately 75 percent of all PVC manufactured is used in construction materials. PVC is the worst plastic from an environmental-health perspective, posing great environmental and health hazards in its manufacture, product life, and disposal. Fortunately, healthier alternatives exist. For a list of alternatives to vinyl, visit www.healthybuilding.net/pvc/.

Looking to Trusted Green Certification Programs When Shopping for Materials

Several wonderful green certification programs have emerged as well-respected, trusted names. Similar to the Good Housekeeping Seal, these programs give you some assurance of product claims.

The Carpet and Rug Institute's Green Label and Green Label Plus

The Carpet and Rug Institute (CRI) has created Green Label and Green Label Plus, an independent testing program that identifies carpets with very low emissions of harmful chemicals, know as volatile organic compounds (VOCs). With all the health issues concerning carpeting, the CRI Green Label is a guarantee of low chemical emissions. The higher Green Label Plus certification (see Figure 5-2) ensures you're getting the lowest emissions available.

You can find out more about the Green Label program at `www.carpet rug.org`.

Figure 5-2: The Carpet and Rug Institute (CRI) Green Label Plus logo.

Courtesy of GLP.

Forest Stewardship Council

The FSC seal of approval is something you'll find on wood products certifying that wood has been *sustainably harvested,* meaning the forests have been protected to last for future generations. Look for the FSC logo (shown in Figure 5-3) as the greenest choice in purchasing wood products. (For more information on the FSC, check out Chapter 8.)

You can find out more at `www.fscus.org`.

Figure 5-3:
The Forest
Steward-
ship Council
(FSC) logo.

The FSC logo identifies products which contain wood from well-managed forests certified in accordance with the rules of the Forest Stewardship Council. ©1996 Forest Stewardship Council A.C.

GREENGUARD

GREENGUARD is an independent organization that has developed standards for adhesives, appliances, ceiling, flooring, insulation, paint, and wall-covering products. The GREENGUARD logo (shown in Figure 5-4) indicates interior materials with low chemical emissions.

You can find out more at www.greenguard.org.

Figure 5-4:
The GREEN-
GUARD logo.

Green Seal

Green Seal's environmental standards for paints, household cleaners, and window products date back to the mid-1990s, and the products are independently tested so there's no bias. The Green Seal logo (shown in Figure 5-5) indicates the product has gone through the rigorous Green Seal testing standards. The seal is used on paints, paper, cleaners, and even on hotels to certify the overall environmental quality.

For more information, go to www.greenseal.org.

Figure 5-5:
The Green
Seal logo.

Scientific Certification Systems

Scientific Certification Systems (SCS) has developed a certification program for environmentally preferable products and services, such as adhesives and sealants, cabinetry and casework, carpet, doors, flooring, paints, and wall coverings. Shown in Figure 5-6, the SCS logo is an independent certification that the product lives up to its environmental claims, including the amount of recycled content and the amount of chemicals released.

Go to www.scscertified.com for more information.

Figure 5-6:
The
Scientific
Certification
Systems
(SCS) logo.

Cradle to Cradle certification

Cradle to Cradle (C2C) certifies a high standard for "environmentally intelligent" design. C2C examines the entire life cycle of a material to ensure the most environmentally friendly material available.

Hundreds of products have been certified. Find the complete list of products at www.c2ccertified.com.

Chapter 6

Material Opportunities: From Cradle to Cradle

*T*he building industry is the biggest consumer by far, requiring the majority of the energy and materials used today. Part of green building and remodeling is examining materials and products and discovering methods to reduce their impact.

In this chapter, I highlight the various methods available for examining products, establish a criteria for selecting materials, and show you how to fight the paper-or-plastic mentality that homeowners typically use when looking at green materials.

Cradle to Cradle: Designing Like Nature

The term *cradle to cradle* (often abbreviated as *C2C*) describes a new way of looking at resources following the principles of natural systems. The concept was developed by German chemist Michael Braungart and American architect William McDonough, and they outlined their concept in a 2002 book called *Cradle to Cradle: Remaking the Way We Make Things*. The book calls for the transformation of industry and manufacturing through what the authors call "ecologically intelligent design."

Most industry follows a simple model: Extract and consume resources, and discard the resources when they're finished with them. This consumption of natural resources follows cradle-to-grave thinking (see Chapter 5), what Braungart and McDonough refer to as a *take-make-waste model.*

Although many industries have tried to change their manufacturing to incorporate recycling, minimize waste, and lower consumption of natural resources, this approach, known as *eco-efficiency,* is not a formula for long-term success. Eco-efficiency simply seeks to make the current, destructive system sustainable and palatable — it's better than nothing, but it's not the best possible approach.

Cradle to cradle is an *alternative* way to look at industry, following the example of nature. As opposed to eco-efficiency, C2C calls for new, more-intelligent materials designed to be recirculated back into use.

In *recycling,* unhealthy materials are processed back into useful materials. This process usually requires a lot of energy and, often, the recycled materials end up being "downgraded" into some lesser form. For example, new plastic water bottles get recycled into gray plastic trashcans. None of these materials was originally designed to be recycled, which is why it takes so much effort and energy to do it. A C2C material starts out as a healthy material, designed to be reused and recirculated back into the same thing it originally was. For example, a chair made from healthy plastics made from corn (not oil) can be recirculated to make that same chair — again and again.

As Braungart and McDonough explain it, if you're trying to drive north to Canada, but you're headed 100 miles per hour south to Mexico, slowing down to 20 mph won't help — you're still headed the wrong way. We can't recycle our way to a healthy environment and economy. Recycling is simply reinforcing the use of unintelligent, unhealthy materials.

Cradle to cradle is designed based on the systems found in nature, where there is no such thing as waste. C2C calls for eliminating the concept of waste entirely. This is Braungart and McDonough's most wonderful innovation and it's changing how people look at materials. In nature, any by-products of waste become food for some other organism. In the book, the authors declare that "waste equals food" (see Chapter 5). Cradle-to-cradle products have relatively no negative impact on the environment and can be returned safely to the earth in a perpetual nutrient cycle.

Table 6-1 compares the pros and cons of recycling with the pros and cons of cradle to cradle.

Table 6-1	The Pros and Cons of Recycling and Cradle to Cradle	
	Recycling	*Cradle to Cradle*
Pros	You can find recycling centers all over the United States and Canada. Recycling keeps materials from ending up in a landfill.	C2C uses natually derived materials. C2C products can be officially certified as Cradle to Cradle.
Cons	Recycling requires a great deal of energy. Recycling makes it seem okay to continue using unsustainable materials such as plastic and aluminum. Recycling returns unhealthy materials to your home. Even recycled plastic releases harmful chemicals. Recycling a mixture of materials together results in the production of less sophisticated products than the original.	C2C is still a new idea, competing with decades of recycling systems.

Products can now get certified in the cradle-to-cradle process, demonstrating their environmental responsibility. Today, nearly 100 products — from water-proof concrete to biodegradable diapers — bear this certification, with hundreds more lined up and ready to be certified. The list of currently certified products is varied and extensive, demonstrating a larger movement toward healthier and more sustainable materials. You can find it online at www.c2c certified.com.

Braungart and McDonough's book itself is a physical example of their concept: It was printed on a synthetic "paper," made from corn-based plastic. When you want to get rid of the book, you can recycle it and the book can be made into more of the same books, without downgrading into something else. This loop is an endless one, and it's an example of true cradle-to-cradle thinking.

The ideas from Cradle to Cradle have spawned a variety of resources. You can find them online at:

✔ **MBDC (www.mbdc.com):** MBDC is a product design firm established by McDonough and Brangart (the same guys behind the book) that helps develop true cradle-to-cradle materials. Exciting new C2C materials are being invented each day, and you can learn more about their design process here.

Biomimicry: Looking to nature for design inspiration

Biomimicry is a new science dedicated to studying the elegant designs of nature to gain insight into how to solve human problems. For example, studying how a leaf converts sunlight into energy can teach us how to invent a better solar panel. Think of biomimicry as innovation inspired by nature.

The core idea behind biomimicry is that nature, imaginative by necessity, has already solved the most challenging design problems. Animals, plants, and microorganisms are skillful engineers. The systems of nature exist as a 3.8-billion-year-old research-and-development (R&D) department.

Our current way of life — consuming all the natural resources and polluting the remaining food sources — doesn't work. Biomimicry offers an opportunity to learn from the sustainable and time-tested systems of nature.

Look at these examples from nature, and the man-made inventions they inspired:

✔ **Abalone mussel nacre (mother-of-pearl coating):** This abalone coating inspired hard coatings for windshields and bodies of solar cars, airplanes, and anything that needs to be lightweight but fracture resistant.

✔ **Antlers, teeth, bones, and shells:** You can now buy a three-dimensional printer, which builds 3D objects layer by layer, as inspired by natural biomineralization.

✔ **Barbs on weed seeds:** Barbs on weed seeds inspired Velcro, perhaps the most well-known biomimetic invention.

✔ **Blue mussel adhesive:** Blue mussel adhesive inspired a man-made underwater adhesive. Unlike traditional glues, this new type of adhesive sets underwater and doesn't need a primer, an initiator, or a catalyst to work. This idea could revolutionize paints and coatings, and enable surgeons to operate without sutures.

✔ **Blue mussel byssus sealant:** The natural sealant (called byssus) that a blue mussel creates inspired an alternative to plastics. This time-release coating for disposable cups, utensils, and plates lasts for a few months and then biodegrades, allowing the material underneath to be composted.

✔ **Dolphin and shark skin:** Dolphin and shark skin inspired Olympic swimsuits. The hydrodynamic texture of shark skin was the inspiration for these swimsuits, allowing less friction from the water and faster swim times.

✔ **Fish antifreeze:** The natural antifreeze in fishes' bodies inspired a type of man-made antifreeze used to freeze human transplant organs without injury.

✔ **Spider web:** Spider webs have inspired ultrastrong man-made wires. Fiber is manufactured without using intense heat, pressure, or toxic chemicals, and it's stronger and more resilient that anything we've used in the past. It has inspired innovative parachute cables, suspension bridges, surgical sutures, and more.

✔ **Bat navigation:** The sophisticated sonar of a bat was a model of modern sonar technology.

✔ **Bird wings:** Vulture wings inspired the invention of the airplane. The Wright brothers were avid birdwatchers, and they modeled the wings of their plane on the shape of bird wings.

✔ **GreenBlue (www.greenblue.org):** GreenBlue is the nonprofit arm of MDBC (see the preceding bullet). GreenBlue educates the public about C2C ideas. This Web site has several resources, including an online training for people to understand C2C.

✔ **MDBC Cradle to Cradle Certification (www.c2ccertified.com):** This is the Web site for the certification program for products wanting to become labeled as cradle to cradle. You'll find the complete list of C2C products here.

✔ **C2C Home (www.c2c-home.org):** A housing design competition to develop a home based on C2C principles. The competition is open to anyone, but you'll enjoy seeing the ideas behind the previous winners.

Setting Priorities and Goals for Your Home

Green building is riddled with contradictions. Take, for example, the following questions:

✔ Should you choose the bamboo that was sustainably harvested, but came from 3,000 miles away? Or should you opt for the wood from trees that *weren't* sustainably harvested but were grown locally?

✔ Should you keep your existing inefficient appliances? Or should you purchase new, Energy Star–rated appliances?

✔ Does a recycled content material work? Or should you buy something recyclable?

✔ Are you better off selecting the durable vinyl trim? Or is painted wood trim better?

There is no such thing as a perfect material, so these questions (and the myriad others like them) don't have any direct answers.

You need to evaluate each question on a project-by-project basis. For example, if you plan on remodeling again in just a few years, using the bamboo would not be the most environmentally correct choice. But if this floor will be around for the next foreseeable decade or so, bamboo may be a wise decision.

Here's my recommended list of priorities when it comes to choosing products for your green building or remodeling project. The items at the top of the list are more important than the ones at the bottom of the list.

✔ **Natural, nontoxic:** These products are healthy, nonsynthetic, and grown (not mixed).

✔ **Low embodied energy:** These products are easy to gather and nonpolluting.

✔ **Sustainably harvested:** These products are gathered without completely destroying the source.

✔ **Recyclable/biodegradable:** These products can be reused or fed back into the earth.

✔ **Recycled content:** These products contain a high percentage of materials that used to be something else.

✔ **Locally harvested:** These products didn't travel more than 500 miles to reach you.

✔ **Durable:** These products are built to last and don't require ongoing maintenance.

Feel free to rearrange these priorities to fit your own values. The key is to set these priorities before you find yourself standing in your home-improvement store or talking about products with your contractor. That way, you'll be prepared for all the decisions you need to make.

Today, you have the option of dozens of green, healthy, and more responsible new materials. For every traditional, unhealthy finish you normally find in a building, a green substitute exists. In most cases, you can play this substitution game on a one-for-one basis. Table 6-2 provides some examples. (*Remember:* This isn't an exhaustive list — these are just a few examples.)

Table 6-2	Green Material Substitutions
Instead of . . .	*Try . . .*
Latex wall paints	Zero-VOC paints
Vinyl floor tile	Natural linoleum
Oil-based floor sealers	Water-based sealers or natural linseed oil
Drywall wall panels	100 percent recycled gypsum panels
Vinyl wallpaper bamboo	Natural fabrics, such as hemp, jute, sawgrass, or
Melamine plastic cabinets (white)	Formaldehyde-free medium density fiberboard (MDF)

Instead of . . .	Try . . .
Carpet with vinyl backing	Carpet with natural fiber backing
Plastic carpet padding	Natural jute carpet padding
Plastic tiles and countertops	Recycled glass tiles, recycled quarry tiles, or recycled paper resin panels

Instead of seeing the lack of simple, straightforward answers about materials as a problem, try to look at them as opportunities. At each stage of the life cycle, you have the opportunity to improve on the impact and save money. Table 6-3 lists some of these opportunities.

Table 6-3	Opportunities throughout a Material's Life Cycle
Stage of the Life Cycle	**Opportunities**
Raw-material source	Choose sustainably harvested wood. Use products made of reclaimed materials. Choose finishes with a high recycled content.
Supply-chain process	Avoid mined materials, such as granite and gypsum. Avoid synthetic polymers.
Manufacturing process	Use fly-ash concrete. Use products with a low embodied energy. Select materials you can create on-site, such as mixed concrete.
Delivery/receiving	Use local materials. Hire local craftspeople.
Installation	Design modular sections to reduce construction waste. Focus on standard sizes (2 x 4, 4 x 8, and so on) to save money and speed up construction time.
Operation	Opt for solar or alternative energy. Install low-flow plumbing fixtures. Avoid painted finishes.
Repair	Use modular fixtures. Use tiles instead of full carpet.

(continued)

Table 6-3 *(continued)*	
Stage of the Life Cycle	*Opportunities*
Reuse	Salvage what's there instead of demolishing it and starting over. Use existing buildings.
Disassembly	Use recyclable materials. Avoid PVC — it's nearly impossible to recycle.

Remodeling an Old Home with Green Materials

Older homes pose certain challenges in remodeling. As an architect in San Francisco, I often work with older Victorian homes with small rooms, undated and unusual additions, and a lack of any insulation in the walls. People are quick to want to simply demolish and build a new building. But not only do older buildings have a certain charm that their newer counterparts can't fake, but you can save thousands of pounds of new materials by remodeling an older home.

In the following sections, I outline some of the common issues that always seem to come up in remodeling old homes. Don't panic! These are normal issues for you to be on the lookout for.

Salvaging the wood

The studs in an older home are typically old growth wood, in true size 2-x-4-inch studs, and they're very easy to salvage and reuse. The walls you remove may be over the existing wood floor and a simple refinishing will revive those old floors.

But watch out! You can't simply take old wood and use it to build a new structural wall. Consult with your architect or structural engineer before doing anything structural with salvaged wood.

Demolishing a few old walls is minor, but you'll probably need a permit from your local building department.

Being aware of asbestos

Asbestos is a durable, insulating, fire-resistant material widely used from the 1950s through the 1970s. When certain unusual cancer cases were attributed to asbestos, the use of it was banned. Lurking under your current carpet or wood floor may be old asbestos tiles. That old resilient sheet flooring in your home may not be vinyl — if it's more than 30 years old, the floor could be vinyl asbestos tile (VAT). Covering the side of your home may be asbestos shingles.

Asbestos is only an immediate threat if the material is broken, releasing fibers into the air. If it's intact, most asbestos-containing products don't pose a significant health threat. But exposure to asbestos dust is dangerous! If you own an older home and you're planning to do any remodeling, check with your local building department for more information on asbestos *abatement* (removal). You may need a licensed asbestos abatement contractor to do the job.

Asbestos cannot (and should not) be recycled. The licensed abatement contractor will dispose of it for you.

Looking out for lead paint

For centuries, lead was used as a pigment and binding agent in most paints. Banned in 1978, lead-based paints were found to cause nervous system damage, hearing loss, stunted growth, reduced IQ, and delayed development. It is especially dangerous to young children whose immune systems are still developing. Lead affects every organ in the body. And children are not the only ones at risk. Adults are not immune from the dangers of lead paint; for example, it can cause reproductive problems in men.

A common misconception about lead-based paint is that it's harmful to children because they eat large flakes of broken lead paint. In reality, the children unknowingly inhale microscopic dust.

The most practical method of protecting everyone in your home from lead-based paint is to keep any old paint intact. Do not sand, scrape, or remove any old paint until you're sure it isn't lead based. You can buy a lead testing kit at your local hardware store. A licensed paint contractor can also help.

A professional lead-abatement specialist can remove lead-based paint in your home. Your local painter can provide referrals for these professionals.

Finding Green Materials

If you want to use green materials in your building or remodeling project, your next step is figuring out where to find them. Given the popularity of green building, finding green materials has never been easier. Here are some fantastic resources to try, in addition to your local home-improvement center:

- ✔ **American Institute of Architects (AIA):** For years, the AIA's Committee on the Environment (COTE) has been a place where architects could discuss how to green their buildings. Today the AIA provides resources and case studies for homeowners to use to green their homes. Contact the local chapter of the AIA (you can find it in the phone book or at `www.aia.org`) and ask about their green resources. You'll also be able to find a local architect familiar with green building through your local AIA chapter.

- ✔ **BuildingGreen.com:** The publishers of *Environmental Building News* and the *GreenSpec Directory* have put all their unbiased and perfectly presented information together in a wonderfully straightforward site. Their reasonable fee (a one-week subscription costs $12.95) provides access to their wealth of research reports and product findings. Organized by construction categories and homeowner categories, BuildingGreen has emerged as the *Consumer Reports* of green building.

- ✔ **GreenHomeGuide (`www.greenhomeguide.com`):** Targeted at homeowners, GreenHomeGuide provides reviews and descriptions of green products by the professionals using them. Their know-how sections provide all the information you need for greening a kitchen or a bathroom.

- ✔ **Manufacturer sales reps:** When visiting product showrooms and talking to the salesperson, communicate to them your desire for green products. Start the conversation and you'll be surprised by the suggestions they provide. Many traditional manufacturers are offering greener versions of their products.

- ✔ **U.S. Green Building Council (USGBC):** The USGBC is a valuable source for data in regard to green building, great for making the argument to skeptical developers and city officials. One of the reasons for the creation of the USGBC was to provide a credible authority on green building, so use them as such. You can point to their combined experience and knowledge to find hundreds of reports and case studies. Visit their online resources at `www.usgbc.org`.

- ✔ **Local showrooms:** Each month, new showrooms open up around the United States offering green materials. Although these showrooms initially opened around the green-building hubs (San Francisco, California; Austin, Texas; Portland, Oregon), new stores are open in Santa Monica, California; Chicago, Illinois; and even Fairfield, Iowa. Your architect or contractor will be able to help you find a local showroom, but the green product manufacturers you find online can also point you to local distributors.

✔ **City offices:** Dozens of cities have a Department of the Environment or something similar. These departments deal with green building, environmental justice, and toxics disposal. If you can't locate one in your city, look at the county and state level. Your local recycling collection company can also point you to a waste-management authority or commission. Such departments are invaluable resources and can provide you with information you never knew existed. Chances are they will carry a directory of local green resources and showrooms.

Knowing Whether Manufacturers Are Telling the Truth

Finding green products is one thing, but knowing which products you can trust is another.

Sustainable building is hot, and a flood of new products tout vague and cryptic claims to be green. When overzealous product manufacturers go from tiny overstatements to outright lies about their products, it's called *greenwashing,* and it can be deceptive or even dangerous.

Determining whether the product you're buying is truly green can be a tricky business. You need to ask questions and look for trusted seals of approval.

Beware of false certifications or pseudo nonprofits. Referred to as *astroturf,* these fake grass-roots organizations are typically funded by the very polluters they promote. Take for example, the Competitive Enterprise Institute (CEI). Calling itself a nonprofit dedicated to "advancing the principles of free enterprise," it has been one of the most vocal naysayers of global warming. In reality, CEI is a front funded by Exxon Mobil, Pfizer, GM, the American Petroleum Institute, and others. Many of these astroturf organizations exist, lending false credibility to harmful products.

In the building world, the Vinyl Institute, a trade association representing the leading manufacturers of vinyl, spends considerable amounts of money to promote the "energy-saving, environmental and health benefits" of vinyl as a building product. The realities of vinyl are somewhat different. Referred to as the "poison plastic" by many, the "asbestos of the 21st century" by others, vinyl is considered one of the most environmentally damaging materials produced. (The Healthy Building Network has developed a drive educating consumers about vinyl; Greenpeace has a campaign showing how to go "PVC-free.") The Vinyl Institute, with an estimated annual budget in the millions, can continue to cloud consumers' judgment through a series of astroturf Web sites implying a scientific basis for the healthy characteristics of vinyl. When a 2002 documentary, *Blue Vinyl,* exposed some of these facts, it was the Vinyl Institute who launched a folksy-looking Web site to dissuade you from believing it.

Don't believe everything you hear. Just remember to follow three simple rules when looking at any material:

- ✔ **Follow trusted certifications.** (See Chapter 5 for a list of respected and trusted green product certifications.)

- ✔ **Get the facts online.** SourceWatch (`www.sourcewatch.org`) is a non-profit with market research on hundreds of corporations and these astroturf organizations. The reporting is impartial and well researched.

- ✔ **Follow the money.** Visit the Web site of the organization making the environmental claims. Look at the "About" section to see where its funding comes from. If it's backed by a corporation with a vested interest, chances are, it's astroturf.

Chapter 7

Green Finish and Construction Materials

In This Chapter

▶ Identifying the hidden health dangers in your home

▶ Finding green alternatives to traditional building finishes

▶ Exploring new wall, floor, and counter finishes

*P*erhaps no other aspect of green building garners more attention or excitement than the finishes inside the home. My clients' faces light up when the time comes to select the multitude of tile, paint, and counter finishes to complete their homes. In this chapter, I fill you in on all the options in covering your floors, walls, and ceilings. In addition, I explore the necessary adhesives, caulks, and other materials lurking and hiding behind your walls. This chapter makes the daunting task of finding and selecting green finishes easier.

As you see in Figure 7-1, a traditional room offers many opportunities for going green with your finishes and construction materials.

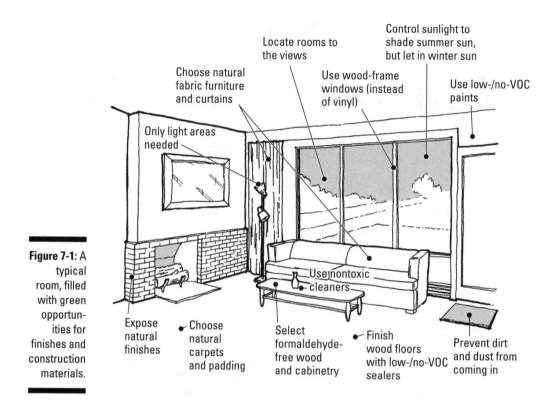

Locate rooms to the views

Control sunlight to shade summer sun, but let in winter sun

Choose natural fabric furniture and curtains

Use wood-frame windows (instead of vinyl)

Use low-/no-VOC paints

Only light areas needed

Figure 7-1: A typical room, filled with green opportunities for finishes and construction materials.

Expose natural finishes

Choose natural carpets and padding

Select formaldehyde-free wood and cabinetry

Use nontoxic cleaners

Finish wood floors with low-/no-VOC sealers

Prevent dirt and dust from coming in

Identifying the Dangers in Traditional Finishes

Most standard construction materials contain a wide array of unhealthy or toxic chemicals. You don't need to put these materials in your mouth to be affected by them. The chemicals in the products *offgas* (release into the room) harmful chemicals.

Figure 7-2 shows some of these common chemicals hidden in your home, lurking behind the walls. Because you can't see the chemicals, preventing them from entering your home is more of a challenge.

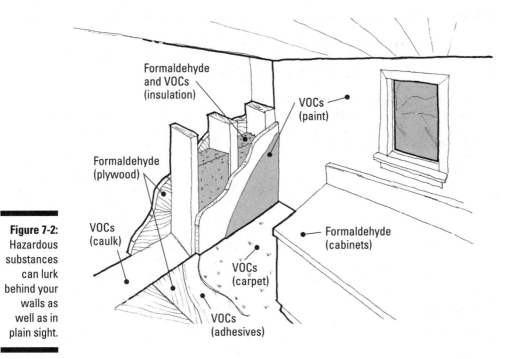

Labels in figure:
Formaldehyde and VOCs (insulation)
VOCs (paint)
Formaldehyde (plywood)
Formaldehyde (cabinets)
VOCs (caulk)
VOCs (carpet)
VOCs (adhesives)

Volatile organic compounds

You know that new carpet or new paint smell? I've got news for you: That smell is not a good thing. In fact, what you're sniffing are harmful chemicals known as volatile organic compounds (VOCs). When you install traditional products, they begin to evaporate and release these VOCs into the air, which results in that familiar odor. Even after the odor goes away, though, these materials continue to release VOCs.

Just because you can't smell anything doesn't mean the air is clear. The drying of paints, stains, caulks, and adhesives all can release VOCs into the air.

VOCs can refer to a large number of potentially harmful chemicals. The long-term effects of exposure to VOCs are still not fully understood. Because the VOCs come from dozens of sources around your house, it's impossible to point to one specific chemical or side effect.

Although you can't see VOCs, if you build or remodel your home with low- or no-VOC finishes, you'll notice a difference. A healthy, green home doesn't smell.

Multiple chemical sensitivity: A possible result of not going green

Thousands of people live with multiple chemical sensitivity (MCS). Generally speaking, MCS is an unusually severe sensitivity to chemicals, including VOCs. Like allergies, people with MCS suffer from:

- Dizziness
- Fatigue
- Headaches
- Irritability
- Itching
- Lack of concentration
- Memory problems
- Muscle and joint pain
- Nausea
- Rashes
- Sneezing
- Sore throat

But unlike simple allergies, these reactions are caused from exposure to the countless chemicals in homes, cars, and offices.

Many doctors don't recognize MCS as a true disorder, but those who have been diagnosed with it will attest to its effects. The U.S. Environmental Protection Agency reports that about one-third of people working in sealed buildings are chemically sensitive.

Here's how it works: You wake up in the morning on synthetic sheets, washed with detergent and bleach. Your windows have been closed all night, so you've been breathing in the chemicals from the VOC paint, toxic adhesives, and formaldehyde cabinetry. You don't give a thought to the synthetic compounds in the makeup you apply to your face. At work, you're exposed to artificial sweetener in your coffee, perfumes from coworkers, and a cloud of cigarette smoke at the front door. The windows don't open in your office building either, so you breathe in toner from the copy machine, mites from the carpet, and plastic from the partitions trapped in the office. When you return home at night, you clean the home with more chemicals, vacuum the synthetic-backed carpets, and sit on a sofa stuffed with chemical foam cushions.

Diagnosing and treating MCS is difficult because it's the combination of all these chemical exposures and not a single product causing the symptoms. Treatment requires removing all these chemicals from your home and living a truly nontoxic life.

For more information on MCS, consult the following resources:

- Multiple Chemical Sensitivity Referral and Resources: www.mcsrr.org
- MCS Survivors: www.mcsurvivors.com
- Debra Lynn Dadd, healthy building expert: www.dld123.com

Formaldehyde

One of the most common indoor pollutants is formaldehyde; the same chemical scientists use to preserve dead bodies. Formaldehyde is a known *carcinogen* (cancer-causing chemical). Formaldehyde-based adhesives are used throughout the construction process, from kitchen cabinets, to insulation, to furniture. Small particles of formaldehyde continue to be released into the air years after these products have been installed.

Hidden Materials: What's Behind the Walls

Hidden within your home, behind the walls and under the floors, lay dozens of materials that you probably don't even think about. But these materials can have a major impact on your health and the environment. Finding healthier and more sustainable substitutes for these unseen materials is important.

Insulation

Inside the walls of your home is some sort of insulation. Insulation helps your home hold in temperature to lower your heating and cooling bills, and it's the best thing you can do in your home to save energy. Generally, insulation is like a coat on a cold day — the thicker it is, the more comfortable you'll be inside.

For a new house, you should add as much insulation as will fit into the walls. For an existing home, adding insulation to finished walls is much more difficult. In either case, choose the insulation best for the health of you and your family.

Many different types of insulation are available. (In Chapter 11, I cover energy conservation and the various types of insulation.) Generally, formaldehyde is used as a binding agent in most insulation products. Look for formaldehyde-free products instead:

 ✔ **Batt insulation:** Choose formaldehyde-free and recycled cotton insulation. Bonded Logic (www.bondedlogic.com) offers recycled cotton insulation made from old blue jeans, making the insulation batts blue in color.

- ✔ **Loose-fill cellulose:** Choose natural cellulose made from recycled newsprint. It's treated with natural chemicals to make it fire resistant. Cellulose is naturally formaldehyde free.

- ✔ **Spray-in foams:** Choose natural soy-based foams. They're healthier and offer all the benefits of spray foam.

Sheathing

No matter what type of siding you have on your home, whether it's stucco or vinyl, underneath it sits a hidden layer of plywood called *sheathing.* Sheathing adds strength to your walls and serves as a barrier to moisture.

The typical type of sheathing used is plywood, which comes from trees and is glued together with a toxic formaldehyde-based binder. As a green substitute, select plywood that's certified by the Forest Stewardship Council (FSC) and is formaldehyde free.

Oriented-strand board (OSB) is an efficient alternative to plywood. OSB is made of small scraps of low-grade wood. As with any wood product, choosing FSC-certified wood with formaldehyde-free glue is a good idea. Because plywood adds strength to your walls, you should check with your architect or structural engineer to see if OSB will provide enough strength for your project.

Caulks and adhesives

In order to fill the thousands of cracks and leaks in a typical home, a sealant called *caulk* is typically used. Sealing these cracks is an important part of saving energy in a building, but these products are typically made from chemicals containing VOCs, and are blown in using ozone-depleting chlorofluorocarbons (CFCs).

Adhesives are also used throughout a building in hundreds of hidden locations. These adhesives typically contain toxic chemicals containing VOCs.

Look for products with non-ozone-depleting blowing agents. Look for the term *ozone-safe* on the label. Also, choose water-based products with low-VOC or zero-VOC content.

Stains and sealers

The countless stains, sealers, and lacquers used in a home typically go unnoticed. Because they're traditionally oil-based, when you use these products you have to wear gloves and a mask. After installation, they continue to give off fumes for years — and unless you're wearing a mask 24/7, you're breathing in those fumes.

Choose water-based and low-VOC or zero-VOC products instead. You'll be thankful for the headache you *don't* get after using it.

All-natural linseed oil (made from flax seed) is a healthy and effective sealant for wall and floor surfaces. Just make sure to avoid linseed oils mixed with drying agents; these add unnecessary toxins into the air. Natural beeswax is a wonderful finish for plaster, concrete, and furniture.

Walls

Whether the walls of your home are constructed out of traditional wood framing, or built green out of straw bales, all your walls must be completed with some protective and decorative finish. In this section, I cover the various types of wall finishes available and let you know what to look for when you're shopping.

Paints and coatings

Some 40,000 years ago, people covered their walls with early cave paintings drawn with natural pigments of red ochre and charcoal. Although we still decorate our walls, paint has evolved into the ubiquitous finish for all our interiors.

Paint poses some potential health concerns because it consists of pigments held together with a binding agent. These binding agents contain VOCs, which are released into the air.

Nearly all the major paint manufacturers now offer a low-VOC line of paints, but be careful: The term *low* is hard to define. Check the labels for the exact content of VOCs. Instead of low-VOC, purchase zero-VOC paints from healthy-paint manufacturers such as AFM Safecoat (www.afmsafecoat.com), Bioshield (www.bioshieldpaint.com), or Auro Paints (www.aurousa.com).

Always wear gloves and a respirator mask while painting, especially if you're using a paint sprayer. After painting, open the windows and flush the home with fresh air for a few days. If you're preparing a nursery for a baby on the way, paint the room at least a month before your little bundle arrives. All these measures will lead to a healthier and happier home.

Recycle or donate all your leftover paint. Your local salvage yard or hardware store may take back your remaining gallons. *Never dump paint down the drain.*

Originally, the pigments in paint contained high amounts of lead, a toxic and persistent chemical linked to damage to the nervous system of children. The use of lead-based paint was banned in 1978 by the U.S. Consumer Product Safety Commission. Unfortunately, if your home was built before 1950, it may still contain traces of this old paint that, if cracked or flaking, is very harmful to your health and especially the health of your children. Kids touch everything around the house. Even tiny amounts of lead paint dust can be picked up by small fingers, and then ingested when they put their fingers to their mouth. If you suspect that your home contains lead-based paint, contact a lead abatement specialist right away.

Earthen plaster

As an alternative to paint, earthen plaster is a beautiful finish for your walls. Made from a pure mix of clay and natural pigments, earthen plaster is also healthy and naturally mold resistant.

The plaster is applied directly onto drywall with a trowel and can be finished smooth or with a heavy texture for a variety of looks. Applying earthen plaster is surprisingly easy to do yourself, and you can keep any leftover plaster and reuse it in the future simply by adding some water.

Plaster works well if used in a damp area such as a bathroom, but you'll want to seal with a water-based sealer any areas that may get splashed.

Wall coverings

For something more interesting than a solid color of paint, wall coverings offer a way to introduce patterns and textures into your home. Unfortunately, most wallpaper is made of vinyl, an environmentally harmful product.

Vinyl, and why to avoid it

When most people think of vinyl, they probably think fondly of their old vinyl LP records. But the truth about vinyl, often referred to as the "poison plastic," is less romantic. Vinyl is the worst plastic from an environmental health perspective, posing great environmental and health hazards in its manufacture, product life, and disposal.

Polyvinyl chloride, commonly known as PVC or vinyl, is one of the most common synthetic materials. PVC is a versatile resin and appears in thousands of different formulations and configurations.

Approximately 75 percent of all PVC manufactured is used in construction materials. It creeps into all sorts of unlikely building products.

For more information on vinyl, I recommend the award-winning documentary *Blue Vinyl* (www.bluevinyl.org), which provides as insightful and often funny look at vinyl. If you can't find it at your local video store, you can get it through Netflix (www.netflix.com). (Check out Chapter 5 for more on vinyl.)

Skip the vinyl and instead look at the large number of beautiful options available. Natural fibers such as jute and raffia create a soft texture on your walls. Natural paper wall coverings are available from several manufacturers, with an incredible assortment of colors and patterns. Old-fashioned wallpaper paste is already natural and healthy, so choose it over synthetic brands.

If you're thinking about putting wallpaper in a damp location such as a bathroom, you may want to reconsider. If water seeps into the wallpaper, mold can grow undetected under the paper, creating a health hazard.

Drywall

Drywall, also known as gypsum wallboard, is one of the most common materials used in construction today. All the walls in your home are likely covered with drywall, which you've coated in paint or wallpaper. Drywall accounts for more than a quarter of all construction waste. Its chief ingredient, gypsum, has to be mined out of the earth and requires an immense amount of energy to produce. All this effort gives off carbon dioxide and other greenhouse gases.

Drywall made from recycled and synthetic gypsum is now readily available; you just have to ask for it. The backing is already made from 100 percent recycled, unbleached paper that is bonded without adhesives onto a gypsum core.

Recycled or natural?

Recycled or natural? This question harkens back to the old "paper or plastic" debate. In reality, most architects and contractors do not want to get into a philosophical (and perhaps even semantic) argument about the pros and cons between these two types of materials.

Although some people would advise you to avoid any and all plastic, certain applications may be appropriate for using recycled plastic. In the walls, perhaps using recycled plastic vapor barriers makes more sense.

Some natural materials release harmful chemicals as well (for example, the natural occurrence of formaldehyde in wood). Just because something is natural doesn't guarantee the healthiness of that material.

Remember: There is no perfect material. All materials have some negative impact on our environment. The key is in setting priorities for the project.

Keep in mind that the boards come in standard heights of 8 feet, 9 feet, and 10 feet. Designing to those ceiling heights will reduce cutting and waste, and save you money as well.

Wood paneling and cabinetry

Wood adds a warm and visually interesting finish to any room. A thin *veneer,* or skin, of real wood is typically glued over a panel of compressed particleboard to create wood paneling. Although this process uses less wood than solid pieces, the particleboard is commonly held together with urea-formaldehyde, a known carcinogen and health hazard.

Request formaldehyde-free particleboard for your panels and cabinets as a healthier option. For the veneer, select woods certified by the Forest Stewardship Council (FSC) to ensure that the wood has come from a sustainable source. Avoid tropical hardwoods — they come from the rain forest and contribute to its destruction. Panels of solid bamboo, a grass, are a greener and more unique alternative.

Wall base and trim

The trim molding lining the walls at the floor, and possibly the ceiling, of your home serves two purposes:

 ✔ Trim adds elegance and style to any room.

 ✔ Trim covers the edges of the wall plaster where it meets the floor
   or ceiling.

Use trim made from small scraps of wood finger-jointed together. After you
paint it, you'll never see the pieces.

Avoid vinyl and fiberglass trim entirely; both are bad for your heath and
the environment.

Floor Finishes

The floors of your home reflect the function and purpose of each room. A
wood floor conveys a more formal feeling, while carpet is more about comfort and walking around with your shoes off. The floor you choose will last
you for 10 to 50 years at least, so be sure to pick something beautiful.

Because the floor covers such a large area, it has a huge influence on the
indoor air quality in your home. Your kids, guests, and pets walk on your
floors, wearing them down and breathing in the chemicals they give off. Here
I explore greener and healthier alternatives for flooring.

Wood flooring

Because they're easy to clean, hardwood floors are great for indoor air
quality and for people with allergies. Traditional wood flooring comes from —
drum roll, please — trees. (Shocking, isn't it?) Although wood is a renewable
resource (people can plant more trees), wood used for flooring is typically
harvested from the clear-cutting of forests. More sustainably harvested options
are available, coming from sources where no trees were clear-cut or harmed to
make your floor.

Look for wood certified by the Forest Stewardship Council (FSC). Anything
certified by the FSC came from a managed forest — not from clear-cutting.
Expect to pay 20 percent more for sustainably harvested wood — but it's
worth the extra money just knowing you've done the right thing.

If you choose floors that have been prefinished at the factory, those chemicals won't have to be brought into your home. If you do stain or seal the floors, choose low-VOC or zero-VOC, water-based products.

Reclaimed wood

Reclaimed wood is salvaged from unusual sources, such as old barns, train trestles, or bridges in the process of being demolished. Although all wood flooring is warm, these recycled woods add particular warmth to a room because of their weathering and flaws. Because it's salvaged from older buildings, reclaimed wood was originally from old-growth trees, so the quality of the wood is far superior to anything available today. The rich wood grain of this old-growth wood is incredibly beautiful. Reclaimed wood commonly contains old rust stains, nail holes, or patched joints, all of which add character and charm to the wood's appearance.

With the rising cost of new wood, more building suppliers now offer reclaimed and salvaged wood options. The energy needed to salvage the wood is still far less than the impact of clear-cutting new trees.

Bamboo

In the past few years, bamboo has become the best known and most popular of the green flooring options. Technically, bamboo is not wood — it's a grass, and some species can grow up to 3 feet in a day. To harvest it, the stalks are cut, leaving the plant intact to continue to grow. Unlike with wood, nothing is killed or destroyed in the process, and this is what makes bamboo such an environmentally attractive option.

Unfortunately, most bamboo comes from Asia, and shipping it such long distances requires a great deal of energy. More local sources are now becoming available.

Although many people imagine an island hut when they think of bamboo, the finished bamboo floor closely resembles traditional wood flooring. It installs in the exact same way and you may not even notice the distinctive knuckle pattern in the bamboo. The grain is incredibly durable and it's stronger than oak, one of the strongest woods.

Like most floors, bamboo flooring is available in a prefinished surface, reducing the need to add sealers or coatings.

Be sure to select water-based and low- or zero-VOC sealers.

Laminated wood

Laminate flooring is a durable particleboard base covered with a plastic photograph of wood grain. The result is an incredibly durable, nearly indestructible floor perfect for high-traffic areas. The planks arrive already finished, so no extra sealing is required.

Although the particleboard is mostly compressed sawdust, it is held together with a binder of formaldehyde, a known toxin. Look for formaldehyde-free wood, sourced with wood certified by the Forest Stewardship Council (FSC). Seal the cut edges of the planks to prevent the formaldehyde from being released into the air.

Laminate flooring options made from bamboo are also available.

Carpeting

Carpeting is the ubiquitous floor covering in the United States, desired as much for its texture as for its ability to cover a variety of hidden sins underneath. Carpet provides a soft, warm, and sound-absorbing surface. Combine all that with carpeting's low cost per square foot and it's the most selected floor covering in the country, covering 70 percent of American floors.

However, in its short life span, carpet attracts dust and allergens. Once considered the status symbol of a luxurious home, carpet is now among a long list of related indoor air-quality problems and material-waste issues. (Nearly 5 billion pounds of discarded carpet end up in landfills each year.)

In the 1990s, after receiving over 500 complaints about carpet-related health effects, the U.S. Consumer Product Safety Commission (CPSC) commissioned a study examining carpet chemical emissions. The landmark study identified dozens of toxic chemicals released from carpets, many of them known carcinogens. That "new carpet smell" is the smell of chemicals being released into the air.

Carpet, especially wall-to-wall carpet, has several inherent environmental issues:

- ✔ **It is typically made from synthetic, oil-based materials.** These materials are considered toxic and release harmful chemicals.

- ✔ **Carpet is typically backed with vinyl (PVC).** Vinyl is harmful at every stage of its life cycle.

✓ **The synthetic and mixed materials make carpet (nearly) impossible to recycle.**

✓ **Carpet requires a great deal of energy to maintain, because it must be vacuumed.**

✓ **Vacuuming alone does not clean carpet, and instead creates an environment in which pests, mold, and mildew can reside.** Carpet is host to numerous indoor air-quality issues, including the spread of asthma.

Luckily, a select group of carpet manufacturers have addressed some or all of these issues. Some of these initiatives include such wonderful ideas as:

✓ Carpet made from natural, renewable fibers and materials

✓ Carpet backed with natural, healthy materials like wool

✓ Take-back programs, where the manufacturers accept the carpet at the end of its use and recycle it back into their supply chain

✓ Carpet tile, which is an environmentally preferable alternative to wall-to-wall carpeting, because damaged tiles can be individually replaced without having to replace an entire floor (Although it takes more energy to produce the tiles, several manufacturers, such as Interface [`www.interfaceflor.com`], produce a recycled content and recyclable carpet tile in a wide array of interesting colors and patterns.)

Used sparingly at entranceways, carpet can be used to control pollutants being tracked into a building.

Look for the Carpet and Rug Institute's Green Label Plus certification as an assurance of sustainability (see Chapter 5).

Padding is installed below the rug as a cushion. Avoid synthetic padding; opt for natural jute padding instead. If installed over concrete, adhesives are often used to glue it down. Skip the glue; it typically contains toxic VOCs and makes replacing or removing the carpet much more difficult. In addition, the glue guarantees that the carpet will be unrecyclable.

Cork

Harvested from the bark of an oak cork tree, cork is considered a *rapidly renewable material,* because it grows back in just five to seven years without harming the tree. Most people imagine a corkboard when they think of cork floors, but in reality, cork flooring comes in a wide array of gorgeous patterns and styles and has been in use for well over 50 years. (The famed architect

Frank Lloyd Wright often installed cork in his kitchens.) Cork flooring is surprisingly durable, providing an attractive, healthy, and biodegradable surface for your home.

The prefinished tiles provide a soft and comfortable walking surface, giving off a pleasant hickory smell. The cork naturally resists water, making it a great choice for kitchens and bathrooms.

Although all-natural cork is sustainably harvested, it typically comes from Mediterranean countries, requiring a lot of energy to transport it. Several manufacturers now offer cork flooring made in the United States from recycled wine bottle corks, reducing the travel distance.

Be sure to avoid cork flooring backed or mixed with vinyl. Choose a zero-VOC adhesive to install and seal the surface with a natural wax twice a year.

Vinyl tile

At first glance, vinyl flooring seems like a great material. Inexpensive, easy to install, and durable, vinyl is one of the most popular flooring choices — 14 billion pounds of it are produced each year in North America alone. But the reality of vinyl shows it to be a health hazard at every stage of its life.

Vinyl releases poisonous dioxins into the atmosphere when it's produced. It gives off very harmful chemicals after it's installed. And it's nearly impossible to recycle.

Vinyl is the most environmentally destructive material used in buildings today. Unfortunately, vinyl is found in hundreds of building products. From plumbing pipes to flooring to wall base, vinyl is everywhere. Because it's so bad throughout its life cycle, avoid it at all costs.

Linoleum

Invented in 1860 by rubber manufacturer Fredrick Walton, linoleum quickly became the floor and wall covering of choice for Victorian homes, and has been in use ever since. Though vinyl tiles replaced linoleum in popularity back in the 1960s, the surging interest in green materials is helping linoleum make a comeback.

Linoleum is a natural product made of linseed oil, pigments, pine rosin, and pine flour (sawdust). It's covered with a natural jute backing. The finished material is thin and incredibly durable. It becomes harder in areas of high traffic. A linoleum floor can last 50 years.

As a green alternative to vinyl, linoleum offers numerous other advantages. The color and patterns are dyed all the way through to the backing, ensuring that the floor will not wear away. Linoleum is natural, making it biodegradable as well. Linseed oil is a natural antimicrobial agent, making it a great choice for kitchens.

Be sure to purchase only "natural linoleum," because the term *linoleum* is sometimes mistakenly used to refer to a generic vinyl or linoleum floor. Avoid installing linoleum in damp areas, such as basements. Use only low-VOC or zero-VOC adhesives to install it.

Concrete

Sometimes you don't need to install any floor at all. Leaving the concrete slab exposed is a great way to save money on additional flooring. Generally, your contractor will take more care in finishing concrete that will remain exposed. In addition, numerous finishing options — from stains to pigments to acid etching — offer a wide variety of design flexibility.

In order to control cracking, a small joint is cut into the concrete every 20 feet or so. You can arrange these cuts, called *control joints,* in interesting patterns and angles for more visual interest.

Earthen floors

Perhaps the most environmentally friendly flooring option is good, old-fashioned dirt or earth. Called an *earthen floor,* it offers some interesting options.

Technically, a true modern-day earthen floor comes in various mixtures. Some are a mix of cement and earth (as in rammed-earth construction). The type of earth chosen makes a large difference in the durability. For example, the more clay content in the earth, the more susceptible it is to cracking from changes in water content (the clay expands and contracts quite a bit).

If you're buying commercial-grade soils for this floor, you can select a "plasticity index," to select the exact amount of clay content. Most single-family houses just collect soil left over from the excavation for the house. The correct soil will stabilize and prevent cracking — but there are no guarantees.

Construction waste

The construction of a typical new home produces enough waste to fill one of the bedrooms of that home, nearly 8,000 pounds of waste. In addition, Americans remodel about half a million square feet of existing space each year. This adds up, and construction waste is responsible for some 35 percent to 45 percent of what ends up in U.S. landfills.

In order to combat the issue of construction waste, many cities are now requiring that a certain percentage of that waste be recycled before it ends up in the landfill. With waste-disposal costs rising steadily throughout the country, many builders have begun to view their debris as something to be managed rather than simply thrown away. In fact, a construction waste-management plan can provide both short-term and long-term payoffs. Disposal is a relatively small portion of the construction budget — only about ½ percent of the cost of the typical home. But with the average builder earning a 5 percent profit margin, this small improvement can make a large difference.

Although hauling waste to the landfill may seem like the path of least resistance, managing your construction waste is easier than you think. Instead of throwing everything into a large dumpster, group debris into neatly organized piles. Not only will this make recycling easier, but these scraps will be reused during construction.

Because wood constitutes nearly 50 percent of construction waste, a separate pile for wood will be put to good use. Other suggested recycling piles include piles for drywall and metals. Any and all fixtures and appliances are easily recycled or sold. Look for opportunities to reuse materials when possible. Here's a breakdown of the construction waste for a typical 2,000-square-foot home.

Material	Weight (in Pounds)	Volume (in Cubic Yards)
Solid wood	1,600	6
Engineered wood	1,400	5
Drywall	2,000	5
Cardboard	600	20
Metals	150	1
Vinyl (PVC)	150	1
Masonry	1,000	1
Containers from paints, caulks, adhesives, and so on	50	-
Other	1,050	11
TOTAL	**8,000**	**50**

Be sure to seal the floor when complete. The best sealer available is simply boiled linseed oil, thinned with turpentine and brushed on in several coats. The odor will be gone in a week.

This system is the perfect complement for radiant heat. The thermal mass of the earth will store up the heat and maintain a nice, consistent temperature all winter long. You could also use the same system for radiant cooling, by running cool water through the same tubes.

Countertops

No other finish seems to get people as excited as countertops. Most people don't have strong feelings about toilet fixtures, roofing material, or exterior siding, but their eyes always light up when they talk about countertops.

People have an intimate connection with their countertops; you touch them and look at them every day. In recent years, countertops have become a bit of a status symbol for homeowners — granite, for some reason, has become the countertop of choice for high-end builders and, thus, for high-end kitchens. Although granite is both lovely and natural, there are many equally beautiful alternatives.

In this section, I fill you in on environmentally friendly countertop materials.

Granite and stone

Stone has a natural and timeless quality. There is a misconception that stone is too expensive for the average person, but the truth is that stone comes in a wide range of varieties and prices. Stone also has varying degrees of environmental impact. Marble and granite are mined deep out of the earth, but other stones (such as sandstone, slate, and soapstone) can be locally quarried without the same damage to the earth.

Natural stone is an elegant and durable finish. Unfortunately, stone is *nonrenewable* (we can't make more of it), and it requires huge amounts of energy to quarry, finish, transport, and install. The most popular stone types — granite, marble, sandstone, and limestone — must be transported long distances, using large amounts of energy. The impact from quarrying, cutting, and polishing the stone requires even more energy. The dust from the stone cutting is irritating and polluting.

As an alternative, look for salvaged stone. Your local salvage yard will carry some countertops saved from demolition. Salvaged stone is much less expensive, but your choice of colors will be limited.

Stone is sold in large slabs, not in pieces. When only a part of a slab is used, the remaining pieces are left behind. Every stone and marble yard has what they call a *boneyard* where these leftovers are placed. These are also cheaper, and you'll have more variety to choose from. As long as you don't need a large amount of the same type of stone, the boneyard is a great place to find stone.

Seal the stone as needed with a low-VOC and water-based sealer, or select stone that doesn't require sealing.

Many types of stone — especially marble, sandstone, limestone, and slate — are surprisingly soft, and they scratch and absorb stains easily. Granite is stronger and more scratch- and stain-resistant.

Dispose of leftover and discarded stone by giving it to a salvage yard. Stone tiles can be reused or crushed into aggregate for concrete.

Terrazzo

Terrazzo is made up of small pieces of marble set into cement and highly polished. Odds are, you've walked on a terrazzo floor. They're common in public buildings — museums, airports, hotels, and so on. When glass is used instead of marble, it's often called Vetrazzo (from vitreous glass), or glass terrazzo, and it reflects light in the most beautiful way. The result is a surface so beautiful you won't notice that this particular glass happens to be made from recycled beverage bottles. You can choose the colors of the glass and the cement binder, giving you an endless list of possibilities. The surface is durable, heatproof, and easy to maintain. The cost is similar to granite, and it can be cut into shapes just like stone.

Paper resin

Made from paper and a resin binder, composite countertops have a warm, neutral look that fits well with most decorating styles. This material looks similar to other popular solid-surface countertops like Corian, but because it's only about one-third plastic, it has a more natural look and feel. Many people compare paper resin to soapstone. The material is also very practical — it's not hard enough to dull knives, but it's dense enough to resist slice marks that can harbor bacteria.

Companies such as Richlite (www.richlite.com) and PaperStone Products (www.paperstoneproducts.com) offer their products out of recycled paper, so ask for the highest recycled content available.

As with concrete or any formed surface, special features can be incorporated into the countertops, such as a drain board next to an under-mount sink, or casting metal rods near the stove, creating a built-in trivet.

Concrete

Concrete is a natural product and, as such, has a natural beauty. A chemical mixture of cement, sand, and water, concrete is durable and will not release harmful chemicals. There's a strange extra benefit of concrete: Your guests will not be able to keep from touching the surface.

Concrete, being a formed material, can have special features incorporated into the countertop, such as a drain board next to an under-mount sink, or a small depression cast into the surface to create a soap dish. With an infinite variety of colors, shapes, and textures, concrete is one of the more unique surfaces you'll see in a kitchen. The drawback is that it can be expensive, depending on the shape.

Solid surfacing

Solid surfacing is a type of acrylic epoxy plastic mixture formed into large, continuous surfaces. Because the entire counter can be formed at once, other elements are often formed into it as well, such as sinks and backsplashes. The color runs through the entire material, so it won't show wear. Both inexpensive and durable, solid surfacing is one of the most popular countertop materials.

Because they are made from plastic, issues around the health and sustainability of these products have been raised. Every major manufacturer of solid surfacing now offers a line of recycled-content products. Typically, the recycled material comes from their own scraps that have been reground back into the mixture (post-industrial content). Obviously, you should pick the brand with the highest recycled content; unfortunately, even the highest percentage is still fairly low, around 15 percent.

As an inexpensive alternative to granite, solid surfacing is now available mixed with chips of real stone, usually quartz. Often called *engineered stone,* the surface looks like granite but feels different to the touch and uses much less energy to produce. The surface has a much more uniform appearance, which gives away that it isn't real stone. Because quartz can't be cut into large slabs, the crumbling bits of quartz are instead used in this mixture.

Although pure solid surfacing is 100 percent plastic, engineered surfaces are mostly stone, usually around 94 percent plastic. Choose the product with the highest amount of recycled stone available, such as those manufactured by Silestone (www.silestoneusa.com). Although engineered stone is not the greenest product available, it is greener than pure solid surfacing.

Plastic laminate

In the 1950s, plastic laminate was all the rage, but by the 1960s, it was beginning to shows its age. Strange patterns, toxic glues, and frayed edges began to show the drawbacks of plastic laminate. Despite its drawbacks, people still continue to ask about it.

To make plastic laminate, slim layers of acrylic plastic are bonded onto a wood backing. This thin sheet is glued down onto a plywood base to create a countertop. The plastic, adhesives, and resins used all pose potential health risks.

If you must choose a laminate, abaca is a wonderful alternative. Made from recycled banana fibers on a hemp backing, abaca laminates have an organic, natural texture. Only use nontoxic adhesives to glue the laminate to the plywood. As a nice detail, place a solid strip of wood along the edge for a more finished appearance.

Other Finishes

From accent tiles to wall panels, countless other green finishes are available to decorate your home.

Be sure to explore the life cycle impact of any product you're considering for your home (see Chapter 5).

Ceramic tile

For thousands of years, ceramic tiles have been used for flooring and wall tiles. Although it requires a great deal of energy to produce, ceramic tile is durable and recyclable, made from natural clay.

Look for locally sourced quarry tiles — they require less energy. Make sure natural glazes have been used; unglazed tiles are course and porous. As a fun alternative, ask your local tile warehouse for any damaged or dropped boxes. You can arrange broken tiles into a mosaic pattern for a beautiful finish.

Set the tiles into cement grout instead of adhesives to avoid adding VOCs into the air. Choose a colored grout instead of white to hide dirt; the grout lines are difficult to keep clean. Seal the completed tile and grout with a water-based sealer.

With careful planning, you can design the bathroom to fit the spacing of the tile. Doing this will avoid cutting, look much better, and reduce waste. If you must cut tiles, do it outside to keep the dust out of the indoor air.

If properly installed, ceramic tile can last 50 years or more, and it biodegrades after removal. Tiles can be reused if carefully removed, or crushed and recycled into aggregate filler for concrete.

Glass

Glass is an all-natural product, made of silica (sand) and melted into a variety of shapes, colors, and types. Because glass is healthy and can be found locally, glass is a fairly green product. Manufacturing glass does require some energy, so recycled glass is an even better option.

Recycled glass tiles are gorgeous and gemlike, and they're a great choice for a backsplash or shower wall. Recycled glass is produced from recycled windshields, bottles, and windows, then crushed to a sandlike texture and mixed with other ingredients, including minerals that add color. This mixture is then heated until the glass particles soften and fuse on their edges. This process uses far less energy than standard glass or ceramic tile manufacturing. Made from a mixture of sources, these recycled tiles contain slight imperfections and bubbles, adding character.

The color of the grout shows through some of the clear tiles, so choose a grout color with that in mind.

Metal

Environmentally speaking, metal is incredibly durable and easily recyclable, making it an attractive choice. Unfortunately, the production of metal is incredibly harmful to the environment. From mining the minerals to the energy needed to melt it down to the greenhouse gases released from this process, metal has a huge negative impact.

Different types of metal vary in their impact. Copper, for example, is destructively mined using slave labor in South America. Aluminum requires mining of bauxite, an incredibly polluting process. Stainless steel is different from steel — it's a combination alloy of steel, chromium, and nickel designed to resist rust, and the chromium is highly polluting and toxic.

Due to the high cost of manufacturing, most metals now contain some amount of recycled content, so just be sure to look for the highest amount available. Several companies produce tiles, sinks, and other finishes made of 100 percent recycled metal.

Both durable and hygienic, metal finishes resist heat and staining. Using flat stainless steel sheeting and adding a natural wood edge will reduce your costs and ease your installation.

Metal scratches and shows fingerprints very easily, so be sure you like that look before you buy.

Resins and plastics

Rigid plastic panels are typically produced from a polyester resin, made from oil, toxic in their production, and difficult to recycle. Several companies now offer greener alternatives with recycled and recyclable options. One company, 3-Form (www.3-form.com), refers to its product as an *eco-resin* to describe its patented, environmentally friendly manufacturing processes.

Choose panels with the highest recycled content available. An infinite array of options, colors, shapes, and thicknesses are available. Panels are a stronger and more colorful alternative to fragile glass, making it a great choice for kid-proof windows, attractive shower enclosures, and even unusual cabinet doors. Ask the manufacturer about standard panel sizes to reduce cutting and waste.

Furnishings

No home is complete without furniture, and several green options are available. Shop carefully and don't be afraid to ask questions. While finding a green floor may be easy, furnishings are more difficult. With so many options available, knowing what to ask or where to look is tough. In this section, I point you in the right direction.

Furniture

Chairs, tables, and sofas are typically made of cheap particleboard, finished with oil-based lacquers, and stuffed with toxic foam. You can smell these chemicals when you unwrap a new piece of furniture.

With any furniture, look for the following green features:

- ✔ **Reclaimed:** Reusing materials salvaged from other uses, reclaimed materials offer old-material quality no longer available. *Example:* Wood from old wine barrels milled into chairs.

- ✔ **Recycled:** Unlike reclaimed materials, recycled materials are put back into the material production and reprocessed into new finishes. Sourced from various materials, recycled materials often have slight imperfections that add to the final appearance. *Example:* Metal tables from recycled metal.

- ✔ **Sustainably harvested:** Yielding materials without completely destroying the chance for future harvesting, sustainably harvested materials will be around for future generations. *Example:* Bamboo furniture, Forest Stewardship Council (FSC) certified.

- ✔ **Natural materials:** Instead of stuffing cushions with synthetic materials containing harmful chemicals, look for natural latex.

- ✔ **Nontoxic finishes:** Most furniture is finished with oil-based lacquers; instead, use water-based finishes and adhesives free of VOCs.

Looking for these options will also ensure a healthier home. Companies such as Vivavi (www.vivavi.com) and Furnature (www.furnature.com) offer only products with these green features.

Draperies and fabrics

The fabrics making up your drapes, curtains, and sofa coverings are typically dyed with polluting pigments on synthetic fabric.

Natural fabrics such as organic cotton, hemp, linen, and natural wool offer healthier alternatives. Exciting new fabrics made from polylactic acid (PLA) are becoming more available. PLA is a natural material made from corn; it's recyclable and biodegradable. Companies like NatureWorks (www.natureworks.com), Interface (www.interfaceflooring.com), and DesignTex (www.designtex.com) all offer PLA-based fabrics.

Exterior Finishes and Trim

Although you don't need to worry about indoor air issues with exterior materials, you have other issues to consider. Anything outside is exposed to the weather, so you need to choose durable materials. Outside, anything painted needs to be repainted every few years, so save yourself the work and choose materials that can be left exposed and unpainted.

Siding

For many people, vinyl siding is considered the best material to use in covering your home. After all, it's durable and cheap, and it never needs painting. Unfortunately, the environmental issues with the manufacturing and disposal of vinyl make it a terrible choice. In the following sections, I fill you in on some other options to consider instead.

Aluminum siding

Popular in the 1940s and 1950s, aluminum siding offered a maintenance-free option for your home. When less expensive vinyl siding was introduced, it forced aluminum siding from the market. Older aluminum siding is easily recycled, but it's difficult to find a source for new siding made of recycled content.

Wood siding

Both vinyl and aluminum siding are designed to copy the look of real wood siding. The best choice is wood certified by the Forest Stewardship Council (FSC) to be sustainably harvested. Instead of paint, finish the planks with a water-based stain to allow the beauty of the wood to show through.

Cedar shingles

Cedar shingles are an attractive and natural option for siding. Cedar forests are disappearing rapidly, so look for shingles made from either reclaimed or FSC-certified wood.

Shingles do not need to be placed in straight lines. Arranging them in curves can be a fun and interesting way to cover your home.

Fiber cement boards

Fiber cement boards are rigid panels made of Portland cement, sand, wood fiber, and clay. They're a durable and attractive siding option. Although they hold paint well, the panels can be left unfinished if you don't mind the gray color. James Hardie (www.jameshardie.com/homeowner) is the largest manufacturer of fiber cement boards, but several other manufacturers offer fiber cement boards as well. The product is available in shingles, boards, and long planks for a variety of design options. Many manufacturers offer a wood grain or sand finish.

Stucco

Stucco is a cement-based product and must be applied or sprayed on by hand. Traditional stucco is really just cement-based plaster — a mixture of Portland cement, lime, sand, and water.

It's typically applied in three coats: a rough scratch coat, a secondary base coat, and then a finish coat, for a total thickness of about ¾ inch. If applying the stucco over a brick or concrete wall, a scratch coat is not needed.

Synthetic stucco, made from acrylic, is now typically used in place of cement-based stucco. If you use synthetic stucco, you have to use a thin fiberglass mesh. Stick with the natural cement stucco instead.

Although stucco can be painted, an integral color can be mixed into the finish coat, making painting unnecessary. Don't be afraid to select bright colors. Stucco is available in much more than tan, with a wide palette of fun colors. Although the cement requires a great deal of energy to produce, the long life and ease of maintenance make stucco a very green choice for your home.

Decking

A well-designed deck can open up a room and allow you the chance to get some fresh air. From staining, to dry rot and splinters, traditional decks can be a maintenance headache. Green options can solve some of these issues. Encourage outdoor living with the durable, low-maintenance decking alternatives in the following sections.

Certified wood

If you go with wood, be sure to use wood certified by the Forest Stewardship Council. The FSC stamp ensures this wood has been sustainably harvested. The most popular traditional decking material, redwood, typically comes from old-growth trees and cannot be replaced. Save these irreplaceable redwood trees and look for FSC-certified redwood instead.

Wood framing used outside is typically pressure treated with chromated copper arsenate (CCA), which is a form of arsenic (not exactly healthy for you or anyone else). The Environmental Protection Agency (EPA) has now banned CCA wood, but it is still in use, especially in children's playgrounds. Look for wood treated with the healthier ammoniacal copper quaternary (ACQ).

Composite lumber

Combining recycled plastic and sawdust, composite lumbers are much healthier and more environmentally friendly than wood. They don't warp, splinter, or need staining.

The maintenance savings alone is reason enough to consider composite lumber. Composite lumber is available from dozens of manufacturers; look for the companies that offer the highest recycled content planks.

Ipe wood

Ipe is a type of wood that is an attractive alternative to the typical redwood or teak decking. The strength and natural water resistance of ipe makes it a great choice for a durable deck. As always, FSC-certified ipe wood is the greenest option.

Reclaimed beams (railroad ties)

Salvaged ties from old railroad tracks are available and attractive, and they don't require any new trees to be made.

Because they were manufactured to be used outside, railroad ties are pressure-treated with CCA. Coat them with two coats of a water-based sealer to seal in the CCA. This will keep most of the harmful chemicals from soaking into your skin when touching it. Maintain the coat every few years to stay protected.

Roofing

The job of a roof is to keep the water out, but the choice of roof can greatly alter the appearance and energy efficiency of your home. Here are some options for keeping the rain out:

- **Asphalt shingles:** Nearly two-thirds of all roofs, both new and existing, are clad in asphalt shingles. Each year, about 11 million tons of asphalt roofing shingle waste is generated in the United States. Although recycled shingles are available, they aren't the best choice. Their dark color absorbs heat in the summer, heating up your home.

If you plan on collecting the rainwater from the roof, the oil in the asphalt shingles will make the water undrinkable. Opt for another type of roofing instead.

✔ **Recycled rubber roofing:** Nearly 300 million car tires are thrown away in the United States each year — that's nearly one per person. Dozens of companies recycle these tires into rubber shingles. These durable and resource-efficient shingles are a good choice.

However, like asphalt, these shingles will contaminate the rainwater as it falls on the roof.

✔ **Recycled plastic and metal shingles:** The large amount of recycled plastic and metal available has prompted manufacturers to create some great roofing products. Recycled plastic shingles look surprisingly like natural slate. Lightweight and affordable, they're a great option for your roof. Recycled metal shingles are also available, offering a reflective and attractive pattern.

When installing metal outside, never mix your metals. A copper roof must be installed with copper nails; a zinc roof with zinc nails.

✔ **Spray-on foam roofing:** Spray-on foam roofing, such as poly-isocyanurate (or poly-iso, for short) is the perfect choice for flat roofs. Once dry, these foams provide a seamless, continuous roof surface that will never leak and that's durable enough to walk on. The light yellow color of the foam is not very attractive, so you'll probably only want to use it on flat roof locations that aren't visible from ground level. But the light color *does* reflect heat to keep your home cool.

No matter what type of roof you choose, select the lightest color available. A dark roof absorbs heat, adding to your cooling costs in the summer. If you live in a warm climate, this issue is even more important.

When rain falls onto a roof, it's captured at the edges by gutters and fed into downspouts. These gutters and downspouts are unattractive and a maintenance headache. Instead consider the following:

✔ **Diverters:** Diverters, which are installed over doors and windows, let the rain run off the edge of your roof and into the ground. A diverter is a thin ramp that directs the water to either side of the opening, preventing the rain from pouring onto your head as you exit through the door.

✔ **Rain chains:** Instead of downspouts, a long, interlocking chain breaks up the water and acts as a wind chime when it rains. It's an attractive alternative to downspouts.

✔ **Water catchment:** Instead of letting the rainwater simply fall into your yard, collect it for later use in your garden. (See Chapter 13 for more information on water catchment options.)

If these options don't work for you, consider recycled plastic gutters and downspouts. They're available from several manufacturers, including RainTube/GLI Systems (www.raintube.com) and Master Mark Plastics (www.mastermark.com).

Remodeling: Bringing Old Materials to Life

Remodeling your home is a form of recycling. Reusing an existing building, instead of building something new, saves energy and resources.

The old appliances you remove are easily salvaged or sold. The sinks and tubs removed can be reused. If your existing toilet is a low-flush model, keep it and reuse it; if not, these old fixtures can be ground up and added as an aggregate into concrete.

Salvage yards offer possible treasures waiting to be found. Antique light fixtures, claw-foot tubs, and historic fireplace mantles are common finds in a salvage yard.

While paint strippers can bring new life to old furniture and fixtures, the chemicals they use are typically some of the harshest you can imagine. Although they require more elbow grease, electric sanders and strippers are a healthier choice. For stubborn or hard-to-clean surfaces, new products, such as SoyGel (www.franmar.com), offer a natural and chemical-free alternative to paint strippers.

Before the remodeling work begins, seal all the existing ducts and vents. This will prevent this dirt from traveling through the home. In order to remove the dust and chemicals stirred up by the remodeling project, tell your contractor to seal off the area to be remodeled with plastic sheeting, and leave it up until the project is finished. Finally, when the project is complete, open all the windows to flush the home with fresh air for a few days; this will remove a large portion of the VOCs and chemicals in the home.

Part III
Green Building Methods

In this part . . .

This part focuses on construction methods. I divide it into three chapters — one on framing (Chapter 8), one on natural building (Chapter 9), and one on manufactured systems (Chapter 10) — and I fill you in on the pros and cons of each. Believe me, you'll be amazed at the variety and benefits of these systems.

Chapter 8

Framing Things Up

*T*he walls of your home serve several functions: They keep out rain, maintain your privacy, and, of course, hold up the floors and roof. All this happens unseen, hidden under a layer of paint or wallpaper. You probably never think about your walls, but they offer some simple opportunities to speed up construction and reduce the amount of materials used.

In this chapter, I fill you in on the most widespread wall system — wood framing — and ways to improve its environmental impact and energy efficiency. Using advanced framing techniques, you can reduce the amount of wood used in building your house by more than half.

Here I show you new, modern materials, such as engineered lumber, that are lighter and stronger than solid wood. Finally, I let you know how substituting steel for wood can save you time and money.

Traditional Wood Framing

Your walls are only about 10 percent to 20 percent of the cost of your home, but they're the most important part. Of the 1.5 million new homes built in the United States each year, nearly all of them (90 percent) are constructed with wood framing.

The history of wood framing

Platform frame construction has been around since the 1830s. And the basic technology of wood platform framing has remained relatively unchanged ever since.

The Industrial Revolution brought new methods of mass production. Standardized nails and lumber allowed any low-skill worker to assemble a wood-frame building. The ease and speed of this system was perfect to meet the needs of a rapidly growing population. New homes could now be built in areas previously considered impossible.

The standard sizes of lumber we know today (2 x 4, 2 x 6, and so on) were first introduced over a hundred years ago. Back in 1902, the assorted lumber mills tried to agree on some standards. Several standards emerged, but lumber still varied from region to region.

The end of World War I brought a vast demand for lumber. By 1921, then Secretary of Commerce, Herbert Hoover, helped push these standards into acceptance by the lumber industry. Hoover was a noted engineer and saw the need and benefits for a national standard.

Coming to an agreement for a national standard was difficult. Arguments over the standard sizes continued for months. Lumber mills located on the West Coast wanted smaller sizes. Every $\frac{1}{16}$ inch they shaved off translated into a weight reduction of 200 pounds per shipment. This would save them freight costs.

Mediating over the bickering lumber mills, Hoover pushed the 1924 American Lumber Standards into acceptance. These are the same standards in use today. Despite improvements in wood drying and grading, we still use the same sizes we did 80 years ago.

If your home was built before 1924, it probably contains nonstandardized, solid studs that are thicker than normal ones. If you're remodeling your home, save these old studs. Although you can't use them for anything structural, the wood can be milled into beautiful trim or flooring.

Looking at how much wood is used

The average-sized home (about 2,000 square feet) uses an acre of forest (44 trees). These trees are typically clear-cut (which leaves nothing for the future). Timber mills take the wood and process it into solid sticks, called *studs*. The studs come in standard sizes (2 x 4 inches, 2 x 6 inches, and so on).

Wood is a big business, estimated at $11 billon per year, with an immense impact on the environment. The lumber industry is the second largest source of greenhouse gas and global warming pollution, after coal production.

To build walls, wood studs are nailed into a line of columns, spaced 16 inches apart. Called *platform framing*, this lightweight construction method was revolutionary when it was introduced because it saved the need for solid walls.

Because most houses are built with wood framing, even the most unskilled person on a construction site knows how to work with it. It's this familiarity that makes wood framing so relatively inexpensive.

Recognizing the problems with wood framing

Wood framing accounts for 90 percent of the homes built in the United States, so you may think it must be a safe, solid method of construction. In reality, wood has some serious concerns and considerations:

- **Fire:** The bottom line: Wood burns, and the biggest threat to your home is fire. Although you can take great precautions, such as installing sprinklers, to prevent fire from destroying your home, fire remains a real concern.

- **Mold:** The empty cavities in a wood-frame wall are the perfect breeding ground for mold to form. The wood and drywall support mold growth, posing a potential health risk for you and your family.

- **Insects and other pests:** Termites thrive on a diet of wood and could ruin your home. The empty chambers inside the walls are also the ideal home for other pests, like mice.

- **Rotting and decomposition:** If water leaks into the house, the wood will warp and eventually rot.

Using wood framing has serious limitations. After you build the frame out of sticks, you still need to insulate, cover, and waterproof it. These weaknesses are all opportunities to reduce the environmental impact and your cost.

Wood framing requires lots of labor and materials to work

You may think of wood framing as a strong, easy way to build. But in reality, it's just a grid of little sticks requiring labor and additional materials to make it work.

In platform framing, walls are formed by nailing studs together to create a hollow frame. Studs are inserted at 16 inches *on center* (measured from the centerline of one stud to the centerline of the next stud). If you want to insert a window or door opening, you have to interrupt the line of studs and frame the new opening. If you want to connect a wall to another wall, you need extra studs at the intersections and corners to make it work. This means each wall wastes wood it doesn't need.

Wood framing must be covered with sheathing

Wood-frame walls can't be left as bare sticks, so they must be covered on the outside with *sheathing,* panels of solid wood. The only reason people build the studs to be 16 inches on center (see the preceding section), is because most sheathing comes 48 inches wide. This allows the sheathing to fit perfectly over four studs. The edges of the sheathing are screwed into the studs below.

I cover some wonderful green sheathing options in the following sections.

Plywood

Plywood is the typical sheathing panel. If you go with plywood sheathing, be sure to choose wood certified by the Forest Stewardship Council (FSC) as sustainably harvested. Look for plywood without formaldehyde-based glues. Avoid using luan plywood, because it comes from the destruction of the rain forest.

In areas with earthquakes or high winds, plywood sheathing is used to add strength to the building. Called *shear walls,* this plywood must be thicker and continuously nailed around all the edges. Check your local building codes for the structural requirements of these shear walls.

Oriented strand board

Made up of small scraps of wood, oriented strand board (OSB) uses less wood than plywood but works just as well. Look for OSB with formaldehyde-free glues or certified by GREENGUARD to have low emissions (see Chapter 5).

Particleboard

A mixture of sawdust and glue, particleboard can be used in some locations as a substitute for plywood. Buy FSC-certified panels or boards made of recycled wood.

Wheat board

Stalks of wheat are compressed with heat and pressure to form rigid panels. The natural starch in the wheat holds the panels together, so no glue or formaldehyde is needed.

Wheat board is the greenest sheathing option, but it may not be available everywhere.

The floor and roof don't line up with the walls

The floors and roof are built in the same way as the walls, but with studs spaced at 24 inches on center. With the wall studs at 16 inches on center and the roof joists at 24 inches, the studs don't align. Because of this, the top of the walls (called the *plate*) must be doubled up to support and distribute the weight.

The spaces between the studs need insulation

The light frame of wood studs has very little insulation value or thermal mass. In order to keep a wood-framed home comfortable, insulation is added to the empty bay between the studs. Rolled insulation comes in standard widths, so it fits perfectly. The thicker the insulation, the more energy efficient your home will be. If your walls are only 4 inches thick, you can only get a minimum amount of insulation value. The thicker the walls, the more insulation you can fit inside. (For more on insulation, check out Chapter 11.)

The walls need waterproofing and siding

Wood sheathing can't be left exposed, so it too needs to be covered. A building paper (or *house wrap*) is used as a waterproof barrier. Choose a breathable house wrap that resists moisture but allows air to pass through the walls. This will help prevent mold from growing inside the walls.

A finish siding must be applied over the wall of studs, insulation, sheathing, and house wrap. Avoid vinyl siding at all costs. Although it's cheap, vinyl is the most harmful construction material produced. Don't fall for claims of recycled vinyl either — a toxic material is still toxic when recycled.

Consider these green siding options (see Chapter 7 for more on siding):

- ✔ **Stucco:** Natural stucco provides a strong, maintenance-free finish. Colored stucco does not need to be painted; uncolored stucco needs painting every three to five years.

- ✔ **Reclaimed wood:** Traditional wood siding is attractive and will last for hundreds of years. Choose reclaimed wood. It's natural and recyclable as well. Instead of painting it, stain the wood to allow the beauty of the grain to show through.

- ✔ **Fiber cement planks:** A mix of cement, sand, and cellulose, fiber cement panels are a durable, long-lasting siding alternative. You can paint the planks or leave them bare. Unlike wood, it won't rot, warp, or burn.

The interior walls must be finished

On the inside of the house, the wood framing and insulation have to be covered with something. Gypsum drywall is typically used, but it's not ideal, because of the energy needed to produce it and the waste is creates. About 12 percent of the drywall used in new construction ends up as scrap in landfills.

Consider the following green alternatives to drywall:

- ✔ **Recycled drywall:** Recycled-content drywall is now available at the same price as regular drywall. The mining of gypsum consumes a great deal of energy and natural resources.

✔ **Paper board:** Paper board products, such as Homasote (`www.homasote.com`), are made of 100 percent recycled newsprint. You can paint, sand, and stain the boards to create a variety of finishes.

✔ **Oriented strand board:** Oriented strand board is a wonderful substitute for drywall, especially if you get the FSC-certified and formaldehyde-free variety.

✔ **Hardboard:** Hardboard, such as Masonite (`www.masonite.com`), is a strong, thin panel. Look for FSC-certified and formaldehyde-free brands.

Check out Chapter 7 for more suggestions on green finishes.

Taking advantage of wood framing

The standardized and rectangular shapes of wood framing present some limitations in terms of design. Consider the following:

✔ **Curves:** Curved walls are incredibly difficult and labor intensive when you're using wood framing. New technologies, such as Flex-C Trac (`www.flexc.com`), allow for curves and arches with much less wood. This hinged wooden track can be bent into almost any shape and screwed into the floor, allowing the wall to follow that shape.

✔ **Insulation:** Because the exterior walls are usually made from 2-x-4-inch or 2-x-6-inch studs, the amount of insulation is limited. The thicker the wall, the more insulation it can hold. Unfortunately, wood-frame walls rarely get thick enough to hold more than a minimum amount of insulation.

Wood-framed homes are built throughout the United States, regardless of climate. But the moderate insulation and lack of thermal mass in wood framing make it inappropriate for very hot or very cold locations. Consider combining wood frame with other construction methods, such as straw bale or structural insulated panels (see Chapters 9 and 10).

✔ **Hidden costs:** Most people think that wood framing is cheap, but the costs quickly add up. When you add in the cost of insulation, sheathing, waterproofing, siding, and interior finishes, your inexpensive wall system gets very expensive.

✔ **Height:** Wood framing is generally limited to around three stories in height. If you want to go higher, concrete and steel have to be introduced.

✔ **Energy leaks:** Small pockets and voids in the walls allow for your heat to leak out of the building. These leaks are hard to avoid and they waste energy and money.

✔ **Flat windows:** The thin walls don't allow for deep-set windows and doors, which makes the front of the house look very flat.

Wood framing does offer some hidden opportunities to speed construction and increase your energy efficiency. If you're going to go the wood-framing route, be sure to incorporate the following techniques:

- ✓ **Stack window and door openings.** Construction will move much faster if you align the windows and doors from floor to floor.

- ✓ **Place windows between studs.** Because you know the studs will be placed every 16 inches, you can plan to locate your windows to fit within these studs. This strategy not only saves time, but eliminates the need for extra wood.

- ✓ **Stack plumbing.** Locate bathrooms and plumbing fixtures over one another on each floor to save money.

- ✓ **Use finger-jointed studs.** Short lengths of wood are stitched together to create one long piece of wood. Resembling interlocking fingers, the finger-jointed studs are cheaper, stronger, and straighter than standard studs. Because they use small pieces of wood, finger-jointed studs save on the amount of wood used as well.

- ✓ **Use modular dimensions.** Design your home to match the dimensions of the wood. Because the walls are built to be 16 inches on center, make the overall length of the walls some even multiple of 16 inches to reduce waste.

- ✓ **Seal the edges.** Place a foam gasket below the edge of each exterior wall to prevent air from leaking out.

- ✓ **Take advantage of advanced framing techniques.** Instead of using 2-x-4s at 16 inches on center, switch to 2-x-6s at 24 inches on center. Using these advanced framing techniques, you can save more than half the amount of wood normally used.

- ✓ **Use engineered wood.** Made up of small pieces of wood glued together, these engineered studs are smaller, lighter, and stronger than solid wood studs.

If you're building your home in phases, plan ahead and make it easier to add later additions. Design the walls to be removed in sections, or preinstall the framing for a future door. This will make it easier when you're ready to move to the next phase.

If there's a chance you may add a second floor to your home project in the future, prepare for it now. Engineer the walls and foundation to support the weight of that future second floor. Doing it now will cost little and save you a lot of money in the future.

The attic is more than a storage space. An attic can later evolve into a spare bedroom or den. Plan for this future expansion now by making the floor of the attic strong enough to be a future floor. If you can't afford to do anything to it now, at least run the electrical and plumbing lines you think you'll need in the future.

Wall costs of wood framing are usually only about 10 percent to 20 percent of the overall cost of construction. When comparing wood to other methods, include the cost of the *entire* wall — including insulation, sheathing, and siding. Also consider the energy costs to heat and cool your wood-frame home.

Certified wood: A look at the Forest Stewardship Council

The Forest Stewardship Council (FSC) is an international agency that promotes the use of *sustainably harvested wood,* which is wood gathered from well-managed forests.

Not all wood is created equal. Although structural lumber is stamped to indicate the quality and strength, you can't determine whether a forest was clear-cut in order to get the wood. The FSC was created in 1993 to provide an independent certification for just this reason. The FSC stamp is a guarantee that the wood came from a sustainably managed forest.

The FSC is an independent, not-for-profit, non-government organization. The FSC sets standards that reflect agreed-upon principles for responsible forest management and accredits organizations that certify the achievement of those standards by specific forests or woodlands. These certifiers track each company and their supply chains back to FSC-certified sources. This *chain of custody* certification assures that consumers can trust the FSC seal (see Chapter 5).

The term *chain of custody* refers to the path taken by raw materials harvested from an FSC-certified source through processing, manufacturing, and distribution until it is a final product ready for sale to the consumer. In the case of a house, this includes framing lumber, trim, or plywood. Any product made of wood is now available from an FSC-certified source.

The FSC has developed the following list of the Ten Principles of Forest Stewardship to address the issues and impacts surrounding forest management:

Principle #1: Compliance with Laws and FSC Principles: Forest management shall respect all applicable laws of the country in which they occur, and international treaties and agreements to which the country is a signatory, and comply with all FSC Principles and Criteria.

Principle #2: Tenure and Use Rights and Responsibilities: Long-term tenure and use rights to the land and forest resources shall be clearly defined, documented, and legally established.

Principle #3: Indigenous Peoples' Rights: The legal and customary rights of indigenous peoples to own, use, and manage their lands, territories, and resources shall be recognized and respected.

Principle #4: Community Relations and Workers' Rights: Forest management operations shall maintain or enhance the long-term social and economic well being of forest workers and local communities.

Principle #5: Benefits from the Forest: Forest management operations shall encourage the efficient use of the forest's multiple products and services to ensure economic viability and a wide range of environmental and social benefits.

Principle #6: Environmental Impact: Forest management shall conserve biological diversity and its associated values, water resources, soils, and unique and fragile ecosystems and landscapes, and, by so doing, maintain the ecological functions and the integrity of the forest.

Principle #7: Management Plan: A management plan — appropriate to the scale and intensity of the operations — shall be written, implemented, and kept up to date. The long-term objectives of management, and the means of achieving them, shall be clearly stated.

Principle #8: Monitoring and Assessment: Monitoring shall be conducted — appropriate to the scale and intensity of forest management — to assess the condition of the forest, yields of forest products, chain of custody, management activities, and their social and environmental impacts.

Principle #9: Maintenance of High Conservation Value Forests: Management activities in high

conservation value forests shall maintain or enhance the attributes which define such forests. Decisions regarding high conservation value forests shall always be considered in the context of a precautionary approach.

Principle #10: Plantations: Plantations shall be planned and managed in accordance with Principles and Criteria 1–9, and Principle 10 and its Criteria. While plantations can provide an array of social and economic benefits, and can contribute to satisfying the world's needs for forest products, they should complement the management of, reduce pressures on, and promote the restoration and conservation of natural forests.

For more information on the Forest Stewardship Council, go to www.fsc.org.

Engineered Lumber

Conventional wood-framing practices consume vast amounts of lumber made out of large pieces of solid wood. More than 95 percent of the old-growth forests once in the United States are gone, increasing the urgency to save what's remaining.

Engineered lumber is a term that refers to an array of new wood products produced with small scraps of wood glued together under intense heat and pressure. These products use half the amount of wood and can have up to twice the strength. Because they are assembled from small pieces of wood from small-diameter trees, engineered lumber is an easy method of saving money as well as wood resources.

What engineered lumber is

Engineered lumber is made by bonding strips, sheets, or particles of wood together with glue. Technically, all the following products fall into the engineered lumber category:

✔ **Plywood:** Thin sheets of wood veneer bonded together with glue, heat, and pressure to form a rigid panel. Each veneer is glued together with the wood grain perpendicular to the other. These alternating layers make plywood incredibly strong. Although solid wood expands and shrinks because of humidity, plywood remains dimensionally stable.

✔ **Oriented strand board (OSB):** Small scraps of wood glued together like plywood. Instead of solid sheets of wood, OSB uses fragments of wood, making OSB nearly as strong as plywood.

✔ **I-joists:** Engineered I-joists are named for their shape, similar to a steel I-beam. Thick pieces of plywood create the top and bottom chords of the beam. The middle part, called the *web,* is made from OSB. These light joists are much stronger than solid wood of the same size, and can be used for framing the floor and roof.

✔ **Glue-laminated lumber:** Glue-laminated lumber, or glu-lams, consists of long strands of wood glued together to form a thick, solid beam. The resulting beam is almost as strong as steel, but much less expensive and more attractive.

✔ **Laminated veneer lumber (LVL):** Similar to plywood, LVL uses thin layers of wood glued together to form dimensional lumber suitable for framing. Think of it as a smaller glu-lam.

✔ **Oriented strand lumber (OSL):** OSL is essentially the same as LVL but uses large flakes of wood instead of solid layers. The appearance of OSL is very different from plywood or LVL.

Although the idea of small fragments of wood may sound weak and brittle, the reality of engineered wood is quite different. Strong, stable, and long lasting, engineered wood works seamlessly with your wood-framed home. Using these engineered products will reduce the amount of wood you need to use in building your home by half. In addition, engineered products never warp or split like solid wood.

As a general rule, any time you need to use a stud larger than a 2-x-8, you should substitute an engineered wood product.

The history of engineered lumber

The history of engineered lumber really dates back to the ancient Egyptians in 3500 B.C. These master builders invented their own version of plywood by gluing thin sheets of expensive, high-quality wood over a core of common wood.

The introduction of the lathe in the 1850s allowed builders to peel thin veneers of wood from a trunk or beam. By 1868, the first patent for structural plywood was issued and it has been in use since.

The remaining line of engineered wood products was finally introduced in the late 1970s and early 1980s in response to the rising costs of solid lumber and steel.

The various engineered wood products come in a range of costs. When looking at engineered wood, don't forget about the important advantages of engineered wood over solid wood: consistent size and greater strength. The initial cost of certain items, such as glu-lams, will be more than a solid beam of the same size. But the glu-lam can go where solid wood would not be strong enough. Other products, such as the I-joists, are about the same cost as solid wood framing, but have a consistent size and quality and can be built much more quickly.

Taking advantage of engineered lumber

Incorporating engineered lumber into your project should be a seamless switch from solid lumber.

In the walls, LVL and OSL can be used in place of solid dimensional studs. Because they are also a wood product, all the same nails, screws, and connectors can be used. (The cost of using LVLs and OSLs as a substitution for all the studs is prohibitive for most homeowners, but if money is no object, you may want to look into this option.)

Engineered I-joists can be used throughout the home. You can use them for the supporting headers over windows and doors, in the floor joists, and in the roof framing. Using the same support hangers and connectors as solid wood studs, I-joists are already in widespread use in home construction.

Although I-joists are perfect for floors and roof construction, their appearance is unfinished and you wouldn't want to see them in a finished room. For exposed beams and areas that need a strong structural support, glu-lams are the ideal choice. Almost as strong as steel, glu-lams can support any structural need you have but are attractive enough to be exposed. Glu-lams are also used when a standard I-joist isn't strong enough. Your structural engineer can help you determine the appropriate engineered wood product to use.

The following suggestions will help you work with the most common engineered lumber, the I-joists:

- Although you can frame your entire roof out of I-joists, you probably won't want to use them where they will be visible. **If you want your roof edges to have that traditional look, consider installing exposed rafter tails.** These beams sit under the eaves of the roof, adding a nice design touch. To use rafter tails with the I-joists, overlap a length of solid wood alongside the I-joist. You can have nice-looking rafter tails with minimal effort.

- When mixing engineered wood with solid wood, remember that solid wood will shrink as it dries. **Allow your solid wood to sit in a dry location on the construction site for 14 days before installing.**

✔ **An easy trick to make the tops of all your I-joists level is to use a taut length of string.** The string will act as a guide so you know you've installed the I-joists to be level.

✔ One of the nicest features of using the I-joists is the ability to run ductwork, plumbing, and wiring through the web of the joists. Many I-joist manufacturers now include premarked or prepunched openings in the web. **Be careful not to cut the holes to be too large; every hole in the joist reduces its strength.**

✔ **To prevent squeaky floors, run a bead of construction adhesive on the top of every I-joist before installing the subfloor.**

✔ The beauty of using engineered wood is the long lengths they can span. A single joist can span up to 28 feet across; a glu-lam can run almost as far a distance. **Take advantage of these spans by designing large rooms without the need for intermediate columns.**

✔ The scraps from the I-joists are perfect for the extra bracing, stiffeners, and fire-blocking you'll need. **Save the scraps in their own pile for easy reuse.**

✔ **Use an automatic nail gun to speed construction.** Special nails precoated with construction adhesive are perfect for working with I-joists. The glue activates when shot out of the nail gun.

Be careful when you're working with nail guns — they can be dangerous!

✔ **Exposed glu-lams and LVLs can be "distressed" to give them a rustic appearance.** Use a sand-blaster or wire brush, but be careful not to cut into the side of the beam.

Advanced Framing Techniques

Advanced framing is a series of techniques to reduce the amount of wood used in building a home. Often referred to as optimum value engineering (OVE), it can reduce the amount of wood in your home by more than half.

What advanced framing is

The 175-year-old tradition of wood platform framing has evolved very little over time. Advanced framing techniques are easy to understand and implement. If the person building your home is familiar with wood framing, then he already has the skills necessary to use advanced framing.

Table 8-1 outlines the differences between advanced framing and traditional wood framing. Figure 8-1 illustrates these advanced framing techniques.

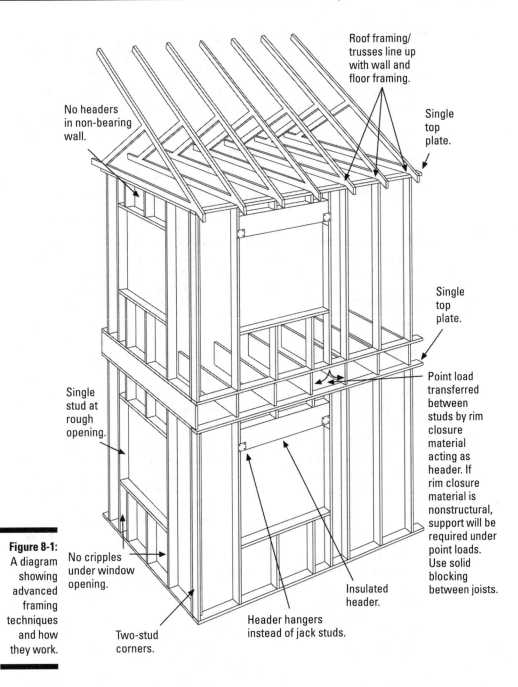

Roof framing/
trusses line up
with wall and
floor framing.

No headers
in non-bearing
wall.

Single
top
plate.

Single
top
plate.

Point load
transferred
between
studs by rim
closure
material
acting as
header. If
rim closure
material is
nonstructural,
support will be
required under
point loads.
Use solid
blocking
between joists.

Single
stud at
rough
opening.

Figure 8-1:
A diagram
showing
advanced
framing
techniques
and how
they work.

No cripples
under window
opening.

Insulated
header.

Two-stud
corners.

Header hangers
instead of jack studs.

Table 8-1	Traditional Wood Framing versus Advanced Framing
Traditional Wood Framing	**Advanced Framing Techniques**
2-x-4 wall studs are spaced on center at 16 inches.	2-x-6 wall studs are spaced on center at 24 inches. The larger studs are stronger, so they can be spaced farther apart. The additional thickness of the wall also allows room for additional insulation.
2-x-8 floor joists are spaced on center at 16 inches.	Use engineered wood I-joists at 24 inches on center for the framing of your floors and roof. The studs and joists now have the same spacing and align to one another.
When two walls meet at a corner, extra studs are placed at each end. These studs are only used as a place to attach the drywall, and these hollow corners create uninsulated voids.	Corners are built using *two-stud corner framing* (where no extra studs are added). Instead of using an entire stud, place a backing strip, called a *drywall clip,* to use as the spot to connect the drywall. Figure 8-2 shows how this works.
Additional studs are used to hold the drywall together.	Inexpensive drywall clips or scrap lumber hold the joints of two drywall boards together without using an entire wood stud.
Extra wood, called a *header,* is placed over openings, such as doors and windows.	On non-load-bearing walls, a single stud is often enough support over a door or opening.
The wall framing does not align to the floor and roof, even when both are spaced at 16 inches on center.	*In-line framing* (where the floor, wall, and roof framing members are all in line with one another) is used. Because the floor and roof framing now line up with the studs in the walls, the weight is transferred directly from the floor to the wall. By aligning the structure vertically throughout the entire house, it makes the building stronger and more efficient.
The top stud of a wood-framed wall, called the *top plate,* is doubled up to distribute the structural loads from the roof and floor above. Two studs are used.	A single stud is used for the top plate of each wall. (Check with your local building codes to see if this is allowed; it usually doesn't present any problems.) Connect the joints of the top plates with a galvanized steel plate. These steel plates should be used on the top plate at all the joints, corners, and intersections (see Figure 8-3).
The home is designed to some arbitrary dimension, often requiring additional cutting and materials.	The home is designed on a 2-foot module to reduce waste and take advantage of the standard size of plywood and sheathing materials (see Figure 8-4).

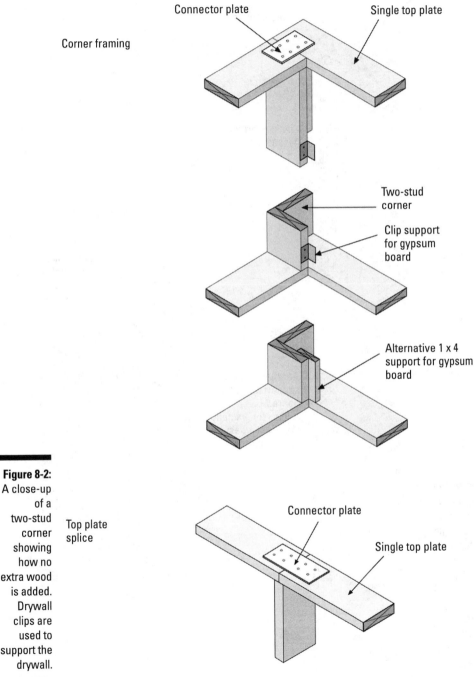

Corner framing

Connector plate

Single top plate

Two-stud corner

Clip support for gypsum board

Alternative 1 x 4 support for gypsum board

Top plate splice

Connector plate

Single top plate

Figure 8-2:
A close-up of a two-stud corner showing how no extra wood is added. Drywall clips are used to support the drywall.

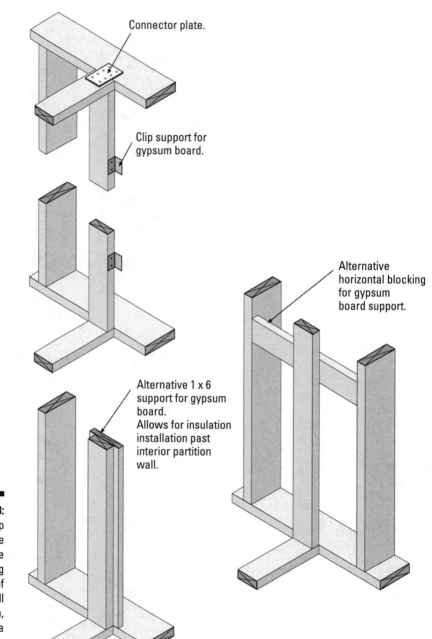

Connector plate.

Clip support for gypsum board.

Alternative horizontal blocking for gypsum board support.

Alternative 1 x 6 support for gypsum board.
Allows for insulation installation past interior partition wall.

Figure 8-3:
A close-up of a single top plate showing how the roof and wall studs align, creating a stronger wall.

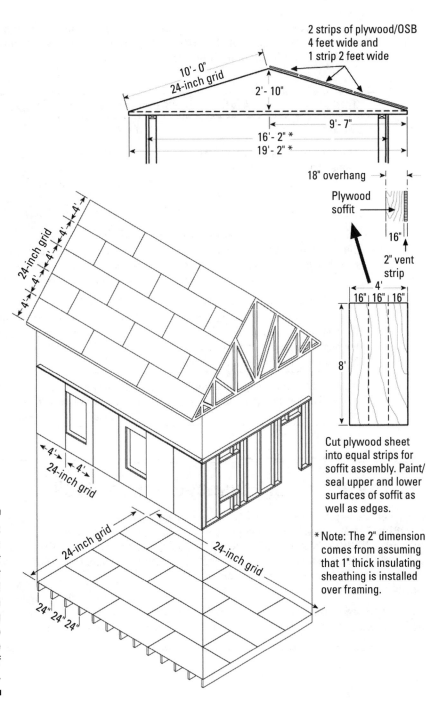

2 strips of plywood/OSB
4 feet wide and
1 strip 2 feet wide

10' - 0"
24-inch grid

2' - 10"

9' - 7"

16' - 2" *
19' - 2" *

18" overhang

Plywood
soffit

16"

2" vent
strip

4'
16" 16" 16"

8'

Cut plywood sheet
into equal strips for
soffit assembly. Paint/
seal upper and lower
surfaces of soffit as
well as edges.

* Note: The 2" dimension
comes from assuming
that 1" thick insulating
sheathing is installed
over framing.

24-inch grid

4' 4' 4' 4' 4' 4'

4' 4'
24-inch grid

24-inch grid

24-inch grid

24" 24" 24"

Figure 8-4:
A diagram
of a modular
layout for
wood
framing with
everything
aligning to
some
measure of
24 inches.

If you've never heard of these advanced framing techniques, you probably have some concerns. Table 8-2 lists some common myths surrounding the use of advanced framing techniques.

Table 8-2	Myths about Advanced Framing Techniques
Myth	**Fact**
The more wood that goes into the frame, the stronger the frame is.	The extra wood only adds to the weight of the frame and tries to make up for the roof and floors not aligning to the walls. Advanced framing techniques will strengthen your home, not weaken it.
The building codes don't allow for the use of advanced framing techniques.	The building codes support advanced framing techniques because they make buildings stronger and remove redundant wood.
If you use advanced framing techniques, the drywall will bow or buckle, because the boards are only supported every 24 inches instead of every 16 inches.	A good contractor uses quality materials and craftsmanship to prevent the walls from bowing.
Attaching the sheathing and drywall every 16 inches makes the building stronger.	Attaching the sheathing and drywall at only 24 inches actually reduces the stress placed on the panels.

The history of advanced framing techniques

Advanced framing techniques came about in the 1970s. The National Association of Home Builders (NAHB) created the innovative approach while constructing a prototypical house for the U.S. Department of Housing and Urban Development.

The NAHB discovered enormous savings in both labor and materials. In its initial study, more than 12 percent of the cost could be saved as compared to a traditional wood-frame home. A third of that cost reduction was in labor savings and two-thirds were in material costs.

The approach behind OVE didn't really start to catch on until the 1990s. Production home-builders sought out new ways to reduce costs, and advanced framing was the ideal solution.

Taking advantage of advanced framing

Advanced framing techniques already take advantage of traditional wood framing. These improvements to the usual practice of wood framing should be done on every home built out of wood. In fact, there is no downside or reason *not* to employ these measures. To compare how advanced framing stacks up against traditional framing, take a look at Figure 8-5.

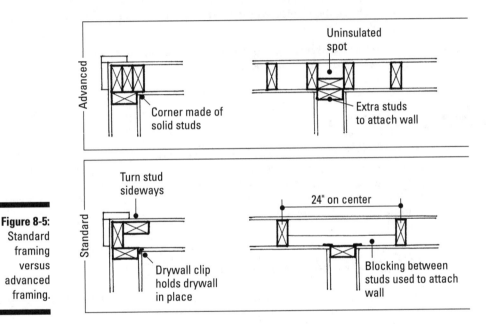

Figure 8-5: Standard framing versus advanced framing.

Standard Framing versus Advanced Framing

Using advanced framing techniques, the National Association of Home Builders (NAHB) discovered a cost savings of over 12 percent when compared to traditional wood framing. These methods can potentially reduce the amount of wood by 55 percent.

In addition to reducing the amount of wood used, follow these other suggestions when designing your green home with advanced framing techniques:

✔ **Substitute oriented strand board (OSB) for your exterior sheathing.** Select boards made from formaldehyde-free glues. If the sheathing is not required for the structure, use nonstructural insulated boards for extra insulation.

✔ **Select finger-jointed studs made from small pieces of wood stitched together to make a full-length stud.**

✔ **Take advantage of the thicker 2-x-6-inch walls and fill them with insulation above the minimum required amount.** (Refer to Chapter 11 for more insulation information.)

✔ **Purchase sustainably harvested wood stamped by the Forest Stewardship Council (FSC).**

Heavy Timber

Traditional timber framing consists of large wooden posts and beams bolted together to create a rigid frame. The ancient art of timber construction creates beautiful, rustic structures. You may be surprised to learn that despite the thick posts, a heavy timber house uses less wood than a house built with traditional wood framing.

What heavy timber framing is

Instead of piecing together a series of little sticks, heavy timber framing uses large posts of wood. Measuring anywhere from 6 inches up to 12 inches thick, the timbers are built into a large frame. The vertical wood is called a *post;* the horizontal wood is referred to as a *beam*.

Traditionally, the posts and beams were held together using elaborate joinery and wooden pegs. With modern tools and equipment, the frame can now be bolted together.

In the empty space between the posts, you can place a wide variety of materials as *infill*. From traditional wood and plaster to straw bale, the infill materials should be green and insulating.

So how could the strong frame of posts and beams use less wood and require less labor than traditional wood framing? The milling of standard lumber requires cutting, so much of the wood is lost. Timber framing uses the *entire* piece of wood, which minimizes the waste. Instead of an average of 400 studs per house, a timber home uses fewer, larger pieces. A timber frame can use up to 30 percent less wood than a wood frame.

The timbers are easily recycled during demolition, and are available from sustainably harvested sources through the Forest Stewardship Council (FSC).

The roof and floors can be constructed out of engineered wood, just as in standard construction. Depending on the infill material you choose for the walls, a timber home can have an incredibly high insulation value.

In a side-by-side comparison to traditional wood framing, it might be hard to see the advantages of timber framing. Consider these benefits:

- ✔ **A timber-framed home uses up to 30 percent less wood than a traditional wood-framed home of the same size.**

- ✔ **Because the timbers are often left exposed, they can dry in the open air, lowering the risk of mold growth.**

- ✔ **With fewer and larger pieces of wood, the timber frame will take longer to rot.** Rot is always an issue with wood, but the exposed timbers will have a better chance of drying out and avoiding rot.

- ✔ **Of course, the wood of a timber-framed home will burn, but if it does, it takes much more time (an additional hour or so) for it to catch fire and it burns slower.** Most building codes show heavy timber buildings have a higher fire resistance. The edges of the posts and beams are shaved off. Removing these edges lowers the risk of fire by eliminating the thinnest portion of the wood.

- ✔ **Even in hurricane- and earthquake-prone regions, timber frames are resistant to the shaking.** Special connections, such as metal connector plates and bolts, are required in these areas.

The history of heavy timber framing

The use of timber framing goes back thousands of years.

You can find timber buildings dating back to medieval times still standing throughout Europe. In Northern Europe, where timber was plentiful and the people were skilled carpenters, timber framing was a great alternative to stone.

As Europeans emigrated to America, they brought their carpentry skills and introduced timber construction to the States. The introduction of mass-produced nails and framing lumber during the Industrial Revolution drew attention away from timber framing.

The natural building movement that began in the 1970s brought about resurgence in heavy timber construction, especially because it works well with many natural building techniques.

Taking advantage of heavy timber

If they're well insulated, the thick walls of a timber-framed home are ideal for most climates. This method is best in regions where the timbers and skilled contractors are available.

Using a simple timber frame offers several aesthetic and structural advantages over traditional wood framing. The frame goes up quickly and allows for a flexible design. And the beautiful wood beams offer some great design opportunities, such as:

- **Infill materials:** Straw bale, adobe, and cob are the perfect complement to timber framing. In areas where a structural frame is required, timber framing offers an effective solution.

- **Exposed beams:** Don't hide the wood — show it off! The exposed beams resemble Tudor-style homes and can be part of the appearance of the wall.

- **Finished beams:** You can stain, carve, or sand the exposed wood to create a variety of appearances.

- **Mixed with wood framing:** Standard wood framing works well with timber construction. The wood-to-wood connections are simple to make, using the same tools.

- **Certified wood:** Timbers are available from the Forest Stewardship Council (FSC) to be certified as sustainably harvested. This is the ideal choice.

- **Open floor plan:** The strong heavy timbers allow you to create an open floor plan without the need for additional columns or supports.

Generally speaking, a timber frame will cost you 20 percent more than a standard wood frame. But when you include the possible savings in construction time and energy efficiency, the price is competitive with wood.

When planning your timber-framed home, consider the following cost-saving suggestions:

- **Prefit the timber frame off of the construction site.** It will speed up the construction in the field.

- **Use mechanical cutting, if it's available.** Because of their size, the timbers are often cut with hand tools. Mechanical cutting can save some money.

- **Use consistent sizes of timbers to lower your costs and reduce field cutting.**

Steel Framing

With forests dwindling, we need alternatives to wood. Steel represents the ideal modern material, a product of the Industrial Revolution. The introduction of steel has changed how we build our buildings.

What steel framing is

Steel is produced by mining metal ore out of the ground and heating it up to thousands of degrees. The molten steel can be formed into a variety of shapes. In this case, the steel is rolled into a C-shape to form a metal stud, or into a U-shape to form a top and bottom track. Holes are prepunched along the length of the stud every couple of feet. These holes allow you to pass plumbing lines and electrical wires through the studs easily, without drilling.

The dimensions of the metal studs are similar to the standard sizes of wood studs. Because the studs are made of thin metal, nails cannot be used. Screws are used to connect the walls and attach the sheathing and drywall to the framing. This slows construction slightly, but makes stronger connections.

The studs are coated with zinc to prevent rust; the end result is called *galvanized steel*. Steel studs offer the following advantages over wood:

- **Steel frames are stronger than wood frames.**
- **Steel weighs significantly less than wood (35 percent to 50 percent less).** The lower weight saves energy on shipping and makes construction easier.
- **The steel studs are consistent in size and quality.**
- **Most steel contains at least some recycled content.**
- **Steel studs are 100 percent recyclable.**
- **Unlike wood, steel is termite resistant.**
- **Steel studs help resist the threat of fire.**
- **It doesn't result in the cutting down of trees.** Perhaps the biggest push to switch to steel studs are the trees. An acre of forest goes into the making of a single home, all of which could be saved by using steel.

Steel framing has the same issues with insulation, sheathing, and drywall that wood framing has. And steel framing has some unique issues you probably haven't had with other building methods. In cold weather, the steel studs carry cold into the building. Plus, connecting wood to steel is more difficult. You can't simply nail the wood to the steel; instead special connectors are needed. (Still, for an experienced builder, this is not an issue.)

The history of steel as a framing material

Like most modern building materials, the use of formed steel goes back to the 1850s and the birth of the Industrial Revolution. Architects were experimenting with iron and steel to rebuild Chicago after the great fire of 1871. Early skyscrapers filled the skyline at the turn of the century.

In the late 1920s and early 1930s, several manufacturers began widespread use of cold-formed steel. It has been used in commercial buildings for decades, but the use of steel framing moved into home construction in the early 1990s.

As the cost of framing lumber has risen, so too has the wide use of steel as a substitute for framing.

Steel is not a perfect material. Be aware of the following issues when building out of steel studs:

- ✔ **Thermal bridging:** In cold weather, the steel studs carry the cold into the building. If it's cold enough, the moisture in the air can form ice on the studs, or water condensation inside the wall.

- ✔ **Thermal movement:** Wood will expand and contract from humidity. Steel is impervious to moisture, but it expands and contracts from temperature. A steel stud can move as much as half an inch if the temperature changes a lot over the course of the day.

- ✔ **Rot:** Although the steel studs will not rot, the plywood and drywall is vulnerable to water. Using steel can mask leaking until it's too late.

- ✔ **Rust:** The galvanized steel studs will not rust, but you'll need to make sure the screws and connectors are also galvanized.

- ✔ **Fire:** Although the studs are fire resistant, they don't perform well once a fire has started. The studs can buckle and collapse in a fire.

Also, the high amount of energy required to produce steel is a concern. The question is, which is better: destroying an acre of forest, or pumping greenhouse gases into the air to make steel? You have to weigh the advantages of each to make a decision. If steel framing can be found locally, with a high recycled content, then you should consider it for your home as a substitute for wood framing.

Taking advantage of steel

As a material, wood is a fairly good insulator. Steel, however, conducts heat and cold. A steel stud will conduct ten times more heat and cold than a standard wood stud. Because of this, steel framing is not recommended for cold climates. The cold weather will creep inside.

The strong, lightweight steel studs are similar to wood framing, but offer the following design opportunities:

- ✔ **Curves:** Curved walls are incredibly difficult and labor intensive. New technologies, such as Flex-C Trac (`www.flexc.com`), allow for curves and arches with much less wood.

- ✔ **Insulation:** As with wood, the thin walls only hold the minimum amount of insulation. Spray-on and exterior insulation is a worthwhile investment.

- ✔ **Height:** Steel framing is generally limited to around two or three stories in height. If you want to go higher, concrete and large steel beams must be introduced.

- ✔ **Consistent sizes:** Although most wood studs vary in size and straightness, the metal studs are perfectly consistent.

- ✔ **Fire resistance:** The steel studs allow your walls to be more fire resistant, important in areas where the building codes require fire-rated walls.

Because the costs of steel and wood often flutter like the stock market, which material is least expensive will depend on the prices at the time you're building. I've often seen contractors switch from wood to steel at the last minute due to the current prices.

For non-load-bearing walls (such as interior walls), the lighter metal studs are generally less expensive than their wood counterparts. For structural walls requiring thicker metal studs, the opposite is true. The labor and time to install is generally the same if the contractor is familiar with both materials.

In colder climates, a steel-framed home will require additional insulation, increasing the overall cost. In temperate climates, this won't be an issue.

In remote areas where the building materials must be shipped, the lighter weight of steel will have a slight cost advantage.

Chapter 9

Natural Building Methods

- -

- -

*T*ypically, a house is built out of sticks of wood (called *studs*) nailed together in a line (called *framing*) to create the floors and walls. Wood framing has been in use for over 175 years, and it remains the most popular method of building homes. Nearly 90 percent of the homes built in the United States last year used wood framing. Odds are, your home is made of wood.

Unfortunately, using all this wood is wasteful and inefficient. Wood-framed buildings require the addition of insulation, waterproofing, and special structural panels. The 13,000 board feet of lumber needed to build the average house also consumes trees and adds to global warming.

In this chapter, I explore several natural construction methods as alternatives to using wood. Consisting mostly of mud, straw, or scrap wood, these methods offer numerous advantages over wood framing. From saving money, to speeding up construction time, to increasing insulation value, natural building methods may be the best choice for your green dream home.

Using natural building methods is not an all-or-nothing approach. You can use a combination of methods and materials. Build the exterior walls out of straw bale, the interior walls out of framing (see Chapter 8), and the garage out of something like structural insulated panels (see Chapter 10).

Check with your local building department before beginning construction using any of the methods covered in this chapter. The building codes favor wood, steel, and concrete. Any time you want to use something else, you may need special approval from the building department.

The history of straw bale

Stories of the first use of straw bale date back to the 1890s when settlers in the Midwest plains of Nebraska had to make do with what was available. Trees were scarce. Because straw bale is really just a waste product, a leftover from their normal farming activities, the farmers had to find a use for it. Several of these buildings are still standing today.

The use of straw bale slowed after World War II due to the surplus of other building materials. Early hobbyist homebuilders started tinkering around with straw bale again in the 1970s in response to the energy crisis. This natural, non-toxic, renewable, and abundant material was quickly embraced by green builders.

Straw Bale

The thick walls of a straw-bale wall have become synonymous with the green building movement. Part low-tech technique, part clever use of a waste material, straw bale is an attractive and popular alternative to wood framing.

What straw bale is

When wheat and rice farmers strip off the husks of the plant during a harvest, long, hollow stalks of straw are left behind. A large machine, called a *baler,* packs this straw into large bricks called *straw bales.* Bales can come from the harvesting of wheat, oats, barley, rice, rye, or flax.

Hay is for horses! The bales I'm talking about are straw, not hay. If you were to use hay, it would attract insects. The strong fibers of straw are pure cellulose (the same material as your fingernails) and contain nothing for the insects to eat.

Measuring around 14 inches wide, 18 inches tall, and 36 inches long, the tightly packed bales of straw weigh about 50 to 60 pounds each — just light enough for a strong person to stack into a wall.

Some 200 million tons of straw are wasted each year in the United States. The annual straw harvest in the United States could build around 4 million average-size homes every year. That's four times the number of houses built each year!

When you hear about a straw house, you may be thinking of something out of the Three Little Pigs. But as you can see in Figure 9-1, the bales are piled up like bricks and cannot be blown down, not even by a big bad wolf. Bamboo stakes or steel reinforcing bars *(rebar)* are used between each row to pin the bales together. Unlike real bricks, mortar is not used between the bales.

Bale Buildings

Straw-bale construction offers high insulation value but can cost more and be difficult to work with.

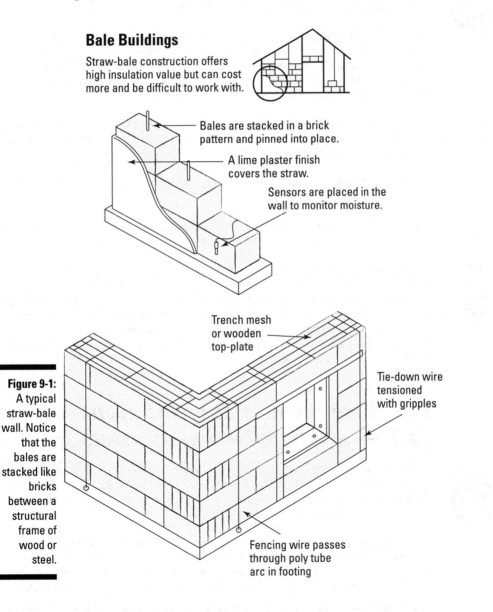

Bales are stacked in a brick pattern and pinned into place.

A lime plaster finish covers the straw.

Sensors are placed in the wall to monitor moisture.

Trench mesh or wooden top-plate

Tie-down wire tensioned with gripples

Figure 9-1: A typical straw-bale wall. Notice that the bales are stacked like bricks between a structural frame of wood or steel.

Fencing wire passes through poly tube arc in footing

After the bales are all stacked up, plumbing and electrical conduits are easily placed in the wall. At the door and window locations, wood is used around the straw bale to act as a place to screw the door and window frames to the wall.

If you forgot a window, don't panic: The bales are very forgiving. Simply take a hand axe and chop out the opening you need.

After the wall is completed, it has to be finished with something to keep the water out. Natural mud-based or lime-based stucco is traditionally used on the outside, with breathable earthen plaster on the inside. The stucco will not stick to the straw by itself, so a wire mesh (called *metal lath* or *chicken wire*) is wrapped over the straw to hold the finish.

The roof is set over the walls and is typically made of wood joists or trusses, just like on a wood-frame home. Because it's built the same way as a typical wood building, the roof can be flat, sloped, or any shape you want.

A straw-bale home has an insulation value that's often triple that of a wood-frame home.

Although there have been several cases of straw-bale buildings going as high as four stories, straw bales are typically kept to one-story buildings.

Although straw bale is strong enough to be load bearing, many states do not allow the bales to be the primary structural element. When this is the case, a structural support frame of wood or steel is built, and the bales fill in between the posts. As you can see in Figure 9-1, the roof is supported by the structural frame, not by the straw bale. Used in this way, the bales are really just glorified insulation. Check with your local building department to see what limitations it has on the use of straw bale.

Dispelling common concerns about straw bale — and highlighting its assets

Straw bale is superior to typical wood framing in many ways, but because it's not traditional, many people have some concerns about using straw bales in their homes. Here are some facts to put your mind at ease if you're thinking about building with straw bales:

- **Although pests such as termites thrive on a diet of wood, straw bales provide no nutritional value to them.** Termites are more likely to eat the wood windows and leave before showing any interest in the straw walls. The dense bales also don't allow much room for larger pests, like rodents.

- **Hay fever, allergies, and leftover pesticides are not an issue.** Because the walls are completely covered, the dry bales inside don't release anything into the home.

✔ **Ordinary rain and moisture are normal and nothing to be worried about so long as you allow the walls to breathe.** Instead of using traditional building paper to cover the walls, use a spray-on sealer. Because splashing water at the ground could saturate the walls, you can use a waterproof barrier (like Tyvek) just at the bottom of the walls.

✔ **Fire testing has shown straw bale to be incredibly resistant to fire.** The densely packed walls prevent any air from feeding a spark. The stucco finish adds another extra layer of protection. Wood buildings are more prone to fire than straw-bale homes.

✔ **As long as water does not leak into cracks in the walls, the straw will last for centuries.** (The ancient Egyptians used straw to pack their tombs.) Besides, leaking water affects any building, not just straw bale.

✔ **Most things can be hung using wooden dowels.** The dense bales will hold them securely in place. For very heavy items, such as cabinets, long bolts can be used through the bales and held in place with a large washer on the other side.

Still not convinced? Here are some advantages offered by straw bale:

✔ **It's nearly free.** Straw bale is available nearly everywhere. In many cases, the bales can be obtained for free or for a very low cost. Because the bales are a waste product, you're doing the farmer a favor by taking the "waste" off his hands.

✔ **Because straw-bale construction requires a simple set of skills, homeowners can often build their homes themselves.** They often invite friends over for a "bale-raising" party (complete with pizza and beer), to get free labor to help build the walls.

✔ **Because the walls have triple the amount of insulation of a traditional home, you can reduce the size of your heating equipment and save money from the start.** Plus, your monthly heating bills will be much lower.

✔ **It's quiet.** The dense, stuffed walls create an incredibly quiet home. One of the first things people notice in a straw-bale home is how silent they are.

Taking advantage of straw bale

The superhigh insulation factor of straw bale makes it perfect for both hot and cold climates. From the hot desert to the frosty mountains, a straw-bale home will keep you comfortable year-round. Damp, humid regions are probably not the best climate for straw bale, but anywhere else is fine.

The modular nature (stacks of large bricks) of straw bale makes it incredibly flexible and versatile in your design. Consider the following when designing for a straw-bale home:

- ✔ **Curves:** Gentle curves are easy to create with straw bale. The plaster finish hides the segments of each bale, creating a smooth, finished appearance.

- ✔ **Deep windows:** The thick bales create thick walls. In hot climates, place the windows on the inside of the wall to create a deep shadow box around the glass. In cold climates, place the windows on the outside of the wall to create interior window seats and deep sills. These deep windows are part of the look of a straw-bale building.

- ✔ **A truth window:** Proud straw-bale homeowners often keep a small area of the wall unfinished to show off the straw below the plaster. Called a *truth window,* these fun details distinguish your home from a typical one.

- ✔ **Deep overhangs:** Although the bales are covered with stucco, you need to keep the walls dry. Use deep roof overhangs to shed the rainwater away from the walls.

Because of their thickness, using straw bale only at the exterior walls is best. The walls on the inside can be made of wood framing (see Chapter 8) or anything you want.

Wall costs are usually only about 10 percent to 20 percent of the overall cost of construction. And straw-bale homes cost the same as, or only slightly more than, traditional wood-frame houses. When comparing the costs to wood, remember to factor in the price of the wood studs, insulation, and higher heating bills. A straw-bale wall goes up much faster than wood, saving you money on labor.

As with any home, reducing the size, keeping it to one story, or cutting back on the number of corners can lower the cost. Find a source for the bales ahead of time. Because they're a farming product, their availability is seasonal and cheaper during the harvesting months. Design the dimensions of the home to match the module of the bales; this will save cutting time and waste.

Adobe

Adobe is the original solar-powered building material. Sun-dried bricks of mud and straw make adobe one of the most abundant and lowest energy materials around. The wobbly walls of an adobe home hold a charm and romance that evokes the spirit of the desert of the American Southwest.

The history of adobe

Adobe is perhaps the oldest building material, dating back thousands of years. Mud-brick buildings have been found all over the world, particularly in the Middle East and North Africa. The word *adobe* can be traced back to the Ancient Egyptian word for *mud brick* from 2000 B.C.

The indigenous people of Central America used adobe to house themselves for centuries. When the Spaniards arrived, they improved the technology by pre-forming the bricks in wooden molds — the same practice we use today.

Adobe was an obvious choice in the rural deserts of Arizona and New Mexico, where material, skilled labor, and money were scarce. Because of the abundance of mud, adobe is often mistakenly considered a cheap material that will wash away in the first heavy rain. The realities of adobe construction are buildings that can last for hundreds of years.

The Great Depression of the 1930s brought widespread attention to adobe construction. The U.S. government sponsored adobe construction projects across the country, particularly in the Dust Bowl regions of the Southwest and Midwest. The low-skill method of forming and stacking mud bricks quickly caught on in these areas. The heat-absorbing qualities of adobe made it the perfect choice for the hot, dry climate. Many of these Depression-era homes are still in use today.

 Many building departments are reluctant to approve adobe buildings, despite its long history (see the nearby sidebar). Although all three of the major national building codes contain some provision for the use of adobe, your local building department will be wary if adobe hasn't been done locally before. Talk with the permit office before planning an adobe home.

What adobe is

Traditional adobe building is incredibly labor intensive. Imagine digging up large piles of dirt, mixing it with clay and straw into mud, and forming it into bricks! If you're building your home by yourself on a shoestring budget, on-site adobe may be a good option. Otherwise, all that labor makes adobe potentially expensive.

Most modern adobe homes now use premade bricks. In the Southwest, where adobe is most popular, adobe brick companies manufacture bricks and deliver them right to your construction site. Premade adobe bricks may only be available in Arizona or New Mexico, however.

Adobe brick manufacturers have made a science out of adobe production. A careful mixture of mud, clay, straw, and water is poured into a wooden frame (like a mold) and left to bake under the sun. The molds are quickly removed and the bricks are dry in a matter of hours. Dung is often used as a stabilizer and natural insect repellant. Once dry, the manufacturer sends the finished bricks out for construction.

If you have to make your own mud bricks, don't be surprised if your local building department asks you to conduct strength tests on your bricks.

Brick sizes vary, but adobe bricks are typically 4 inches tall, 10 inches wide, and 14 inches thick. The way in which you turn the bricks will create either a 10-inch- or a 14-inch-thick wall. The bricks are light enough to be lifted with two hands and stacked into the wall. Just like real bricks, a cement mortar is used to hold the bricks together.

Sun-baked adobe bricks offer a seemingly endless supply of building material, requiring only manual labor to create. No other energy is used, making adobe an incredibly green building option.

The concept of using mud bricks may make you think of dust, cracking, or even melting walls. Here are the realities of an adobe home:

- **Dust, allergies, and dirt are not part of the adobe experience.** Because the walls are completely covered with plaster, the encapsulated bricks will not spread dirt around your home.

- **Although rainwater will soak into the stucco, the insulation and the clay content in the brick resist the moisture.**

- **Adobe doesn't burn.** In fact, if your home catches fire, the wood roof, windows, and doors will burn away leaving the charred adobe walls intact.

- **Minor cracking is part of any masonry material like adobe.** *Major* cracks are a potential source of leaking or structural problems. Avoid these by using quality adobe bricks from a respected manufacturer. Ask the manufacturer for references of contractors who have used their products.

- **If you want to hang pictures on the wall, just use simple hangers.** For heavy items such as cabinets, you need to install some wood, called *blocking*, into the wall. The blocking acts as a secure spot to screw or nail into the wall.

How adobe works in a home

Like most construction methods, the stacked adobe-brick walls are finished with stucco on the outside and plaster on the inside. The process is straightforward. After the foundation is poured, the adobe bricks are stacked row by row, as shown in Figure 9-2. A layer of mortar is placed between each row of bricks. The mud bricks are slightly imperfect and misshapen, so they don't create neat bands the way fired bricks would.

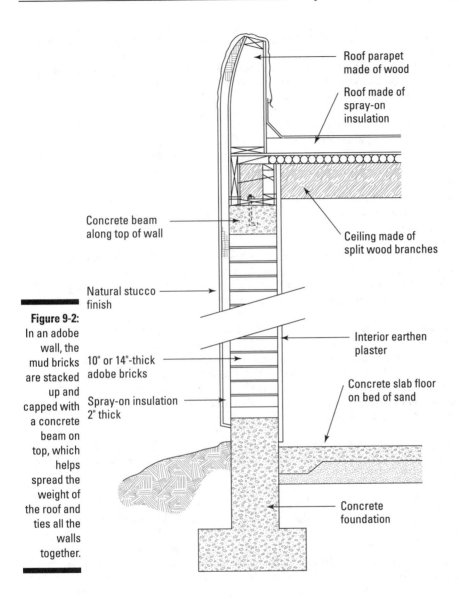

Roof parapet
made of wood

Roof made of
spray-on
insulation

Concrete beam
along top of wall

Ceiling made of
split wood branches

Natural stucco
finish

Figure 9-2:
In an adobe
wall, the
mud bricks
are stacked
up and
capped with
a concrete
beam on
top, which
helps
spread the
weight of
the roof and
ties all the
walls
together.

10" or 14"-thick
adobe bricks

Interior earthen
plaster

Concrete slab floor
on bed of sand

Spray-on insulation
2" thick

Concrete
foundation

At window and door openings, a wood beam called a *header* is placed over the opening to hold up the bricks above it. Wooden blocks are placed around the openings. These blocks are where the windows and doors are screwed into the wall.

Where a wood-frame wall has large empty voids inside it for things like plumbing and wiring, an adobe wall is solid. But adobe is very forgiving and flexible. You simply take the back of a hammer and lightly chop out a channel for the pipes and electrical conduits to run. If you forgot to install a switch or an outlet, just grab a hammer and cut out a path for the wires.

When the wall is complete, a concrete cap, called a *bond beam,* is poured along the top of the entire wall. The bond beam ties all the walls together and helps distribute the weight of the roof over the adobe wall below. In addition, this bond beam creates an even and level surface for the roof because the adobe blocks are uneven and irregular.

The roof is built directly over the concrete bond beam. The thick adobe walls are strong enough to support any type of roof: pitched or flat. For a traditional-looking flat roof, place large, round, wooden beams (called *vigas*) across the ceiling. Smaller branches of wood called *latillas* are often placed between the vigas to decorate the ceiling. Plywood is placed over the latillas, and any type of roofing material can be used over that. An insulating spray-on roof, such as icynene or polyisocyanurate, is a great choice. This is the traditional roof for Southwestern-style adobe buildings.

For pitched roofs, the construction is the same as with any pitched roof. Wood joists or trusses are put into place to support the roofing material of your choice. You can finish this tall space as an attic or leave it open to create rooms with high, sloped ceilings.

Adobe has a wonderfully high thermal mass (see Chapter 11). It stores up the heat from the sun all day, and releases it at night when it's cool. Using this mass, an adobe wall will keep you comfortable year-round, and reduce your energy bills. Although adobe has a high thermal mass, it has almost no insulation value. You have to add insulation by spraying it on the outside with the same material used for flat roofs. A finished adobe house is incredibly energy efficient and comfortable in both hot and cool climates.

When the walls and roof have been installed, metal lath or chicken wire is wrapped around the entire wall. This supports the stucco finish and plaster, which won't stick to the bare adobe or the insulation.

In dry climates, the adobe blocks can be left exposed and just sealed with a waterproof sealer. The finished wall will look like brown-colored bricks.

An adobe building is typically only one story, although there have been many two- and three-story adobe buildings throughout history. The thick (10- or 14-inch) walls of adobe are strong, but their heavy weight will limit the height of the building. As with most load-bearing brick buildings, the walls are thickest at the ground floor and get thinner at each floor to reduce the weight.

Taking advantage of adobe

You've probably seen the adobe buildings scattered around the Southwest. The influence of Native American and Mexican cultures inspired their use throughout parts of Arizona, New Mexico, and Texas, where the hot, dry climate is perfect for maintenance-free adobe houses. But you may be surprised to know that adobe has historically been found throughout the United States, from Oregon to Pennsylvania, using abundant mud bricks dating back to pre-Revolutionary times. The high thermal mass walls of adobe work well in any climate with seasonal changes. Don't think it's just for the desert — adobe could be the perfect solution for you.

The small adobe bricks offer incredible flexibility in both the construction and final appearance of the home. Consider the following when designing an adobe home:

- **Curves:** Tight curves are easy with adobe, though it adds to the cost. The final plaster finish creates a smooth, unified look.

- **Deep windows:** The wide bricks produce thick walls. To prevent water from damaging the building, push the windows to the outside, which creates deep window sills. Make the sills match the floor, or use brick for a traditional touch.

- **Embrace the mud:** The imperfect bricks create walls with a distinctive, wavy feel. Don't try to make the walls completely straight — enjoy the wackiness. It's part of the final look and charm of adobe.

Due to their thickness, it's best to use adobe only at the exterior walls. The interior walls can be made of wood framing or anything you want (see Chapter 8).

When comparing the cost of an adobe wall to a wood-framed wall, it really comes down to the labor cost. If you're doing all the work yourself, you could build your adobe house for as little as $40 per square foot. Contractor-built adobe homes can be up to twice the cost of wood framing.

The real cost savings comes from the energy saved in the heating and cooling of the building.

If doing any work yourself, always remember to factor in the money lost from reduced time at work.

Use a consistent size of windows around the home. Making these openings the same will save on your labor. Consider using salvaged wood beams for the roof to save on costs.

Rammed Earth

The first thing you'll notice about a rammed earth wall is how beautiful it is. The massive walls, with vivid waves of rich color, are striking and unique. Beneath the stunning surface lies a clever building system, offering energy efficiency and strength.

The history of rammed earth

The tradition of packing earth to build a wall dates back to the Great Wall of China in 220 B.C. Similar to adobe or cob, rammed earth is a mixture of clay and sand. But the tightly tamped material is a big difference from those other materials.

The tradition of using earth to build homes has been around for thousands of years. Large ancient structures, such as temples and mosques, were built of rammed earth throughout the Middle East. The pharaohs of Ancient Egypt ruled over cities constructed of rammed earth.

In the United States, rammed earth was popular from 1780 until around 1850, when the introduction of mass-produced bricks and cut lumber became readily available. These industrial materials allowed easier, faster construction of homes to meet the needs of the growing population.

Rammed earth had a brief resurgence during the sparse 20-year period after World War I through the Depression, when people could build their own homes using nothing but local dirt.

The demand for manufactured housing at the end of World War II brushed natural methods like rammed earth aside. It wasn't until the energy crisis of the 1970s that builders rediscovered using packed earth to build homes. Green builder David Easton single-handedly popularized the modern use of rammed earth through his many books on the subject.

What rammed earth is

Rammed earth is essentially just man-made stone. But instead of being compressed for hundreds of thousands of years like sedimentary rock, rammed earth is formed in mere minutes through the compaction of dirt.

Rammed earth construction is a simple, yet labor-intensive, process that begins with the erection of formwork over the foundation. The foundations are the same as they would be for any home, but they must be sized to support the weight of the finished wall.

Forms can be made of plywood, metal, or fiberglass. The forms are held together with large bolts or bracing on the outside (see Figure 9-3). Formed to be at least 1 foot thick, finished rammed earth walls have a very flat surface because they take on the shape of the formwork mold.

Rammed earth walls are formed by packing, or *tamping,* a mix of soil with a tiny amount (around 3 percent) of Portland cement. The cement acts as a binding and strengthening agent. This mix is dumped into large wall molds, called *formwork,* in 7- to 8-inch-high rows, called *lifts.* A device that looks like

a jackhammer with a manhole cover stuck on the end, called a *tamper,* is used to compact the soil into the formwork. Each lift is tamped down to half its height.

The wall rises slowly — an 8-inch lift at a time — until it's complete. The forms are reused over and over again. The packed forms can be removed almost immediately and moved to the next portion of wall.

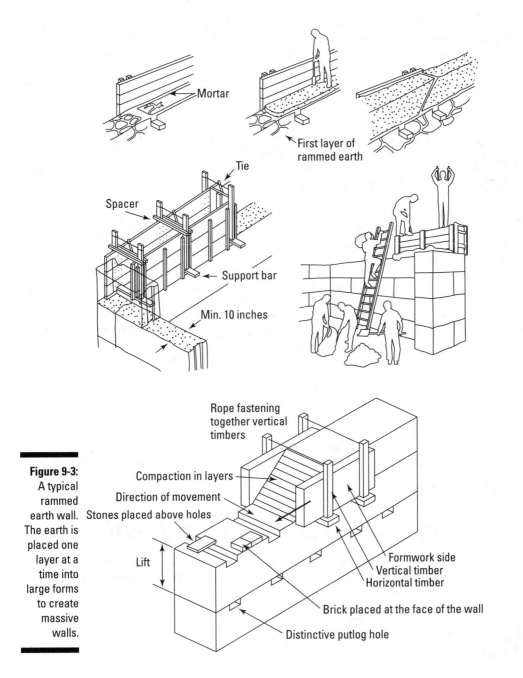

Figure 9-3:
A typical rammed earth wall. The earth is placed one layer at a time into large forms to create massive walls.

Because the mixture is really a very light version of concrete, the walls grow continually stronger as time passes, just as concrete does. The finished rammed earth wall is nearly as strong as concrete.

The mixture of the wall can affect the strength and appearance. Too much clay, and the wall will shrink and crack; too much soil, and the wall will not be as strong. A structural engineer will be able to help you balance the right mix.

The finished walls are treated with a clear sealer to prevent dust from coming off the walls and protect them from the rain. Interior walls can be finished with natural linseed oil. The walls feel and act similar to stone.

Although you can apply plaster directly to the surface of a rammed earth wall, you shouldn't. The walls show off the layers of each lift, creating wavy bands of vivid colors. Show off the labor of building that wall by designing it as a visible feature of the house.

All the plumbing and wiring must be planned ahead of time. Adding a forgotten outlet is incredibly difficult (if not impossible), so often builders will place empty conduits into the wall to allow you to come back and add something later.

Because the soil is pressed into place, rammed earth is incredibly strong and dense. The 12- to 24-inch-thick walls have a high thermal mass, so they maintain a consistent temperature throughout the day. The high thermal mass can potentially reduce your energy bills by 80 percent as compared to a wood-frame home. But the earth has little insulation value, so it's often sprayed onto the outside, similar to adobe (see the preceding section).

The walls of rammed earth have several advantages over traditional wood frame construction: They're fireproof, rot resistant, and impervious to insects.

Given the amount of effort needed to make the walls, you may want to reserve them only for areas where these beautiful walls will be visible. Make the other walls out of straw bale or wood.

Taking advantage of rammed earth

Rammed earth homes can be designed for most climate regions, including damp areas with cold winters. Consider them as an alternative to adobe for wet climates.

Place the wall in the path of the sun to absorb the heat and take advantage of the thermal mass.

Despite the effort involved in building a rammed earth wall, the beauty and strength offer some unique advantages. Consider the following:

- **Flat walls:** Because the walls are molded from forms, they're typically flat. Although, theoretically, curves are possible, creating the forms would be prohibitively expensive. If you want to create some excitement, consider flat, angular walls instead.

- **Texture:** Just like a Jell-O mold, the walls will take the shape and texture of the form. Plywood creates a rough surface, while steel or fiberglass forms create a polished finish.

The strength of rammed earth (similar to concrete) makes it strong enough for tall buildings, but due to the labor involved, they're typically only used in one-story buildings.

Given the labor needed to form a rammed earth wall, the final cost will depend on the price of labor for your project. For do-it-yourselfers, your free labor and dirt can build a wall for practically no cost. Using your own labor, you can budget a rammed earth wall to cost less than half that of a traditional wood-frame wall. The majority of that cost goes toward the reusable formwork materials. Using a contractor, plan on the initial construction to be about 5 percent more expensive than wood.

Here are some suggestions to help you save money in building your rammed earth home:

- **Reuse the formwork as much as possible.** Because the forms can be removed right after tamping the soil, you can easily reuse them.

- **If you're using plywood forms, make the walls some even module of the plywood.**

- **Instead of setting the windows into the wall, create breaks in the wall and build a wood wall above and below.** It will speed up the construction and make installing the windows easier.

Cob

If you're looking to build a sculptural fantasy home, cob is for you. With cob, any shape, flourish, and feature can be accomplished to create something unique and artistic.

The history of cob

Cob houses have been standing for centuries. The concept of living in a mud hut has probably been around since the dawn of Man.

The word *cob* comes from the Old English meaning, "a lump or rounded mass." The technique has been in use for hundreds of years throughout Europe, where the thick walls can keep you warm and dry. Cob was especially popular in England, with roots going back to at least the 13th century. The scarcity of stone and wood made using the abundant sandy clay soil perfect for cob construction.

By the 15th century, cob houses became the standard method of construction in England — that is, until the industrialized methods of brick and lumber took over around 1880.

What cob is

Cob construction is just like a ceramic sculpture — a really large one. A mixture of clay, sand, straw, water, and earth, cob is very similar to adobe in raw material. Instead of being formed into bricks, cob is built up a handful at a time. The strong, fireproof walls can create artistic and sculptural earthquake-resistant walls. Requiring little money or skill, a cob home can be built by homeowners willing to get their hands dirty.

Before you start thinking it's like living in a mud patty, keep in mind that the finished cob wall is covered with plaster, similar to adobe. Where adobe uses same-size bricks to create flat walls, cob lends itself to organic shapes, including arches, vaults, and curves.

Cob walls contain no steel reinforcing or cement, so they're typically sculpted to be 1 to 2 feet thick for stability. The thick walls create a cozy and surprisingly dry home.

The process of using cob is simple to learn. Cob is also cheap to build with. No bricks, forms, or wood are needed.

Cob construction uses sand, clay, and long strands of straw. Cob walls are built over a standard foundation by applying layer after layer of this mixture. These layers (called *cobs*) are placed by hand and then stepped on to pack it into place. Each layer must be dry before the next one can be applied. The walls rise slowly depending on how long the drying takes. Anywhere from 6 inches to 3 feet of wall may be completed in a day, but then it needs to be left alone for up to two weeks to dry completely. To reduce the weight, the walls taper and get thinner as you build up, from 24 inches at the bottom to 12 inches at the top. As they dry, the walls are trimmed and shaped to keep them straight.

Doors and window openings are simply set into the wall as it takes shape. If you forget to place a window, you can set in a wood header at the top and cut out the opening. The continuing layers build up around their wooden frames. Once dry, the walls are strong and load bearing, able to easily support the weight of the roof.

Earthen or lime-based plaster is applied directly to the wall to seal and protect it. The walls hold up surprisingly well in rainy climates. Still, be sure to waterproof the bottom couple of feet of the wall, and have deep roof overhangs to shed the water away from the house.

Cob houses require a tremendous amount of labor, so they're perfect for people wanting to build their own home (because the cost of paying someone else to do it may be prohibitive).

Living in a mud patty may raise some eyebrows, but the low-cost, owner-built technique makes a lot of sense. If you're worried about your cob house washing away during the first heavy rain, remember that the walls are porous and surprisingly dry on the inside. The plaster finish protects the walls. And, like adobe, cob is fireproof.

Taking advantage of cob

Traditionally, cob has been used in the cold, wet climates of England and Europe, but it's an appropriate material for most locations. The earth provides a high thermal mass, and the straw provides good insulation value. Plus, cob offers unlimited artistic opportunities. The shapely, organic material is unlike any other building material you've seen.

The layers of cob can be used in some clever ways. Consider the following:

- ✔ **Curves:** Organic, irregular curves are easy with cob. In fact, making curves is easier than making perfectly straight walls.
- ✔ **Relief:** Cob lends itself to being shaped and molded, allowing decorative wall reliefs, built-in shelves, light coves, and wall benches built right into the walls.
- ✔ **Fixed windows:** Embed regular windows and doors directly into the cob as you build each layer. For fixed windows, you can use a single piece of glass implanted into the cob and sculpted into any shape. Creative ideas such as using glass bottles can also be used.
- ✔ **Fireplaces:** The cob is completely fireproof, so your fireplace can be built into the wall as part of the sculptural design.

Because cob can only be considered for houses you build yourself, the costs are incredibly cheap. Skipping the need for formwork or steel reinforcing saves a great deal of money. The flexibility and forgiveness of the material speeds up changes and omissions in the walls.

Made from local earth, clay, and straw, cob is one of the cheapest building materials imaginable. The dirt removed during excavation is usually enough to build the walls. Combine this with your free labor, and you have a house that can be built for much less than a wood-frame building. The walls of a home are only about 20 percent of the total cost of construction, but still a considerable amount.

Because the walls allow for random sizes of doors and windows, you can use salvaged ones from your local salvage yard. Even a broken piece of glass or colorful glass bottles can be inserted into the walls to create a unique window.

Pneumatically Impacted Stabilized Earth

A refinement of rammed earth, pneumatically impacted stabilized earth (PISÉ) creates a beautiful wall made of only natural and healthy materials. PISÉ shares the beauty of rammed earth but is much less labor intensive.

What pneumatically impacted stabilized earth is

Technically, PISÉ is a type of rammed earth. A mixture of mud and cement is packed into a form. Rammed earth requires you to build formwork into which you pack earth, and PISÉ improves on this process. With PISÉ, you only build one side of the formwork and spray the earth into the form. PISÉ offers all the environmental benefits of rammed earth, but with a much shorter construction process.

The history of PISÉ

In the late 1700s, Paris builder Francois Cointeraux created a school dedicated to the study of rammed earth construction. Called *pisé de terre*, it translated to "puddled clay of earth."

Nearly 200 years later, author and rammed earth pioneer David Easton developed a new version of rammed earth construction, which he called *PISÉ* in honor of the old French school. Instead of tamping the earth into a form, Easton realized he could use a high-pressure spray gun to shoot the soil into the mold.

This spray technique is four times faster than traditional rammed earth. By reducing the labor, you also reduce the cost.

A one-sided form is placed over the building foundation (see Figure 9-4). Think of it as an open-faced sandwich. A watery mixture of earth and Portland cement (3 percent) is sprayed through a *pneumatic* (pressurized) spray hose into this form. This method is the same one used to form swimming pools.

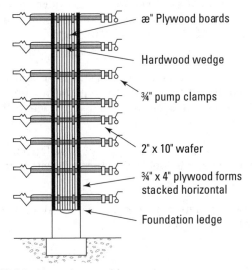

- æ" Plywood boards
- Hardwood wedge
- ¾" pump clamps
- 2" x 10" wafer
- ¾" x 4" plywood forms stacked horizontal
- Foundation ledge

Wall framing using wood forms

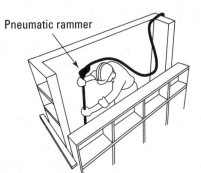

Pneumatic rammer

Temping using pneumatic rammer

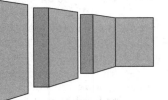

Finished walls

Figure 9-4: Similar to rammed earth, PISÉ uses mud sprayed into a form. Because it's sprayed in, only one side of the form is needed.

The mix is light and sticky enough to adhere to the side of the form without slumping. The PISÉ mix is sprayed in 2- to 3-foot-high layers and left to dry. In 30 minutes to an hour, another layer is added. Unlike rammed earth, the form must be left in place for a few hours until the PISÉ dries.

The single-sided forms are easy to set up and take down, and can be reused over and over again. The open face makes installing plumbing and electrical conduits, as well as adding steel reinforcing for earthquake resistance, much easier.

In case you're wondering why anyone would still use rammed earth if PISÉ is so superior: PISÉ requires specialized spray equipment and can't be installed by the typical homeowner. Also, although PISÉ is attractive, it lacks the wavy colors of a rammed earth wall.

You can apply plaster directly to the face of a PISÉ wall to finish it, although the exposed surface has a beautiful look. Finish the walls with a natural linseed oil instead.

The strong PISÉ walls are superior to traditional wood framing. They are resistant to fire, rot, and insects.

Taking advantage of pneumatically impacted stabilized earth

PISÉ buildings work in most climates, including damp areas with cold winters. The thermal mass of the walls works well in passive solar design to maintain a consistent temperature in the home.

Regardless of the special tools and skills needed to build a PISÉ wall, they do offer some distinctive advantages. The flat, formed walls of PISÉ allow for:

- **Flat walls:** The one-sided forms make it easiest to create flat walls. Because you spray into the form, curves and more elaborate molds are possible, but they do add to the cost.
- **Texture:** One side of the wall picks up the texture of the formwork. The other side can be finished with any texture you choose.

Constructing a PISÉ building requires access to spray tools and skilled workers. Depending on where you live, this can greatly affect the cost. Research these issues before beginning your PISÉ project.

The cost savings from the speedy construction allows PISÉ to be about the same cost as traditional wood framing. The finished building is as strong as concrete and energy efficient, making PISÉ far superior to wood.

To save money in building your PISÉ home, follow these suggestions:

- **Reuse the formwork as much as possible.** The PISÉ mix dries quickly, allowing you to strip off the forms and reposition them.

- **Size your walls to allow you to use the same piece of formwork.** Think of it as a reusable mold.

Cordwood

The ancient method of cordwood building produces beautiful, rustic-looking homes. The simplicity and charm of a row of stacked logs makes great use of a waste material to build your home.

What cordwood is

Cordwood construction stacks up short, round lengths of wood into a wall. Using what would normally be cast aside for firewood, cordwood looks like a stack of wood you'd have behind your fireplace.

The ends of the logs are left exposed, making efficient use of these leftover scraps of thick branches. The cordwood is held together with mortar, creating a wall with both high insulation and high thermal mass.

As with straw-bale walls, cordwood is not typically allowed to be structural and support the wall. Instead, the stacks of wood are used to fill in the wall between the pieces of a structural frame, even though the cordwood is incredibly strong on its own.

A variety of cordwood, from 1 to 6 inches across, is stacked up in a random pattern (see Figure 9-5). The wood protrudes from the wall about an inch or so, giving the wall a textured look. The finished walls are anywhere from 12 to 24 inches thick.

The history of cordwood

Cordwood structures can be found around the world, with the oldest standing ones in Greece dating back nearly a thousand years. In heavily wooded areas, using the scrap wood just made a lot of sense. Like most natural building methods, the tradition of cordwood had a rebirth with the green building movement.

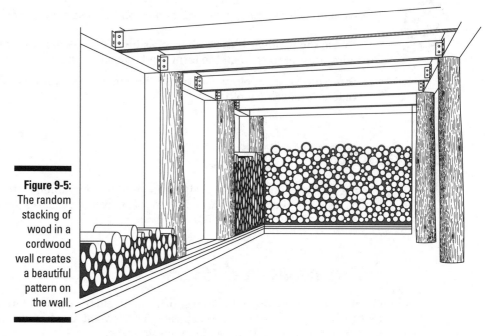

Figure 9-5:
The random stacking of wood in a cordwood wall creates a beautiful pattern on the wall.

You can find your own cordwood from a variety of sources, including fallen trees, timber mills, sawmills, and split firewood.

No matter where you find the cordwood, you'll need to remove the bark to prevent water from sneaking into the home. Nearly any type of wood can be used, but the best choice would be the naturally rot-resistant woods, such as cypress, cedar, or juniper. Choose a light wood to keep the logs from swelling and shrinking.

Ideally, you should use the same species of wood on each wall. This ensures that the wood will react to water and temperature the same way.

The process of building a cordwood wall is a lot like laying rows of brick (refer to Figure 9-5). The logs are set with their ends sticking out, and mortar is placed between each piece. It's similar to the Lincoln Logs you played with as a kid.

You may be surprised to know that the logs are not treated or coated with anything. The ends are left to breathe naturally. If you like, you can use lime plaster, linseed oil, or sand to finish the exterior of the wall.

Cement-based mortar is typically used to hold the logs together, mixed with sand and sawdust to help it bond to the bare logs. Many green builders have been using cob (see the preceding section) as a mortar instead. The natural clay and straw of cob mortar is a more sustainable alternative, but you need to take the same waterproofing measures discussed in cob construction.

Practical needs, such as electrical wiring and plumbing, must be planned ahead of time and built into the wall.

Although a cordwood wall is incredibly dense and strong, most building codes will not allow you to use them to support the roof. In these situations, a structural frame of heavy timber or steel is used, and the cordwood is used as a fill in the structural frame. For load-bearing cordwood walls, the logs need to be woven together at the corners.

The logs are stacked up by hand, and a 3- to 4-inch bead of mortar is placed at each end. The mortar is kept about an inch away from each end and doesn't continue all the way through the wall. An air space is left inside the wall to insulate and to prevent water from soaking indoors.

The insulation value of cordwood varies based on the type of wood, the thickness, and the mortar. Generally, the finished wall is about the same as a traditional wood-frame wall. The mortar adds a thermal mass, which will keep the home comfortable year-round.

Taking advantage of cordwood

The thermal mass and insulation of cordwood allow it to be used in most climates. The walls are surprisingly dry, permitting you to use cordwood even in wet climates. Extreme cold or hot climates are not appropriate for cordwood walls, however.

The simple process of cordwood building does provide some special design opportunities. Very different from wood framing, cordwood creates a richly textured and rustic wall.

The individually stacked lengths of wood allow you some fun and creativity. Consider the following when building your cordwood home:

- **Placement:** Cordwood builders typically take great care in the arrangement of the logs. The goal is to accentuate the differences in the wood and have a random placement of sizes. The beauty of a cordwood wall comes from the exposed wood ends.

- **Decoration:** Homeowners usually decorate the mortar between the logs with anything they can find. Marbles, seashells, and pebbles are often pushed into the still-wet mortar to decorate the home.

> ✓ **Bottle windows:** Just as with cob, glass bottles can be inset into the wall to create a unique window. Place mortar between a stack of bottles to make a bigger window.

The random (almost sloppy) method of cordwood construction makes it a labor-intensive, but fun, way to build. The cheap (or even free) materials must be stacked by hand but go up quickly.

If you're doing the work yourself, a cordwood home will cost less than a wood-frame home of the same size. Compared to straw bale or cob, cordwood is the most affordable.

In addition to a lower construction cost, cordwood walls are maintenance free, eliminating the need of painting or siding.

Here are some tips to lower your costs:

- ✓ **You'll save time and money if the source of the wood is nearby.** Cordwood requires a lot of small pieces of wood, and it's easy to underestimate how much you'll need. Transportation wastes money and energy, so stick with local sources.

- ✓ **Rainwater splashing off the ground can cause the wood to rot.** Run foundation walls 18 to 24 inches off the ground. Start your cordwood wall high to protect it from moisture and splashing rain.

- ✓ **Get the rain away from the walls.** Broad eaves at the roof at least 12 inches deep will shed the water away from the house and keep your walls dry.

- ✓ **Practice makes perfect.** The arrangement of the cordwood is the key to creating beautiful walls. Practice on some test walls before embarking on the real thing. It will give you a chance to experiment with the patterns and get a feel for placing the walls.

- ✓ **Weave the corners of the cordwood walls together for added strength.** It takes a little longer but saves you money in the end.

Earthships

An *Earthship* is not just a method of construction, but a radical approach to how you live in relation to nature, energy, and water. As a construction method, the walls are earth-filled tires set into the ground. As a philosophy, Earthships promote energy-independent, cheap construction for the masses.

The history of Earthships

The concept of the Earthship was the visionary idea of architect Michael Reynolds. In 1969, Reynolds moved to Taos, New Mexico, where he began building homes out of the junk he could find lying around. He continues to live today in an Earthship community he founded in the outskirts of Taos.

Reynolds has since written several books on the subject, educating people on how to build their own Earthship homes. Earthships generate their own electricity, collect their own water, and clean their own waste — what people refer to as living "off the grid" (because they're disconnected from the public utility companies). The low-skill, low-cost idea of living completely off the grid has attracted thousands of eager homeowners looking to build their own homes.

What Earthships are

Combining passive solar design with a waste material, Earthships are a unique approach to building environmentally friendly homes. If you're looking to build your own house, an Earthship is an attractive and energy-efficient option.

In reality, Earthship construction is a simplified form of rammed earth. Instead of building elaborate formwork, discarded tires become the form into which you pack the dirt. These earth-filled tires are strong enough to be the foundation and support the roof.

The Earthship is set into the ground and turned toward the sun. Because the house is buried on three sides, it's well insulated. The side open to the sun is designed to control the sun to allow it in during the winter, and keep it out in the summer. Using these methods, an Earthship heats and cools itself without consuming any fossil fuels.

The roof of an Earthship is typically a *green roof* (covered in plants), and is used to collect the rainwater (see Chapter 13). The plants on the roof naturally clean the water, which is used in the home.

Most Earthships incorporate solar panels or wind turbines to generate all the electrical needs for the home, making an Earthship a completely self-contained, sustainable home.

The primary building block of an Earthship is of one of the world's most abundant and troublesome waste products: used automobile tires. Americans throw away nearly 300 million tires each year — nearly one per person. Ten percent of those tires end up in landfills and can be put to good use. In an Earthship, the tires stack up to create 30-inch-thick walls. Because earth is packed into each tire, the walls are structurally stable and have a very high thermal mass, similar to rammed earth.

The assembly of an Earthship (see Figure 9-6) is a random assortment of scrap materials and found objects, most of which are dug out of the local landfill. Instead of a traditional foundation, tires are stacked into an excavated trench. Each tire is packed firmly with dirt. The next layer of tires is staggered, like brick, and filled again. This process is repeated until the wall is completed.

Used soda cans are wedged between the tires. The metal flip tabs on the cans will support the final layer of plaster, the same way chicken wire does with adobe or straw bale. There is no order — the cans can be shoved into any convenient location.

Plumbing and electrical runs fit neatly in the grooves between the tires. Adding additional outlets or pipes is easy.

For curving walls, the recycled soda cans are placed like bricks with mortar to create a lightweight wall. The finished wall — whether straight or curved — is coated with stucco or plaster.

The roof can be made out of wood (as in traditional wood construction) or with large timbers (as in adobe construction). The roof must be strong enough to support the weight of the plants that will eventually live on top.

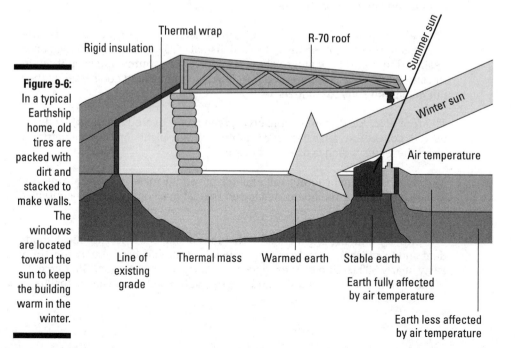

Figure 9-6: In a typical Earthship home, old tires are packed with dirt and stacked to make walls. The windows are located toward the sun to keep the building warm in the winter.

Traditional building codes do not contain provisions for using Earthship construction, so check with your local building department. Many of these buildings are built without government approval, but I can't officially condone this.

If the thought of building your walls out of tires makes you think of an auto-body shop, don't worry. Tires have a funny smell, but the finished walls are covered with stucco, so there's no odor. And, although tires do burn, it takes a lot to get them started. The earthen fill and stucco finish protects the walls even more.

You may be worried about using tires in your home, but the finished Earthship walls will be safe. Plus, they make good use of something that would otherwise have ended up in a landfill.

Digging your own Earthship

The thick walls of an Earthship home will work in any climate. The high thermal mass and insulation value will keep you comfortable year-round.

The unusual tire construction of Earthships presents some interesting design opportunities for you. Built entirely by hand, the Earthship will be more sculptural and individual. Enjoy this part of the process and let the uncommon methods inspire some cool designs.

The large walls of tires create a thick and cozy home. Consider the following when designing an Earthship:

- ✔ **The walls will be rounded at the ends to match the tires. Gentle curves can be formed with the tires.** For tighter curves, use the soda-can method.

- ✔ **Work with other methods.** You don't need to build the entire home out of one construction method. Earthships work well with adobe, cob, and straw bale. Save the thick tires for the exterior walls and foundations.

- ✔ **The tire walls are best suited for single-story homes.**

Although the wall materials are free, the intense labor almost demands that you build your Earthship by yourself. Prepackaged floor plans are available for purchase to help you design the perfect Earthship and get permit approval. You can find more information at www.earthship.org and www.earthshipbiotecture.com. Plan packages start at around $3,000.

With the trade between your free labor and the time it takes to build, an Earthship will cost about the same as traditional wood framing. The real savings will be in your monthly utility bills.

Earthships have been around for nearly 40 years, so take advantage of that. Talk to other Earthship homeowners for more advice. Visit the forums at www. earthship.net or at www.dennisweaver.com, the Web site of actor Dennis Weaver, who discusses his own Earthship home on the site. The introductory books *Earthship: Volume 1, Earthship: Volume 2,* and *Earthship: Volume 3,* by Michael Reynolds (the founder of Earthships) are invaluable if you're considering building an Earthship home.

Ceramic Earth

Originally developed as a low-cost method for building homes in poor communities, ceramic earth is a method of creating strong houses — fast. Like adobe and cob, the walls are made of the local earth. A large fire is burned inside the house to bake the walls like ceramics in a kiln. The finished buildings are sculptural works of art.

What ceramic earth is

Think of ceramic earth like a giant ceramic kiln. Ceramic houses are adobe houses made with very high clay content. The finished walls are fired in place to become hardened ceramic. These permanent, waterproof, and earthquake-resistant homes use all four natural elements: Earth and water are used to make the bricks, while fire and air are used to finish them. The result is an affordable, strong home made of natural materials.

There are two types of ceramic earth:

- ✔ **Fired adobe:** Fired adobe uses stacks of clay bricks to create the walls. After they're set into place, a fire is set inside the home to bake the bricks into a hard ceramic shell.

- ✔ **Earthbag construction:** Earthbag construction uses long tube bags filled with dirt and sand. The long bags are wrapped in coils, similar to a ceramic pot, spiraling upward into a dome.

I go into greater detail on these two types of ceramic earth in the following sections. Check out Figure 9-7 for an example of earthbag construction.

The notion of using bags filled with dirt may make you think of dirty rooms. In reality, because the walls are completely covered with plaster, the covered earthbags will not spread dirt around your home. Plus, the ceramic earth has already been fired and doesn't burn; the shape of the domes resists fire as well.

The history of ceramic earth

The concept of ceramic earth is the work of visionary Iranian architect, Nader Khalili. In his native Iran, poor people lived in small adobe houses that were prone to collapse in an earthquake. Khalili discovered that, if the walls were fired, they would bake together the same way a ceramic pot acts in a kiln. Through experimentation, Khalili perfected his techniques. In addition to strengthening old adobe buildings, Khalili built new buildings using the same process.

When Khalili moved to California in 1984, he discovered that the homes of poor people were not made of adobe, but of wood. His ceramic firing technique would not work, so he began experimenting with sandbags filled with earth.

Earthbag shelters have been used in the military for decades as a lightweight, low-cost, and quickly built solution. The infantry constructed bunkers from sand-filled sacks as far back as World War I. Several architects have explored earthbag structures, but Khalili improved on the system to create what he calls *superadobe*.

Working with the National Aeronautics and Space Administration (NASA), Khalili has proposed using his earthbag technique to create human settlements on the moon. He has since created developments of his superadobe around the world.

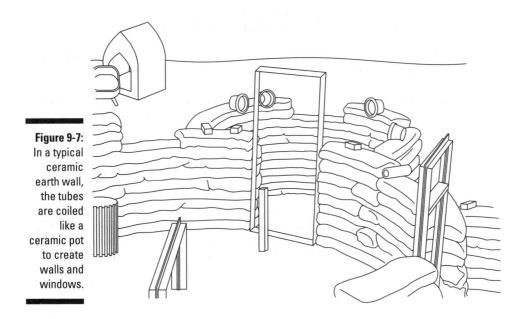

Figure 9-7: In a typical ceramic earth wall, the tubes are coiled like a ceramic pot to create walls and windows.

Fired adobe

The basic technique in building ceramic houses is very similar to adobe. Instead of mud and straw, the bricks are made with a high clay content. The mixture has the consistency of ceramic clay when it's pressed into forms and left to dry for a week or two.

Instead of using cement mortar, a clay mortar mixed with glass is used. This mortar fuses better to the clay bricks. The bricks are stacked by hand, one by one, with a new layer of mortar over each row. The joints between the bricks are left open to allow them to expand during the fire.

The roof is made of domes, vaults, and arches out of the same material so it can be fired. To create arches and vaults, mortarless blocks are used to support the arch; they're taken away after firing. Because there is no mortar holding it in place, these temporary bricks are easily removed.

After the walls and roof are in place, a burner is installed to create the fire. The type of burner used depends on the fuel available. Oil, gas, and wood can all be used. A chimney, or *flue,* is built into the walls and roof to allow the fumes to escape and allow air to feed the fire. These holes will be filled in later.

The building is heated to over 1,000°F to bake the adobe clay. After the firing, the ceiling flues are opened to allow a slow cooling over the next two days.

After they're cooled, the exterior walls can be finished with earthen plaster or ceramic tile. These finishes are applied directly to the fired brick.

Many of the early ceramic houses had no plumbing or electricity. But spaces for electrical wiring and plumbing can be made using unmortared bricks, which are removed after the firing.

Like adobe, the ceramic bricks have a high thermal mass to keep you comfortable year-round. Heating and cooling a ceramic home is inexpensive.

Earthbag construction

Earthbag construction really lives up to its name. A basic earthbag home uses simple sandbags stacked up into arches like an igloo. Clay or regular barbed wire is used to hold the layers of earthbag together, like a mortar.

Like a coiled clay pot, earthbag construction fills long, snakelike sandbags and coils them up to make walls. The walls are wrapped around in a coil, with each successive layer on top. On top of each layer, strands of barbed wire are placed to prevent slippage between each row of earthbags. The weight of the bags pushes down onto the barbed wire, locking the rows together.

Wrapping the bags into these coils allows you to create curvy, organic shapes with dramatic arches and domes. The technique is very sculptural and fluid. As you see in Figure 9-7, the earthbags produce homes with no corners. The walls curve into one another and into the roof to craft a *monolithic* (all the same material) building.

The long bags can be made of polypropylene plastic or burlap fabric, available through construction supply sources. The bags (or tubes) come in several sizes, from 12 to 26 inches wide. Keep them out of the sunlight, because the UV light breaks down the bags.

Start building your earthbag home by digging a trench 1 foot deep for the foundation. Two or three layers of earthbags will fill up the trench and work as your foundation. Fill the tube bags with pretty much anything you like: earth, clay, sand, gravel, or rice hulls — whatever is locally available will usually work, but earth is preferred. Wet materials work best and help the walls fit together better.

To create the perfect round room, anchor a long rope to the floor in the center of where you want the room to be. Mark the rope with the size of the circle you want to create. Using it like a compass, the rope will trace the outline of the round room and create a circle! To create the perfect dome, use that same rope trick to maintain the perfect radius of the curved wall of the dome. Several ropes can be used to create a variety of complex domed shapes and forms. Leave the very top of the dome open for a round skylight.

Create arched windows by rolling the filled tube back on itself. If you forget a window or door, wait for the bags to set and use a saw to cut an arched opening. The arch shape is important because it helps hold the building together structurally.

Because the earthbags will disintegrate in the sunlight, you'll need to cover the walls with plaster or stucco right away. If you fill the tube bags with something permanent like concrete, then you can leave the walls bare and allow the bags to fall apart. You can coat the entire dome as a green roof, covered with grass.

The finished building is almost solid earth and sand, giving it an incredibly high thermal mass (from the earth) and high insulation value (from the trapped air).

The building codes do not support many of these alternative construction methods, but the strength of this earthbag building should convince your local building department.

Sculpting your earthbag home

Although ideal for the hot desert, the low-cost materials of ceramic earth are perfect for most climates. You probably wouldn't want it in a very wet or very cold climate, however.

The unique technique of using ceramic earth allows you to be artistic and sculptural with your design. So different from a typical wood-frame house, ceramic earth provides you the freedom to design anything you can imagine. Embrace the ceramic qualities of your home with arches, vaults, and dome shapes.

The curves and coils of ceramic earth offer incredible flexibility in both the construction and final appearance of the home. Consider the following:

- ✔ **Just as you would with ceramic pots, adding different types of sand and clay will create different finishes.** Glazes made of salt or ground-up, recycled glass bottles will add a beautiful color and finish to your fired walls.

- ✔ **Whether you're using the fired brick or earthbags, ceramic earth construction is perfect for creating dramatic domes and arches in your design.**

- ✔ **Features such as built-in benches and shelving are easily added to the walls because they're fired with the rest of the house.**

- ✔ **Insert glass-capped pipes or salvaged bottles into the walls to create unusual windows and stained-glass decorations.**

Ceramic earth is an incredibly labor-intensive method, but it encourages the use of free materials and your own labor. The raw material costs are so low you can build simple structures for a few hundred dollars.

Assuming the labor costs are your own free effort, ceramic earth will cost about half the amount of traditional wood framing. This method quickly forms the foundation, walls, and ceiling with cheap materials.

Consider building your ceramic earth home in stages to reduce the amount of work you have to do all at once. This low-skill technique is perfect for gathering a group of friends together to help out in building the home.

Chapter 10

Manufactured Building Methods

● ●

In This Chapter

▶ Finding out about structural insulated panels

▶ Looking at insulated concrete forms

▶ Analyzing the benefits over traditional wood framing

▶ Exploring the cost advantages over wood

▶ Considering design issues with manufactured building methods

● ●

*E*very year, 1.5 million new homes are built in the United States, nearly all of them out of wood framing. And 1 acre of forest (about 44 trees) goes into the building of a typical home. With demand for wood soaring, builders are turning to alternative methods of construction.

In this chapter, I fill you in on two manufactured building methods: structural insulated panels and insulated concrete forms. Both of these clever building methods offer numerous advantages over traditional wood framing. I discuss the pros and cons of each system, as well as the things you need to know to take advantage of each. The techniques outlined in this chapter will show you how to get the most out of each of these construction methods.

Structural Insulated Panels

A structural insulated panel (SIP) is a panel of thick, rigid, foam insulation sandwiched between two structural skins of plywood boards. SIPs can be used for walls, floors, and roofs in both residential and commercial buildings. The SIP panel looks like a rectangular sandwich, with the two layers on the outside and the filling in between (see Figure 10-1).

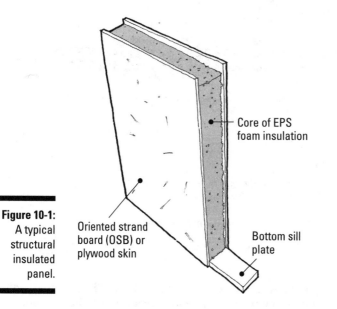

Figure 10-1:
A typical
structural
insulated
panel.

Core of EPS
foam insulation

Oriented strand
board (OSB) or
plywood skin

Bottom sill
plate

This structural sandwich is typically made with an inner core of expanded polystyrene (EPS) insulation between two structural skins of oriented strand board (OSB), which is made up of small scraps of wood glued together into a panel. The OSB uses less wood than standard plywood, and the EPS is inflated without ozone-depleting chemicals, making this a greener product than the typical wall of wood framing and plywood.

SIPs are available in a variety of alternative insulation cores and skin materials. They are manufactured under strict factory-controlled conditions. Because they're premade, the panels arrive at the construction site strong, precisely cut, and very dimensionally stable. That means they won't shrink or warp from water or temperature the way that traditional wood does.

The sandwich of a SIP is equivalent to the wood framing, sheathing, and wall insulation of a traditional home, all in one simple panel. Because each panel is a preformed structural wall, the finished building is much stronger than a traditional wood-frame house and can be put together much faster. Building with SIPs can speed up your construction time, reduce waste, and decrease the amount of labor.

The history of structural insulated panels

The first foam-core panels appeared in the 1930s, when they were called "stressed skin panels." They were the product of research by the U.S. Forest Service. The panels were created to reduce the use of wood resources. First Lady Eleanor Roosevelt dedicated a small stressed-skin house in 1937, bringing attention to this new technology.

Although standardized SIPs have been around since the 1950s, they didn't catch on in the construction industry until the 1980s. Production

and tract-home builders have recently fallen in love with the technology, and the use of SIPs has grown steadily.

Early SIPs were made up of plywood skins glued to both sides of Styrofoam insulation. Today's SIPs are made with either $\frac{7}{16}$-inch or $\frac{5}{8}$-inch oriented strand board (OSB) skins factory glued to expanded polystyrene (EPS) insulation cores.

The pros and cons of structural insulated panels

SIPs offer numerous benefits to homeowners, but no product is perfect. In this section, I fill you in on the pros and cons of structural insulated panels.

The pros

SIPs offer numerous advantages:

- ✔ **SIP homes go up much faster than traditional wood-frame buildings.** An experienced contractor trained in SIP installation can save a significant amount of construction time.

- ✔ **With proper planning and coordination with the manufacturer, SIPs can be precut and partially assembled to speed construction even more.** Panels are typically 4 feet wide and come in lengths of 8 feet up to 24 feet. Entire walls can be put up immediately, with the openings for the windows and doors already cut.

- ✔ **Because the window openings can be precut into the panels, a separate header over the openings may not be needed.** Just be careful to figure out the correct sizes for your windows and doors. Although it's only slightly difficult to make an opening larger, you won't be able to make a precut opening smaller!

- ✔ **The foam cores of a typical SIP panel are predrilled for plumbing and electrical wiring.** The panels already have spaces to run plumbing or electrical chases. Unlike with traditional wood walls, the pipes and wiring must be fed up through these predrilled holes, making it like adding plumbing to an existing wall. Working with the panels takes some getting used to. Making new chases for pipes is more difficult than in traditional wood-frame walls, but it's still easy to do.

- ✔ **Because SIPs are solidly filled with a high-density foam insulation, without any of the voids, gaps, or mistakes found in wood-stud walls, SIP buildings are much more energy efficient.** Your monthly heating bills will be up to 50 percent lower than in a similar wood-frame building.

Because they're nearly airtight, you have to take some extra steps to ventilate your new SIP home. Be sure to follow the manufacturer's installation recommendations for venting.

- ✔ **In addition to removing air gaps and leaks, a SIP building has a higher R-value (insulation value) than traditional wall construction.** Building with SIPs can cut your home energy consumption by up to half, lowering your energy bill and saving you money. SIPs are one of the most energy-efficient construction methods available. Conserving this energy not only saves you money, but reduces greenhouse gas emissions, air pollution, and dependency on oil.

- ✔ **Because the foam insulation is 98 percent air, SIPs are very resource efficient.** The blowing agent used to spray the foam doesn't hurt the earth's ozone layer.

The OSB uses small pieces of wood from fast-growing, small-diameter trees, instead of large, solid pieces of lumber. Be sure to use formaldehyde-free and low-VOC adhesives for the OSB panels.

- ✔ **Because SIPs are prefabricated and precut in the factory, constructing a SIP building generates far less waste.** The same panels can be used for the walls, floors, and roofs, saving the need for several other materials, and allowing you to use leftover scraps in other parts of the construction.

- ✔ **Because every wall is a structural wall, a SIP building is up to twice as strong as a conventional wood-frame home.** If you live in an area prone to hurricanes, earthquakes, or tornados, a SIP building will offer you better protection than a wood building.

The cons

The primary concern with SIPs is that the chemicals from the OSB panels contaminate the indoor air quality. Be sure to select SIPs made with formaldehyde-free OSB panels. Formaldehyde is used as an adhesive and is a known carcinogen. Avoiding it is healthier for you and your family.

I also suggest that you purchase panels certified by the Forest Stewardship Council (FSC) to ensure that the wood came from sustainable sources.

Comparing the cost of structural insulated panels to traditional wood

SIPs include the framing, the insulation, and the sheathing, so when it comes time for you to compare the cost of SIPs to traditional wood framing, you want to make sure you're comparing the costs correctly. When you factor in all these other materials, SIPs are cost competitive to standard wood framing, adding only 5 percent to 10 percent to the material costs. But when you factor in the labor savings and construction waste savings, the cost is about the same as wood construction.

The real savings with SIPs will appear in the savings in heating and cooling the finished building. Factor in these operational costs when considering SIP construction.

Buying advice for structural insulated panels

With dozens of national SIP manufacturers out there, you may find it hard to choose. When you're deciding on a SIP manufacturer, consider the following:

- ✔ **Where is the manufacturer located?** Choose a manufacturer as close to you as possible to reduce shipping costs.

- ✔ **Is the product healthy?** Choose a manufacturer that uses formaldehyde-free and low-toxic adhesives. Some manufacturers are switching over to soy-based adhesives, which are better for your health and are the superior choice.

- ✔ **What type of foam does the manufacturer use?** EPS foam is the most common type used (choose EPS over polyurethane), but look for alternatives such as polyisocyanurate or recycled content foam.

- ✔ **What type of boards does the manufacturer use?** Although OSB is most common, look for wood certified by the Forest Stewardship Council (FSC). Consider alternatives such as Agriboard (www.agriboard.com), made of compressed straw panels.

✔ **What type of backing does the manufacturer use?** Alternative panels are available with one side covered in fiber cement siding for exterior use, drywall for interior use, or waterproofing for exteriors. All these options potentially speed up construction, but they require more planning.

✔ **Does the manufacturer precut the panels?** Choose a manufacturer that precuts the panels based on your architect's computer drawings.

✔ **What does the manufacturer do with its own waste?** Choose a company that uses scrap pieces of panel and recycles unusable waste.

Due to their solid insulation core, SIPs offer superior energy efficiency, providing an insulating value from R-15 to R-45. Choose the thickest SIP panel you can use to maximize this high R-value. The panels come in a nominal thickness of 4 inches, 6 inches, and 8 inches. Although thicker panels cost more, you'll see a dramatic savings on your energy bill if you use them. For every step up in thickness, expect a 20 percent drop in your heating and cooling bills.

Taking advantage of structural insulated panels in your home

The quick assembly and energy efficiency of SIPs makes them a great choice for building your green dream home. In this section, I cover how to design with SIPs, and how to educate your contractor on using them.

Considering design

A typical SIP comes 4 feet wide. You can really benefit from these standardized sizes by designing your home to be some unit of 4 feet. By designing to this module, you'll reduce the need for cutting, and speed construction time.

A typical SIP also comes in heights of 8 feet to 24 feet. Size your building to the widest span possible without the need for interior walls or columns; this will create open spaces in your plan. The SIP manufacturer or your structural engineer can tell you how far a distance the panels can be used as a floor or roof.

The panels themselves are very boxy, so SIP buildings tend to be boxy. If you want to do curving walls, SIPs are not the right choice. Consider making openings fit within the 4-foot module of the SIP, instead of punching holes for windows and doors.

After they're erected, the SIPs must be covered with siding. You can use any green siding you want — stucco, board siding, shingles — allowing the building to be either very modern or traditional, based on your tastes. (You can find suggestions for siding in Chapter 7.)

Convincing your contractor

If your contractor is unfamiliar with SIP construction, contact the Structural Insulated Panel Association (`www.sips.org`) for a list of workshops in your area. These workshops educate builders and homeowners on how to build with SIPs. If your contractor is reluctant to go, offer to pay for the workshop or to go with him. The Structural Insulated Panel Association can also steer you toward certified installers around the country.

When your contractor tries SIPs, chances are he'll see the logic and efficiency of them and want to continue building with SIPs. If he's new to the SIP world, you may want to share the following tips with him (or just show him this book):

- ✔ **Seal all the joints with a special sealing mastic or an expanding foam sealant.** Fill the space between the panels and in any unused electrical chases with low expanding foam. Proper sealing between the panels is very important in a SIP building.

- ✔ **Although a 4-foot-wide-by-8-foot-high panel can be lifted by two people, longer panels can require a crane to install.**

- ✔ **Take the time to plan the building properly and precut the panels.** When the SIPs arrive at the construction site precut, they can be rapidly assembled.

- ✔ **Store panels under cover, out of the sun, and off the ground.** Keep them dry and cool.

- ✔ **Set aside panel scraps for later use for headers, filler sections, and anywhere small pieces are needed.**

- ✔ **Recycle your scraps whenever possible.** Some SIP manufacturers will accept scrap panels back for recycling.

- ✔ **Use vented panels for roof applications, or install roof venting as required.**

- ✔ **Always provide mechanical ventilation in a SIP house.** The nearly air-tight construction keeps out drafts, but also prevents fresh air from coming in.

- ✔ **Use the thickest panels possible to maximize insulation.** Use at least 6-inch-thick wall panels and 8-inch-thick roof panels.

- ✔ **Select panels with special foam-sealing channels for sealing between panels during construction.** Apply an expanding foam sealant as suggested to provide a tight seal. Without proper sealing between panels, water can penetrate into the panels.

 ✔ **To further seal the panels, tape the interior joints with construction tape.**

 ✔ **In seasonal climates (warm summers and cold winters), treat panels against insect infestation with boric acid.** It's effective and harmless to people and pets.

 ✔ **Does the company offer any technical support or training?** Look for a company with helpful customer service to answer your technical construction questions.

Insulated Concrete Forms

An insulated concrete form (ICF) is a lightweight hollow block. ICFs are designed as a stay-in-place formwork for poured-in-place concrete walls. Think of them as fancy LEGO blocks. The hollow block forms are typically stacked up, and concrete is poured inside. Although a typical concrete wall needs elaborate formwork to act as a mold, the ICF *is* the formwork. As you can see in Figure 10-2, the ICF looks like a hollow mold.

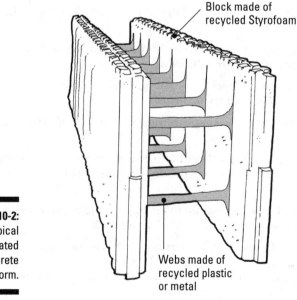

Block made of recycled Styrofoam

Webs made of recycled plastic or metal

Figure 10-2:
A typical insulated concrete form.

ICF blocks are typically made of EPS, separated by plastic or metal spacers that hold the block together. The ICFs serve as a cavity for the structural walls of a building. Usually, reinforcing steel (rebar) is set into this cavity, and then concrete is pumped in. The concrete *cures* (firms up) inside the ICFs, which are left in place permanently, providing insulation. The result is a super-strong, very energy-efficient wall.

The pros and cons of insulated concrete forms

Insulated concrete forms offer all kinds of advantages over traditional construction, but no material is perfect. So in this section, I fill you in on the pros and cons of ICFs.

The pros

ICFs offer numerous advantages over traditional building methods:

- ✔ **Stacked as interlocking blocks, ICF homes are faster to build than traditional wood-frame buildings.** An experienced contractor familiar with ICF construction will be able to save time and money in construction.

- ✔ **When installed, an ICF wall offers superior energy efficiency and thermal comfort.** ICFs combine the *thermal mass* (ability to store temperature) of concrete with the *insulation* (ability to hold temperature) of the ICF block. The concrete walls have a high thermal mass, which regulates the daily temperature swings, keeping your home more comfortable throughout the day.

- ✔ **Because the ICFs are solidly filled with concrete, the walls don't have any openings or gaps found in wood-stud walls, making ICF buildings much more energy efficient.** Your monthly heating bills will be up to 50 percent less than in a similar wood-frame building.

- ✔ **Owners of new ICF homes almost always comment on how unbelievably quiet their new house is, compared to their old wood house.** The mass and insulation of the walls have a deadening effect to outside noises. It's similar to the quiet you find in your basement.

- ✔ **An ICF building is more secure than a wood-frame building.** The strong and durable walls are perfect for areas where earthquakes, tornados, and hurricanes are commonplace. Unlike wood-frame houses, an ICF home is more fire resistant. ICF homes are safer for you and your family.

  In fact, many insurance companies provide a discount on a homeowner's policy for an ICF home. Ask your agent about these benefits.

The history of insulated concrete forms

Early ICFs first appeared in the late 1960s, with the growth of concrete construction. Conceived of by engineers as a "perfect" building material, ICFs combined simplicity, strength, and energy efficiency.

By 1972, a Swiss company developed Rastra, using recycled polystyrene and cement. This combination offered several advantages, including strength and ease of adding a stucco finish. Today, Rastra is one of the best-known ICF manufacturers available.

Production homebuilders have embraced the technology, and the use of ICFs has grown steadily, especially in areas where the strength holds the biggest benefit.

Although Rastra blocks use recycled polystyrene and cement, most of today's ICFs are made of pure polystyrene, making them lightweight, easy to cut, and easy to stack.

Cons

Because the walls are solid concrete, you need to plan for your plumbing and electrical chases as you would in a regular concrete building. You can add chases for forgotten pipes after you pour the concrete, but you'll have to cut into the ICF, reducing the insulation value.

Choose a contractor with ICF experience, or at least experience with concrete construction. After the walls are poured, you can't afford to punch holes through the wall to add a forgotten window.

Comparing costs of insulated concrete forms to traditional materials

So how does an ICF building stack up to its wood-frame and concrete counterparts?

Wood

ICFs eliminate the need for wood framing, structural walls, and insulation, so don't forget to factor these savings into your estimates. Taking all this into consideration, an ICF home will cost around 5 percent to 10 percent more than a conventional wood-frame home.

In comparing costs, keep in mind that an ICF home is stronger, more comfortable, and more energy efficient than even the best insulated wood-frame building. The real savings with ICFs comes from the savings you get in heating and cooling. Don't forget to factor in these savings when looking at ICF construction.

In recent years, concrete prices have increased, raising the total cost of ICF construction. Be sure to correctly estimate the cost of the concrete so you have an accurate estimate.

Concrete

An ICF home will cost about the same as, or even less than, a poured-in-place concrete building. The savings in labor costs and the added insulation will factor into these savings.

Compared to precast concrete blocks, ICFs will cost about 5 percent more due to the added costs of the poured concrete.

Buying advice for ICFs

With so many ICF manufacturers in existence, you may find it difficult to choose one. To help narrow the list, consider the following:

- ✔ **Where is the manufacturer located?** Choose a manufacturer as close to you as possible to reduce shipping costs.

- ✔ **What type of web does the manufacturer use?** The *web* (the thing that connects the ICF block together) comes in a variety of materials. Consider only buying an ICF made with recycled plastic webbing.

- ✔ **What type of foam does the manufacturer use?** EPS foam is the most common type used, but look for alternatives such as Rastra, made from recycled polystyrene and cement.

- ✔ **What is the thickness of the insulation?** Some manufacturers offer thicker insulation than others. Although the thickness of the inside of the ICF doesn't affect insulation, the thickness of the foam on the *outside* does. The thicker the ICF insulation, the better your energy efficiency.

- ✔ **What type of interlocking grid does the manufacturer use?** Each manufacturer has a different type of stacking and interlocking method. Look for an ICF with interlocking blocks that will speed construction. Interlocking blocks are much easier to work with than blocks that only stack together.

- ✔ **Does the company offer any technical support or training?** Look for a company with helpful customer service to answer your technical construction questions.

Using insulated concrete forms to your advantage

The lightweight and modular ICF blocks provide you an easy way to build a strong and energy-efficient home. The blocks allow you some fun design opportunities, so in this section, I outline some suggestions for designing with ICFs. I also offer recommendations on how to convince your contractor to use them.

Considering design

Most ICFs come in the same size as actual concrete blocks — 16 inches long and 8 inches high. You can benefit from these standardized sizes by designing the size of your floor plan to be some measure of 16 inches. By designing to this module, you'll reduce the need for cutting and speed up construction.

ICF homes can be designed in any style and will accept any traditional exterior finish including wood siding, stucco, board siding, shingles, and brick. (You can find a full list of suggestions for siding in Chapter 7.)

Their small, modular size makes ICFs a great option for creating curving or angled walls. With a handheld rasp, you can sand and round out the edges of the forms to create a softer appearance.

The strength of the concrete gives you the ability to create large openings as well. Just as you would with LEGO blocks, make the openings fit within the spacing of the blocks, rather than just randomly punching holes for your windows and doors. As with any building, window and door openings are made slightly bigger than the window or door you want to put into the wall. Simple wood pieces (called *blocking*) can be used to fill in the extra space around the windows and doors.

Most ICFs come in standard sizes of 4-inch, 6-inch, 8-inch, and 10-inch widths. The insulation is on the outside, so although a thicker wall will be stronger, it will not give you any added insulation value. As a minimum, use at least a 6-inch-thick wall form.

Convincing your contractor

Although it looks new and different, anyone with construction experience can quickly get up to speed on ICFs. It's more important that your contractor have concrete experience than direct experience working with ICFs. One person with ICF experience can easily train the rest of the crew. (For information on working with ICFs, contact the Insulating Concrete Form Association at 888-864-4232 or go to www.forms.org.)

When the crew has some practice, each ICF home requires less skilled labor and less total labor than a wood-frame home. Plus, ICFs are very lightweight, so crews stay fresh through the day.

If your contractor still isn't convinced, show him how easily chases are cut into ICFs with a knife, even after pouring the concrete. Fastening drywall or siding is simple; you do it with screws instead of nails.

When your contractor tries ICFs, he'll soon see their benefit and want to continue building with them. If he's new to ICFs, you may want to share the following tips with him (or just show him this book):

- ✔ **Cut the ICF blocks with a simple hand saw, and be sure to wear a mask when cutting the forms to prevent inhalation of the dust.**

- ✔ **Make sure all your openings are correct before pouring the concrete.** After the concrete is poured, it will be incredibly difficult (and expensive) to jackhammer a new opening.

- ✔ **After the concrete is poured and cured, any forgotten electrical or plumbing conduits are cut directly into the form using an electric hot knife.** Plumbing and electrical lines are inserted into these grooves and covered by the drywall.

- ✔ **Although two people can easily lift the blocks into place, special equipment may be required for tall installations.**

- ✔ **Fill the joints between the blocks with expanding foam to create an airtight wall.**

- ✔ **Store forms under cover, out of the sun, and off the ground.** Keep them dry and cool.

- ✔ **If using the ICF below grade and against soil, treat the forms against termite infestation.** It's not dangerous if you don't, but the insects can reduce the insulation slightly.

Part IV

Green Building Systems and Site Planning

"Of course, when we landscape the place, we'll get rid of that old washing machine and replace it with one that's indigenous to these parts."

In this part . . .

In this part, I offer a detailed picture of the wonderful world of sustainable systems that go into a building. Chapter 11 begins with a look at the variety of energy systems available. In Chapter 12, I cover the heating and cooling systems that keep you comfortable. I discuss water systems in Chapter 13. And Chapter 14 is a look at the landscape and orientation of the building, where you see there is more to landscape than just grass.

Chapter 11

Energy Systems

. . . .

. . . .

*B*uildings are energy hogs. A whopping 40 percent of all the world's energy goes into the operations of homes, offices, and factories. From maintaining the light level to keeping them a comfortable temperature, we use copious amounts of energy just to keep things running.

In this chapter, I explore the source of this energy, how it's used, and the numerous ways you can conserve it. This chapter will forever change how you look at your light switches!

Our Growing Energy Need

The energy released from the burning of natural resources (to provide heat and power) is a precious commodity. People are all dependent on this energy. Think about the last time there was a power outage at your home and how difficult it was to function. Remember digging through drawers for a flashlight or some candles, unable to use the microwave, or praying that the batteries on your laptop would last a few more minutes? Our entire lives are wrapped around this addiction to energy.

Despite all we now know about the importance of reducing energy use, the demand for energy keeps going up. The oil Americans now consume in six weeks would have lasted an entire year in 1950. But it's not just oil. American demand for electricity will rise by 45 percent in the next ten years.

Buildings: The biggest energy hogs

In order to keep lights on, rooms comfortable, and hot showers flowing, buildings are the biggest users of energy. The majority of the world's energy goes into keeping our buildings running and comfortable. In reality, most of this energy could be saved with building improvements. Smarter planning, better insulation, and solar panels are all examples of how to reduce the energy use in buildings.

So what do we do with all this energy? More than two-thirds of the energy in a building is used for lighting, heating, and cooling:

- **Heating:** 34 percent
- **Appliances and lighting:** 34 percent
- **Water heating:** 13 percent
- **Electric air conditioner:** 11 percent
- **Refrigerator:** 8 percent

Each of these areas is a potential place to conserve energy. I discuss all these and more later in this chapter. You can see a simple overview of where to save energy in your home in Figure 11-1.

Our current sources of energy

If you turn on a light switch, somewhere in the world, a generator has to produce that electricity. Utility companies did too good a job of making our use of energy simple and seamless. Most people don't know where this instantaneous energy comes from, or the journey it takes to get to them. In the following sections, I give you a quick look at our current sources of energy.

Oil

Americans love cars. Cruising down the open highway is woven into American life, like apple pie and baseball. But all this driving comes with a huge price. The gasoline that Americans use to move these cars is part of a 20-million-barrel-a-day oil habit. More than 55 percent of the oil Americans use is imported from other countries, many of which are economically and politically unstable.

Americans' consumption of oil continuously increases, while the supplies of oil around the world are slowly running out. The pollution from cars and trucks produces more global warming and more air-quality issues. A third of greenhouse gas emissions are from gas burned in automobiles.

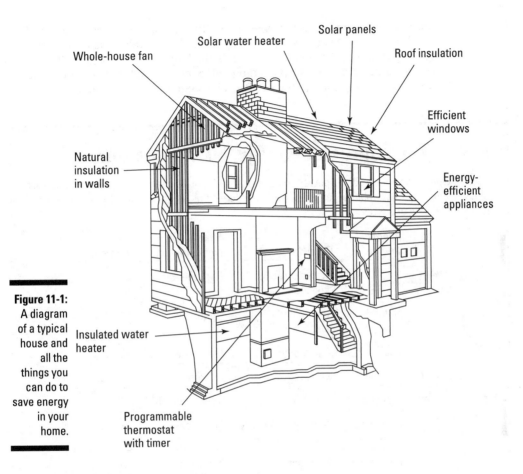

Solar panels

Solar water heater

Roof insulation

Whole-house fan

Efficient
windows

Natural
insulation
in walls

Energy-
efficient
appliances

Figure 11-1:
A diagram
of a typical
house and
all the
things you
can do to
save energy
in your
home.

Insulated water
heater

Programmable
thermostat
with timer

Natural gas

Like coal (see the following section), natural gas is a fossil fuel found in large
underground deposits. Because it was created millions of years ago, we can't
create more.

Although natural gas is clean burning and gives off lower levels of air pollution than coal, gas still has the same issue that all fossil fuels have — what
happens when we run out?

Coal

Coal is a combustible mineral found buried deep in the earth. Because coal is
a *fossil fuel,* formed from the ancient remains of plants and dinosaurs, we
can't produce more when we run out. Unlike some of the other energy
sources, the United States actually has an overabundance of coal — enough
to last for centuries. In fact, the United States has so much of the stuff that it
exports coal to other countries.

Coal generates more than half the electricity used in the United States, and is the nation's largest single source of energy. Unfortunately, coal is also the biggest polluter in the United States. It is the largest source of greenhouse gas emissions and mercury poisoning in U.S. air and water. In addition, coal mining is one of the most destructive things people can do to an area.

The source of energy, by the numbers

If you're wondering where all this power comes from, you're not alone. Most people are unaware of how we feed our daily hunger for energy. In the following table, you can see the sources for all our various forms of energy.

Energy Source	Used In	Renewable or Nonrenewable?	Percent
Oil	Transportation and manufacturing	Nonrenewable	38.1
Natural gas	Heating and electricity	Nonrenewable	22.9
Coal	Electricity	Nonrenewable	23.2
Nuclear	Electricity	Nonrenewable	8.1
Propane	Heating	Nonrenewable	1.7
Biomass	Heating, electricity, and transportation	Renewable	2.9
Hydropower	Electricity	Renewable	2.7
Geothermal	Heating and electricity	Renewable	0.3
Wind	Electricity	Renewable	0.1
Solar	Light, heating, and electricity	Renewable	0.1

If it seems a little off balance, that's because it is. We rely heavily on nonrenewable, fossil-fuel-based energy. We suck these fossil fuels out of the ground, and it continues to get harder and harder to find new sources of fossil fuels. In addition, the burning of these fuels causes global warming, pollutes the air and water, and continues to get more expensive. The money spent on finding new sources of oil can be better used to invest in renewable energy.

New technologies are being developed to reduce the pollution from coal production and burning. Sometimes incorrectly referred to as "clean coal," the process crushes the coal into a gas, and uses steam to treat the pollution and gas coming out of the flue. The nonprofit watchdog organization Greenpeace has labeled clean coal technology as "greenwashing" and not solving the real problems associated with coal.

Nuclear

Think of nuclear energy as a fancy way to boil water. Nuclear energy uses radioactive materials to create steam, and that steam powers a generator, which then makes electricity.

Nuclear energy is the second largest source of electricity in the world. It's cheap and doesn't give off any air pollution. Unfortunately, dealing with the radioactive waste created by the creation of nuclear energy is a big problem — no one knows where to put it (or how). Plus, nuclear incidents, like Chernobyl and Three Mile Island, rare as they are, raise safety issues.

Hydropower (dams)

Hydropower comes from building a large dam across a river. To make electricity, the dam is opened and water flows into it, spinning the turbines to generate electricity.

Because it uses water, hydroelectric power is considered to be a clean, renewable source of energy. Unfortunately, when the dams are built, low-lying rivers get turned into deep lakes and entire habitats are destroyed.

Global Warming

Global warming (also referred to by terms such as *climate crisis, climate chaos,* or *climate change*) is the slow warming of the earth caused by a buildup of air pollution in the atmosphere, which traps heat from the sun. Burning millions of tons of coal to produce electricity for our homes or gasoline for our cars is responsible for the release of this global warming pollution. There are several different gasses that contribute to global warming. Carbon dioxide, methane, and nitrous oxide all contribute to this greenhouse effect that causes global warming.

The impacts of global warming are severe, causing everything from rising sea levels to the extinction of entire species to crazy weather (stronger hurricanes, more severe drought, and intense heat waves). Many of the effects of global warming are already being felt today.

A brief history of global warming

In a relatively short time, awareness of global warming has gone from theory to scientific fact. Here is a brief look at how scientists uncovered the problem and how people and nations have reacted.

1827 French mathematician Jean-Baptiste Fourier discovers that the earth's atmosphere is similar to a "glass vessel," trapping heat from sunlight. The phenomenon later becomes known as the *greenhouse effect*.

1896 While scientists are theorizing that industrial burning of fossil fuels could raise the earth's temperature, Swedish chemist Svante Arrhenius is the first to measure the amount of carbon dioxide emissions. "We are evaporating our coal mines into air," he writes.

1870–1910 Second Industrial Revolution. Electricity and discovery of new chemicals create economic growth around the world.

1890s–1940 Average surface air temperatures on earth increase about 0.5°F. Several scientists see the American Dust Bowl as a sign of the effect of global warming.

1920 Opening of oil fields in Texas and the Persian Gulf inaugurate an era of cheap energy.

1938 Scientists argue that global warming is underway, raising interest in the subject.

1939–1945 World War II becomes a power struggle to control the world's oil fields.

1956 Scientists create an early computer model of the global atmosphere, allowing them to study the effects of global warming.

1957 The Soviets launch the Sputnik satellite, prompting an era of satellite exploration to help study the global climate. Scientist Roger Revelle discovers that man-made carbon dioxide cannot be absorbed by the oceans.

1967 The International Global Atmospheric Research Program is established to gather data on short-range weather prediction, including changes to the climate.

1968 Studies predict the possibility that Antarctic ice sheets could collapse, catastrophically raising sea levels around the world.

1969 Americans land on the moon, permanently altering the perception of the earth. The idea of "away" (as in throwing something away) goes away.

1970 The U.S. National Oceanic and Atmospheric Administration (NOAA), the world's leading funder of climate research, is established.

1970 The first Earth Day is held on April 22. Environmental awareness grows and green movements gain ground as this annual tradition kicks off. It continues to this day.

1972 Scientific study of ice cores allows measurement of carbon thousands of years in the past. The connection between carbon levels and temperatures can now be proven.

1976 Chlorofluorocarbons (CFCs) are shown to contribute to the destruction of the ozone layer and add to global warming. They are later banned.

1981	Ronald Reagan becomes 40th president of the United States, bringing with him a backlash against environmental protection. Political conservatism is linked to skepticism about global warming. That same year becomes the warmest year on record.
1985	Scientists declare a consensus on global warming and call for the governments of the world to restrict greenhouse gas emissions.
1985	British and American scientists discover a hole in the layer of ozone over the Antarctic. Other environmental disasters, such as the African famine, capture the public's attention as global warming becomes more prominent in mainstream politics.
1987	The warmest year on record. The 1980s becomes the hottest decade on record, only surpassed by the 1990s.
1988	The Intergovernmental Panel on Climate Change (IPCC) is created by the United Nations. The Global Warming Prevention Act is introduced by Representative Claudine Schneider (a Republican from Rhode Island), but Congress passes only half the bill.
1990	The first IPCC report is released and finds that the earth has warmed 1°F in the past century. Though it remains uncertain whether warming is due to human activity, the report leads to negotiations toward an international agreement on climate change.
1992	The first global-warming treaty, the Framework Convention on Climate Change (FCCC), calls for reversing warming and sets the goal of cutting carbon emissions to 1990 levels by 2000.
1997	The Kyoto Protocol is proposed by the United Nations, asking countries to limit the amount of their greenhouse gas emissions. President Bill Clinton signs the treaty but never submits it to the Senate, which says it must first see "meaningful participation" from developing nations before ratifying.
2005	The Kyoto Protocol takes effect in August. The United States and Australia are the only industrialized nations to not participate. The impact of Hurricane Katrina raises awareness of the connection between global warming and the unusually severe hurricane season.
2006	*An Inconvenient Truth,* a documentary on former Vice President Al Gore's campaign to draw awareness to climate change, is released. It quickly becomes the third-highest-grossing documentary of all time and goes on to win the Academy Award for Best Documentary.
2007	An IPCC report says, with at least 90 percent certainty, that global warming is man-made and will "continue for centuries." A second report predicts that, in the coming decades, rising temperatures and rising sea levels will cause floods and mass famine.

Talking about global warming is a lot like talking about dieting. No one really wants to accept the truth about what needs to be done. To lose weight, you really just need to eat less and move more. To combat global warming, we really just need to eliminate the burning of fossil fuels and switch to renewable energy sources, such as solar and wind. In order to get to this next step, you can reduce the energy used in your home by following the methods discussed in this chapter.

Because buildings are the largest users of energy, reducing the energy your home uses is the best place to fight global warming. Each dollar you save off your monthly energy bill is a step toward slowing down the effects of global warming.

Renewable Energy Systems

Given the issues around fossil fuels, carbon emissions, and air pollution, more and more states are requiring their public utilities to generate a percentage of their power from renewable sources. *Renewable energy,* unlike fossil fuels, is any type of energy derived from resources that are regenerative and cannot be depleted. Because fossil fuels are remnants from ancient plant deposits from millions of years ago, we can't make any more. Renewables, however, come from clean sources — such as the sun, wind, and plants. The sun and the wind aren't going anywhere, and we can grow as many plants as we want. The result: less pollution and reduced global warming.

Photovoltaics (solar power)

Green architect William McDonough has a funny story about solar energy. Someone asked him, "What do you think of nuclear energy?"

"Oh, I love it," he said, surprising the person. "I love it so much I think we should implement large-scale nuclear energy immediately."

Shocked, the person asked, "Really?"

"Sure," McDonough continued, "We already have a wonderful nuclear reactor located 93 million miles away, and it already provides much more energy than we would ever need."

He was talking, of course, about the sun.

Using solar panels, we can convert our abundant sunlight into electricity. The sun currently provides 5,000 times the amount of energy people need. Let me say that again: *The sun currently provides 5,000 times the amount of energy people need.* More sunlight energy hits the earth each hour than the world's population consumes in an entire year. It's clean, it's free, and it'll never run out.

All of California's electricity could be produced in just 200 square miles of sunshine. (That's equivalent to an area the size of Lake Mead, behind the Hoover Dam.) All the electricity needed for the entire United States could be produced in an area equal to about three-fourths of the island of Manhattan.

How solar panels work

Solar panels (also known as *photovoltaic [PV] panels*) have no moving parts and emit no waste. When sunlight strikes the thin panel of silicon, the electrons get excited and start moving, which produces an electrical current.

Because they require sunlight to operate, the panels only work in the daytime. Instead of storing energy in batteries (as was done 10 or 15 years ago), the panels now use a grid-tie system. During the day, the panels produce energy, and excess electricity is pumped back into the electrical grid. (Your electric meter actually runs backward!) At night, when the panels are dormant, your home simply pulls energy off the power lines as usual. The net result is a monthly utility bill of $0.

In addition to saving you the cost of the monthly electricity bill, a solar panel system on your house can actually increase the value of your home. For example, a $20,000 solar system will add anywhere from $20,000 to $50,000 to your home's resale value. This reason alone is enough to consider solar panels for your house.

Be sure to explain the added value of solar panels to your appraiser when he's estimating your home's value.

Buying green power

If you think you can't afford or find a proper spot for making your own renewable energy, consider buying your own. Depending on where you live, you may be able to purchase clean, renewable energy from your local utility company. Look for companies certified with the Green-e logo, shown here. The seal indicates that you can trust the source of the energy.

Courtesy of Center for Resource Solutions.

Where to put solar panels

Solar panels need an unobstructed and south-facing area of your roof. If your roof is pitched, the panels are at the mercy of the angle of your roof and may not be as effective as they could be. On a flat roof, the panels can be turned and angled toward the south-facing sun.

Find a spot that is not shaded. And because the panels you install on your home could be there for 25 years or more, keep in mind any trees around it that could shadow the panels in the future.

Although they're not very heavy, the weight of solar panels is about double that of typical shingles. Be sure to ask your architect, contractor, or structural engineer whether your roof can bear the weight of solar panels.

If you believe solar is only possible in places like Arizona, think again. Solar panels require light, not heat. A cold and sunny location works just as well as a warm and sunny location.

Technically, the panels don't have to be located solely on the roof. Any sunny location within 1,000 feet of your home works just as well. If some pesky neighbors complain about the appearance of the panels, you can conceal them on your property instead of putting them on the roof.

Several manufacturers produce solar cells designed to integrate into the building. The most popular of these are solar panels designed to double as roof shingles. Although their cost is about 20 percent higher than regular solar panels, the solar shingles blend seamlessly into your roof, which means most neighbors (and design review boards) will be unaware of their presence.

The cost of solar panels

Solar panels have an average payback of five to ten years (meaning, in five to ten years, you should have saved enough in your electricity bills to cover the cost of the panels in the first place). The payback for a solar panel system will vary greatly based on:

- ✔ The amount of power you use
- ✔ Where on the roof they're located and how much roof space you have available
- ✔ Your geographic location (which affects how much sun exposure your home gets)

Different states offer various rebates for solar panels. Call your local building department for information on these incentives. It could save you thousands of dollars on your solar panels.

The number of solar panels needed to power your home is not dependent on the size of the building — it depends on the amount of power you use. So, your first task is to determine how much energy you need. Start by gathering a year's worth of your electricity bills. Add up your total annual kilowatt hours (kWh) from the utility bills. Then divide that number by 1,930. This will give you the approximate size (in kilowatts) of the solar system you need. Each kilowatt will cost between $5,000 and $9,000 installed (before rebates). *Remember:* Cost and available rebates vary by region.

Let's say your annual electricity costs are $2,000, and you're using 13,300 kWh per year.

13,300 kWh ÷ 1,930 ≈ 6.9 kW

You would need a 6.9 kW system to produce 100 percent of your power needs.

Going with the high end of the price range, $9,000, the installed cost of a 6.9 kW system would be around $62,100. Rebates would reduce that by $19,300. And your final cost would be $42,800 (out of pocket). If you factor in tax credits, that net cost drops to around $22,000. Which means that, in ten years, your solar panels will have paid for themselves, and you'll be able to reap the rewards of solar panels (zero electricity bills) without any additional cost.

If $22,000 sounds like too big an upfront cost for you, remember: You don't need to size your system for 100 percent of your power. Start small and add to your panels in a few years. Every little bit helps!

If you can't afford solar at all right now, then the next time you repair the roof, install just the conduit for a future solar panel system. It will save you time and money when you're ready for solar.

For every 100 square feet, solar panels produce between 1 and 1½ kW. For example, a 5 kW system would require about 500 square feet of roof space. Make sure to check to see if your roof is big enough for the size of the system you have in mind.

For more information on solar panels, consult the following:

- **Million Solar Roofs Initiative (www.irecusa.org):** This initiative hopes to help businesses and communities install solar systems on 1 million rooftops across the United States by 2010.

- **The Photovoltaic Performance Calculator (PVWatt; http://rredc. nrel.gov/solar/codes_algs/PVWATTS/):** Calculates the typical performance of solar electric arrays for more than 200 locations in the National Solar Radiation Database.

> ✔ **The Database of State Incentives for Renewable Energy (DSIRE; www. dsireusa.org):** A comprehensive source of information on state, local, utility, and selected federal incentives that promote renewable energy. DSIRE now includes state and federal incentives for energy efficiency.

Wind

It's possible that the electricity for your light bulb came from a wind turbine in California. Large fields of these wind turbines spin and pour electricity into the energy grid, all with no greenhouse gas emissions or air pollution. Each of these turbines provides enough electricity to power 400 homes. The United States has enough wind potential to produce three times more energy than it currently uses.

The blowing effect of wind is created by weather. As the sun warms the air, that air rises. Cooler air then rushes in to fill the space. Using a wind turbine, we can capture this force from the wind to spin the turbine and create electricity.

A typical wind turbine looks a lot like the propeller of an old plane set on top of a tall mast or pole. Wind energy is the fastest growing form of electricity generation in the United States. Smaller and more efficient wind turbines are being released, potentially allowing anyone to add wind power to his own home.

In order to work, wind power requires, well, wind! You need to live in a gusty, windy area or it won't work. In order to maximize the wind around your home, raise the turbine above the height of surrounding buildings and trees.

The cost of wind energy has dropped in the past decade and will continue to decline. Personal wind turbines can be had now for under $3,000, for a 1 kilowatt system. (Most homes use 3 to 6 kilowatts.) Just as with solar (see the preceding section), you don't need to rely on the wind for all your energy. Even just generating a fraction of your electricity with wind is a great investment.

In the early days of wind power, wind farms were located along the windiest routes. It is no coincidence these wind paths turned out to be migratory routes for birds. As a result, some of these older wind farms unintentionally kill several hundred birds a year. Today, wind farms are located to avoid bird flight paths.

Microhydropower (mini dams)

Solar power has sleek, shiny panels, and wind power has futuristic propellers, but microhydropower may remind you of muddy shoes and damp clothes. Microhydropower is a small generator powered by the force of running water.

If you have a flowing river or creek on your property, you may want to consider adding a microhydro energy system. Like a dam, only much smaller, microhydro power produces electricity from water turning a small turbine. Because the entire system sits below the water, microhydropower doesn't create the same environmental issues as a large dam does.

If you have flowing water on your property, microhydropower might give you the most power for the least amount of upfront cost. The cost of a microhydro system starts as low as $5,000.

Hydrogen fuel cells

A *hydrogen fuel cell* is a device that converts the chemical energy stored in oxygen and hydrogen into electrical energy. This electrochemical reaction combines the hydrogen with oxygen in the air. The only thing it gives off is the combination of the two, also known as water. A hydrogen fuel cell located in your basement could produce energy and drinking water for everyone in the building.

Hydrogen fuel cells are still, as of this writing, a new technology and not widely available in the United States. Japan has been experimenting with fuel cells for homes with great success. By 2020, you'll be seeing more of these.

Introducing Energy Efficiency

Although solar and wind power offer a clean and exciting way to *produce* energy, probably the best thing you can do is to reduce and save the energy you already use. You can save energy and money with no loss of comfort or convenience by taking some simple, energy-efficient steps.

The refrigerators, heaters, and air conditioners sold today need only about half the amount of energy they did 20 years ago. Homes built using these techniques will use a fraction of the energy needed to heat, cool, and light conventional buildings. Most of them can be applied to existing buildings, cutting the building's current energy bills in half.

Insulation

There is almost nothing you can do that will have as big of an impact on your home energy bills as insulation. *Insulation* is the ability of your home to store temperature. Just as your coat can hold in your body temperature on a cold day, insulation holds in the temperature of your house. And just as the thick walls of your freezer hold in the cold, so can insulation hold in your air conditioning. The more insulation you have, the better it works, and the lower your heating and cooling bills.

You spend a lot of money to heat your home. Hot air rises and leaks out of your home through the walls and every crack and crevice. The walls, floors, and ceilings are the biggest sources of leaking in a home.

Each year the amount of energy lost through uninsulated homes in the United States is equivalent to the amount of fuel delivered through the Alaska Pipeline. The costs of adding insulation to your home will pay for itself in a matter of months in a mild climate and in just weeks in a severe climate.

When to insulate your existing home

For a new house, you should add as much insulation as will fit into the walls. Adding insulation to finished walls is much more difficult.

If any of the following is true about your home, then you should consider insulating your home:

- ✔ Your home was built before 1981.
- ✔ You have a room that is too hot in summer or too cold in winter.
- ✔ Your heating and cooling bills are too high.
- ✔ You have sound issues from neighbors or other outside noise.
- ✔ You're remodeling. (A remodel will be the easiest and best chance you have to add insulation to your existing home.)

The key to insulation is making sure it's installed properly. Make sure the insulation is not compressed, especially on the edges and around wiring. Make sure it's in contact with the wall or ceiling — even small gaps will have a massive impact on the insulation's effectiveness.

Insulation doesn't just go in the walls. Be sure to include insulation in these areas, too:

- ✔ **Attic:** Be sure to insulate the floor and roof of your attic.
- ✔ **Crawl space:** An average of 80 percent of the air in a moldy, dank, cold crawl space will end up in your house. Insulate the floor to prevent this.
- ✔ **Foundation:** More than half of your heat leaks out of the edges of your foundation slab. Insulate the edges prior to erecting the walls.
- ✔ **Hot water pipes:** Adding insulation wrap to the hot water pipes is simple to do and especially important for pipes in crawl spaces.

Types of insulation

The effectiveness of insulation is measured in terms of the *R-value,* which is its thermal resistance. The higher the R-value, the greater the effectiveness of the insulation. Many different types of insulation are available:

- ✔ **Batt insulation (R-value: 2.9 to 3.8):** Loose, fluffy batts of pink fiberglass are the most common type of insulation. Batts fit neatly between the studs of your wall framing. Unfortunately, the fiberglass is filled with chemicals and can irritate your lungs.

  As an alternative, choose formaldehyde-free and recycled cotton insulation.

- ✔ **Loose-fill cellulose (R-value: 3.1 to 3.7):** Dry, loose fill is sprayed into closed up walls, or into attics and hard-to-reach places. It works great for existing walls that you don't want to open up completely. Unfortunately, loose-fill insulation tends to settle like flour in a jar, leaving areas uninsulated.

  As an alternative, choose natural cellulose made from recycled newsprint. It's treated with natural chemicals to make it fire resistant.

- ✔ **Spray-in foams (R-value: 3.6 to 6.2):** Spray-in place foams are sticky and expand to fill the entire wall cavity. Although they cost more than other forms of insulation, the have a much higher R-value. Because they expand to fill every nook and cranny, they work much better at insulating your home. Avoid any foam that uses chlorofluorocarbons (CFCs) to expand.

  As an alternative, choose natural soy-based foams. They're healthier than spray foam and offer all the same benefits. This is my favorite choice.

- ✔ **Rigid foam board (R-value: 3.9 to 7.0):** Stiff boards of insulation are used at the edges of a concrete slab, over concrete basement walls, or anywhere space is tight. They're more expensive per inch than other types, but rigid boards get a much higher R-value. Avoid formaldehyde products.

  As an alternative, choose polyisocyanurate or extruded polystyrene (EPS).

Lighting controls and features

Lighting accounts for one-third of the energy used in the average home. By changing bulbs, adding some sensors, and bringing in sunlight, you can cut this energy use in half.

Compact fluorescent bulbs

Compact fluorescent (CFL) bulbs are a type of fluorescent lamp that fits into a standard light bulb socket. Traditional incandescent bulbs waste energy, give off a lot of heat, and constantly burn out — all of which adds up to added maintenance and air-conditioning costs.

CFL bulbs use a fraction of the energy of their incandescent counterparts, produce 70 percent less heat, and last ten times longer. All this saves you $30 or more over the life of each bulb.

If every American home replaced just one light bulb with a CFL bulb, we would save enough energy to light more than 2.5 million homes for a year and prevent greenhouse gases equivalent to the emissions of nearly 800,000 cars.

Some things to consider before you run out to the store to buy new CFL bulbs:

✓ **Most fluorescent bulbs use a tiny amount of mercury in order to work.** Because mercury is unhealthy, make sure to purchase low-mercury fluorescents. Several manufacturers (including Philips and Sylvania) now offer them.

✓ **Mixing and matching bulbs from different manufacturers can create color issues.** One bulb might be yellowish, while the one right next to it might be more bluish. This presents a challenge if you're slowly upgrading the bulbs one at a time as they burn out.

✓ **Many people complain that CFL bulbs cannot be dimmed.** Dimmable CFL bulbs *are* available — for a little more money.

✓ **Because they contain mercury, CFL bulbs should not be thrown away.** Send them to your local hazardous waste disposal program (where you send batteries and tires).

LED bulbs

A *light-emitting diode* (LED) is a tiny semiconductor that emits light. It looks like a small bulb but contains no filament to burn out. Although LEDs are twice as energy efficient as incandescent bulbs, they're still not as efficient as CFL bulbs.

LEDs have an incredibly long life — 30,000 to 50,000 hours. (The typical CFL bulb lasts about 10,000 hours; the typical incandescent bulb only 800 to 1,000 hours.) New types of LED bulbs are being released, making them affordable for common household use.

Occupancy sensors

Occupancy sensors turn on the lights when someone enters the room and shut off after a set period of no movement. Switch sensors replace the traditional light switch and fit into the same space. Occupancy sensors are perfect for mud rooms, powder rooms, kids' play rooms, garages, basements, and anywhere else you may forget to turn off the lights.

Kill switches and plug strips

Even when they're turned off and not running, appliances still continue to use energy. Always-ready devices like TV sets, stereos, DVD players, and microwaves use even more energy while waiting for you to click your remote. If you plug those appliances into a power strip with an on/off switch, and you switch off the power strip when you're not using the appliances, you could save $50 a year.

A *kill switch* shuts off everything connected to that circuit. It's great for infrequently used rooms, like guest rooms and workshops. Your electrician can install these just like any other switch to shut off electricity to an entire room.

Clever switches and dimmers

Small plunger-type switches can be hidden in the side jamb of a closet door. When the door opens, the closet light comes on; it turns off when you close the door. These are a simple and fun way to make sure the closet light is never left on.

Dimmer switches can save energy and extend bulb life. However, the energy saved is not quite proportional to the amount you dim — a light dimmed down to one-quarter of its output still uses half the energy.

Daylighting

People love natural light. Subconsciously, we seek out sunlit places and enjoy spending time in natural light. Beyond fulfilling this desire, however, there are some tangible benefits to adding natural daylighting into your home.

Studies have proven that daylighting speeds up recovery from illness. Also, kids will have better concentration while studying under natural daylight, and it reduces eyestrain.

In the following sections, I cover your daylighting options.

Skylights

Skylights are rooftop windows. They bring in twice the light of a traditional window of the same size. Skylights eliminate the need for electric lighting during the day.

To reduce the heat gain from too much sun, install skylights on the north side of the roof. Double-glazed skylights have two layers of glass to help insulate the skylight. Choose operable skylights to capture passing breezes.

Sun tunnels

A sun tunnel (like the one shown in Figure 11-2) uses a small dome skylight on the roof and another on the ceiling of a room. A flexible tube, similar to a clothes-dryer vent, connects both domes. Also called a "sun tube," "sun pipe," or "solar tube," light bounces around the inside of this tube, creating a bright skylight inside. Sun tunnels are inexpensive and easy to install, and they're perfect for existing homes or houses with tall attic spaces.

Mirrors

Because a mirror reflects light, well-placed mirrors can be used to reflect the light, doubling the amount of ambient light in a room. You can use bulbs of half the normal wattage, or half the number of fixtures, with no loss in light level. The potential energy savings is enormous (50 percent in this simple example).

The typical mirror is a sheet of flat plate glass coated with aluminum or silver on one side. The opposite side is a highly reflective surface. Because the coating is on the backside, it's protected from scratching and will typically last a very long time.

Figure 11-2:
A sun tunnel loops through an attic space to bring light down to the room below.

Courtesy of Solatube International, Inc.

Today, the modern mirror uses less than 3 percent lead content in the paint coating. In fact, lead-free mirrors are now commonly available. Because glass itself it a natural material, mirrors are inherently green materials.

Mirrored glass cannot be recycled, but if protected, it can last many years with minimal maintenance. It does not release chemicals, and glass is one of the most commonly recycled materials in the world.

Light shelves

The principle behind daylighting is simple: By using natural light, you reduce the need for electricity. In practice, however, bringing daylight deep into a home can be challenging. Enter light shelves.

Light shelves are horizontal fins located above eye level at the windows to bounce the light back up onto the ceiling. This diffuses the light and brings it deeper into the building. Well-placed light shelves also act as a shading device and reduce glare.

In order to work effectively, both the light shelf and the ceiling need to be white (or at least a light hue).

You may be thinking, "Hey, if mirrors reflect light so well, why not top the light shelf with a mirror surface?" Unfortunately, reflecting direct sunlight into a building can create enough heat to burn the ceiling. Remember as a kid when you would use a magnifying glass to burn leaves? A mirror can potentially create the same heat! Be careful when using horizontal mirrors that would reflect large amounts of direct sunlight.

Caulking and sealing

If you added up all the cracks in a typical house, they would be equivalent in size to leaving an entire window wide open all winter. Much of the heat in your home is leaking out through the ducts, pipes, and outlets in your exterior walls. You can fill the cracks with caulk, sealants, and weather stripping — this is one of the easiest and quickest things you can do to improve your home's energy efficiency.

In the following sections, I give you a rundown of the major sources of leaks in your home, and what you can do to stop them.

Penetrations

Water pipes, gas lines, and electrical conduits penetrate the walls of your home. Over time, cracks form around the penetrations, allowing a lot of heat to escape. When you're caulking the cracks around these penetrations, be sure to select a water-based caulk. If you're doing a remodel, this is your best chance to get access to some of these areas.

Outlets and light switches

Those little plastic covers over your light switches and electrical outlets don't insulate at all. Insert foam gaskets below these covers to help keep warm air from leaking out of these spots.

Recessed lights

Recessed lights in your ceiling are expressways for warm air to escape and for cold air to come in. Wrapping the fixtures in insulation is a possible fire hazard, so make sure these lights are *IC-rated,* which means they *can* have direct insulation contact. Also, be sure to caulk between the light housing and the drywall ceiling.

Wood framing plates

Seal the top and bottom plates of a wood wall with a foam gasket or weather stripping between the wood and the foundation or roof. This will seal a large, continuous crack that goes around your entire home.

Ducts

The average home has a 30 percent leakage in its ducts. All the joints in your ductwork should sealed with low-toxic *mastic* (a water-based joint compound you can find in the heating, ventilation, and air-conditioning [HVAC] aisle at most hardware stores).

Avoid using duct tape; ironically, duct tape is not good for ducts.

Thermostats

The thermostat is another large hole in your wall that allows air to leak out. Put a foam gasket behind your thermostat so it reads the actual room temperature instead of the colder temperature inside the wall.

A programmable thermostat is inexpensive and ensures that you run the heater or air conditioner only during specific times. Instead of running the heater all night, a programmable thermostat can turn on the heat a couple of hours before you get up. This can save you 30 percent off your heating bills. It can do the same in the summertime with your air conditioning, turning it off while you're away at work and turning it back on before you come home at the end of the day.

Energy-efficient windows

Windows are the eyes of your home. They provide views, sunlight, ventilation, and solar heating.

Your walls are stuffed with insulation, but your windows are not so efficient. In fact, 10 percent to 25 percent of your heating and air conditioning are leaking out of the windows' uninsulated frames. If your home has single-pane windows, as nearly half the homes in the United States do, you're losing even more energy; consider replacing single-pane windows with double-pane ones.

Don't throw away your old windows. Your local salvage yard will gladly take them and keep them from ending up in the landfill. Old windows can also be used to create an interesting interior partition.

When remodeling your home, the issue with energy-efficient windows is the cost. You could spend $20,000 replacing all the existing windows in your home, or achieve the same energy savings by spending just $2,000 for insulation. Although new windows will reduce your energy bills, think about this when looking for the biggest bang for your buck.

If the cost and effort to replace all the windows in your home is too great, consider the following:

- ✔ **Hang heavy curtains on every window.** Heavy curtains will prevent warm air from leaking out of the windows in the winter and block the hot sun in the summer.

- ✔ **Wash the windows often.** Keep the windows on the south-facing side of your house clean to allow the winter sun in for warmth.

- ✔ **Put tinted window films on the south and west sides of your home to block the heat gain from the summer sun.**

- ✔ **Install awnings and overhangs over south-facing windows.** This will help block the heat gain from the summer sun as well.

- ✔ **Mount plastic sheeting over your windows and use a hair dryer to shrink the sheeting until it's taut.** The plastic sheeting will serve to insulate the windows in the winter months. You can find easy-to-install plastic sheeting for windows at any hardware store. A low-budget trick: Recycled bubble wrap (from packages) works just as well as plastic sheeting and creates an interesting pattern over your windows.

- ✔ **If you can't afford to replace every window, consider just focusing on older windows or on windows in the coldest rooms of your house.**

If you're building a new home, some of the cost of installing more efficient windows will be offset because you'll be able to use a smaller, less expensive heating system.

If you live in a cold climate, you'll need different windows than your friends in Florida or Arizona. Generally, you'll want to buy double-pane windows with low-emissivity (or low-e) coatings on the glass. Most manufacturers offer windows filled with argon gas between the two panes of glass. This will add to the cost but increase the insulation value of the window.

If you live in a warmer climate without a harsh winter, it's important to buy windows that will block the hot sun from coming in. Look for windows with tints and films to reflect UV light.

Several materials are commonly used to make the frame of the window:

- ✓ **Fiberglass:** Fiberglass offers the best energy efficiency. Look for recycled-content frames.

- ✓ **Wood:** Wood is fairly energy efficient. Although wood is a renewable resource, request FSC-certified wood. Wood frames need to be painted, so consider clad wood frames — they're attractive and more insulating.

- ✓ **Vinyl:** Although similar to wood in energy performance, vinyl window frames are made of, well, vinyl (an environmentally dangerous material). Vinyl window frames are the least expensive option — but not the best.

- ✓ **Metal:** Metal frames conduct heat and cold, making them poor for energy savings. Only get metal frames with a thermal break, to keep the metal from freezing on the inside.

Only purchase Energy Star–rated windows.

The insulation value of windows is not measured in R-value, it's measured in U-value. U-value (which is the inverse of R-value) measures the ability to hold in temperature. The lower the U-value, the better the insulation, so look for the lowest U-value available. If you live in a colder climate, only buy windows with a U-value at least 0.35 or lower.

Correctly installed windows should have no air leakage around them. Consider using a water-based expansion spray foam between the frame and wall framing. Do not stuff insulation in there; compressed insulation has no benefit.

The Internal Revenue Service (IRS) and your local utility company offer tax credits for installing energy-efficient windows in your home. Ask your accountant about the requirements.

Energy-efficient appliances

The major appliances in your home — refrigerators, clothes washers, dishwashers — account for a big chunk of your monthly utility bill. If your appliances were purchased before 1990, you're spending a lot more on energy than you need to and it's time to upgrade them.

Be sure to buy only Energy Star–rated appliances, which have met a minimum federal energy standard. Purchase the highest Energy Star–rated appliances you can find — it will save you a great deal of money. (Go to www.energy star.gov for details on the Energy Star ratings.) Check out Figure 11-3 for the Energy Star logo, which you'll see on all Energy Star–rated appliances.

Figure 11-3:
The Energy
Star logo.

Courtesy of www.energystar.gov.

Bigger isn't always better when it comes to appliances. Bigger appliances will only cost you more money and waste energy. Get just what you need.

Some states and local utility companies offer rebates for buying new Energy Star appliances. You can save hundreds of dollars off the purchase of that new refrigerator or washer!

If you have solar panels on your home, choose electric appliances. Otherwise, pick appliances that run on natural gas. It's a cleaner and cheaper alternative.

Here are the major appliances you may want to look at replacing:

- **Refrigerator:** If you're thinking of replacing an old appliance, the refrigerator is a great place to start. New refrigerators consume 75 percent less energy than those produced in the late 1970s. Upgrading to a modern refrigerator can save you more than $100 a year on your utility bill.

   If possible, locate the refrigerator away from direct sunlight and the oven. This keeps the refrigerator from having to work that much harder to stay cool. Also, keep in mind that refrigerators with upper freezers use 10 percent to 15 percent less energy than side-by-side models.

- **Clothes washer:** Energy Star washers use half the energy that standard models use, saving you about $110 a year. Also, front-loading washers use less water than top-loaders.

- **Clothes dryer:** A $5 clothesline is free to operate and leaves your clothes smelling fresh. Save the dryer for rainy days. Only run the dryer when full. Because most of the energy is used to create heat, it's better to run it for a longer time at a lower heat setting.

✔ **Water heater:** Water heating is typically the third largest energy expense in the home, accounting for about 13 percent of the average home's energy bill. If your gas water heater is more than ten years old, it probably operates at less than 50 percent efficiency and it's time to replace it. Choose a model with a timer so it only heats water when your family needs it. Be sure to insulate it with a heater wrap; this can save you even more money on your energy bills.

Chapter 12

Heating and Cooling Systems

. . . .

. . . .

*O*ne of the best ways to make your home healthy, comfortable, and energy efficient is to choose the correct heating and cooling system. Just keeping yourself comfortable uses up to two-thirds of the energy in your home. In this chapter, I cover the various types of heating systems, from mechanical to natural ones. In addition, I show you ways to reduce the need for heating and cooling in the first place.

Mechanical Systems

Mechanical systems are machines that heat water or air using gas or electricity. Whether they use fans to blow hot air, or pipes to pump hot water, all these systems must:

✔ Provide heat when it's cold outside.

✔ Provide cooling when it's hot outside.

✔ Provide moisture when the air is dry.

✔ Absorb moisture when the air is wet.

✔ Bring in fresh air from outside.

✔ Filter the air that is brought in.

In the following sections, I show you your options when it comes to mechanical heating and cooling systems.

Forced-air systems: Heating and cooling

A *forced-air system* (also called a *whole-house system*) is one of the most common types of heaters used in homes. Gas or electricity is used to heat air, which is then blown around the house via metal ducts and into different rooms through vents on the floor or ceiling. The same system can be used for cooling your home as well. A thermostat controls the air flow. The vents are usually located in the draftiest parts of the room, typically near the windows and doors.

Although this sounds simple enough, forced-air systems have some disadvantages:

- **Uneven heating and cooling:** Air is blown into the room, causing some areas to be warmer or cooler than others.

- **Pollen and dust:** Forced-air systems bring in fresh air from the outside, carrying with it pollen and allergens. These systems also spread dust around the home — especially if the home has floor vents, where dust and dirt are easily trapped. If you have asthma or allergies, a forced-air system is the worst choice for controlling the air around you.

  If the air coming out of the vents smells funny, consider having your ducts cleaned by a licensed mechanical contractor. Not only will your system operate more efficiently, but you'll also notice an immediate improvement with dust and allergies.

- **Noise:** You can hear when the fan is on because of the sound of the air blowing through the vents.

- **Inefficient:** Most homes have only one thermostat monitoring the system, resulting in some rooms being warmer or cooler than others. Plus, you typically have to heat and cool the entire home rather than just the room you're using.

If your current heater was built before 1980, it's time to upgrade to a new system. Even if you stick with a forced-air system, current models are much more efficient than older ones; the upgrade will pay for itself in energy savings in less than three years.

Heating systems

Most building departments will require you to install a heater in your home, but a cooling system (or air conditioner) is not required. Even in warmer climates, you'll need to install a heater, even if it never gets used. In this section, I cover a variety of energy-efficient heating systems for your home.

Electric baseboard heat

Instead of a large system for the whole house, individual room units are often a great alternative. Small electric baseboard heaters run along the base of the wall and are relatively inexpensive to operate.

If your home is well insulated and doesn't require a lot of heating, electric baseboard heaters are often the best option. Each room can control the heat, allowing for great flexibility.

Gas room heaters

Similar to electric baseboard heating, individual room heaters are usually wall-mounted, self-contained units. Running on natural gas, they're an efficient option for small homes or for heating one room at a time.

Select a model with an automatic ignition instead of a pilot light. Pilot lights waste energy and often blow out, potentially leaking gas into your home.

Solar thermal water heater

A solar heater is a wonderfully simple device. This 2-x-4-foot box sits on your roof. There are no moving parts, just a coiled pipe entering at the bottom and exiting at the top. As the sun shines on this box, the water in the pipe is heated. The heated water rises through the coiled pipe automatically, where it is stored in a standard water heater tank. You can see how this works in Figure 12-1.

Although you can use the heated water to meet the hot water needs in your house (showering, dishwashing, and so on), you can also use it for heating your home. The hot water can be converted into heat in the form of:

- ✓ **Radiators:** Hot water is sent through pipes to a typical radiator.

- ✓ **Forced-air fan:** A fan blows air over copper tubes filled with the hot water. The hot water, in turn, heats the air.

- ✓ **Radiant heat (see the following section):** The hot water is used for a radiant heating system.

Powered solely by the sun, the solar thermal heater provides hot water for free, greatly reducing the operating costs for all these heaters. Because it relies on the light and not heat to warm the water, the system even works in the winter. When the sun sets at night, the hot water is stored for later use. If carefully planned, this system can provide for all your hot water and heating needs.

Be sure your roof is strong enough to support the weight of the solar heater before you install it. If your home was built before 1980, ask your architect or engineer to confirm the strength of your existing roof.

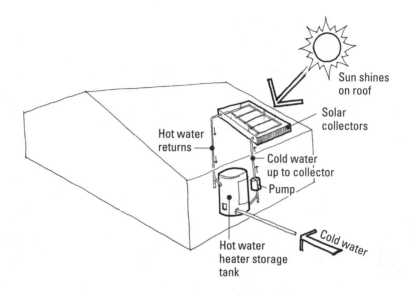

Figure 12-1:
In a solar water heater, sunlight hits the box on your roof, slowly heating the water and sending it back into your home. This even works in the winter.

Radiant heat

A *radiant heating system* (also called *hydronic*) uses an efficient combination of hot water pumped through tubes to warm the floor. Unlike traditional forced-air heating, where hot air blows to heat the air, radiant heat uses the principle of radiation to heat the surface. As shown in Figure 12-2, radiant heat warms the occupants, not the space — an important distinction. The result is a wonderfully comfortable and cozy feeling of warmth.

Here are the advantages that a radiant heating system offers:

- ✔ **Comfort:** Because the heat source is under the floor, temperatures are warmer at floor level (where you are) and the heat rises to the ceiling. Because the floor is warm, walking barefoot and sitting on the floor are cozy possibilities.

- ✔ **Dust-free:** No air is pushed around in radiant heating, which means it offers a dust and pollen-free alternative for those suffering from allergies or asthma.

- ✔ **Not drying:** Unlike forced hot air, radiant heating will not dry out the air.

- ✔ **Safe for kids:** Children are safe from contact with hot radiators or dirty vent ducts.

- ✔ **Quiet and maintenance free:** A radiant heat system is virtually noise and maintenance free.

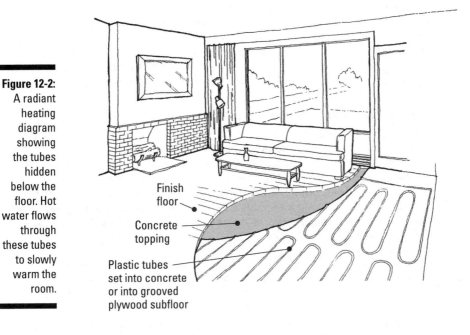

Figure 12-2:
A radiant heating diagram showing the tubes hidden below the floor. Hot water flows through these tubes to slowly warm the room.

Finish floor

Concrete topping

Plastic tubes set into concrete or into grooved plywood subfloor

The hot water in the tubes can be produced through a gas or electric boiler or hot water heater. If you're generating your own electricity with solar panels, the electric version is a better choice. The best and most energy-efficient option would be the addition of a solar water heater on the roof to preheat the water and reduce the operation of the boiler.

Although you can adapt a radiant system for any floor type, an earthen floor or concrete slab works best. The thermal mass of these floors holds in the heat from the tubes and will maintain a much more consistent temperature. Radiant heat can be installed in both floor-joist systems and slab floors, but installing it into a slab will be slightly less expensive because it's easier. When installing over wood floor joists, special products are now available to make installation easier. Products such as Warmboard (`www.warmboard.com`) are plywood panels with precut grooves. The tubes are set into the grooves, hastening installation.

As a general rule, a radiant heating system will cost about $1.50 to $1.75 per square foot installed, not including the heat source.

The advantages of radiant heat have brought it to the mainstream market in the United States (it's already commonplace in Europe).

For areas where tubing is not an option, electrical radiant heat companies such as Nuheat (www.nuheat.com) provide a thin wire mesh you can install in the thin space under tile or carpeting. These warm the floor slowly, just as with a tube system, and are a great addition to a single bathroom. Although electric radiant heat systems are expensive to operate normally, your costs are free if you're producing your own electricity with solar panels.

Ground source heat pumps (geothermal)

Ground source heat pumps (also called *geothermal systems*) are a fairly new and innovative method of heating and cooling a building, but the idea is relatively simple: The earth below ground maintains a consistent temperature of around 57°F. Instead of heating the building from the freezing air outside, or cooling the building from the blistering air outside, you heat it or cool it from this 57°F. Because this geothermal temperature is much closer to people's normal comfort zone, it requires much less energy to use. In Figure 12-3 you can see how this system works.

The U.S. Environmental Protection Agency (EPA) credits geothermal as "the most energy-efficient, environmentally friendly heating and cooling technology available."

The only by-product of using a ground source heat pump is warm water. With this ground source water, you can heat both the air and the water needs for your building.

Generally speaking, geothermal systems come in two standard configurations: vertical closed loop or horizontal closed loop.

When in Rome . . .

Those innovative ancient Romans used radiant underfloor heating in A.D. 670 using terra-cotta pipes. Already masters of plumbing and irrigation, the Romans heated their villas and baths by directing flue gases from wood fires in pipes beneath stone slab floors.

Rediscovered early in the 20th century, modern radiant heat substituted copper pipes for terra cotta and hot water instead of hot gas. Frank Lloyd Wright often employed this method of comfortable heating. The tract homes of Levittown featured radiant heat. In the 1970s, plastic tubing replaced the often faulty and leaky pipes.

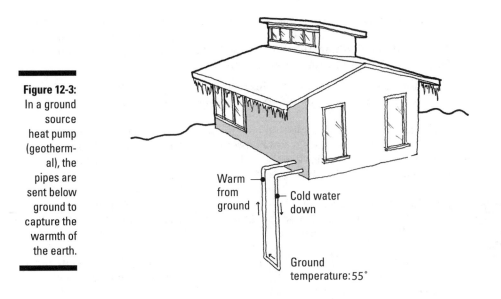

Figure 12-3:
In a ground source heat pump (geothermal), the pipes are sent below ground to capture the warmth of the earth.

Warm from ground ↑

Cold water down ↓

Ground temperature: 55°

✔ **Vertical closed loop:** The most common system is the vertical one. In this system, loops of piping are fed several hundred feet into the earth, which requires a great deal of boring. Given the depth, the ground source temperature remains consistent throughout the year. On a site with expansive soils or bedrock, the vertical systems are too expensive.

✔ **Horizontal closed loop:** Horizontal closed loop systems are installed in trenches only 5 feet below the surface of the earth. Due to this shallow installation, the ground temperature changes seasonally. Although horizontal loops are much easier to install and work with for bedrock sites, they do require significantly more surface area (approximately 2,500 square feet of surface area per ton of cooling) in order to work effectively.

The advantages of geothermal include the following:

✔ **Cost savings:** Homeowners with geothermal units typically realize energy savings of 25 percent to 50 percent over conventional gas, oil, or heat pump systems. As a general rule, a typical 2,000-square-foot house can be heated or cooled for as little as $1 a day. Because a geothermal system also produces hot water as a by-product, it's up to 30 percent less expensive to operate than a traditional gas or electric water heater.

✔ **Pollen and dust free:** A geothermal system does not draw spores and pollen into the building as a forced-air heating system does. If you have allergies or asthma, this is a welcome change and you'll notice a marked improvement in your indoor air quality.

✔ **Fume free:** Because the geothermal system does not involve combustion, a pilot light, or a chimney, no odor or fumes will be added to the house.

For smaller buildings, installation cost is the main drawback. Drilling the holes for the vertical system can be prohibitive for single-family homes. Another possible roadblock is the lack of qualified contractors who know how to properly design, install, and service these systems.

Look for equipment certified by the Air-Conditioning and Refrigeration Institute (www.ari.org), a nonprofit organization that rates residential and small commercial systems.

Given their affordable installation cost, low operating costs, low maintenance costs, and overall energy efficiency, geothermal systems are an excellent choice to consider for your home.

Fireplaces

No other feature provides as strong an image of home as a fireplace does. When they think of holidays and family gatherings, many people picture people sitting around a hearth. For centuries, a fireplace was the sole source of heat in a home; today, it's used only occasionally.

In the following sections, I cover your fireplace options.

Be sure to close the chimney flue of your fireplace when not in use. If you don't, valuable (and expensive) heated or cooled air will fly right up and out of your home, wasting money.

The early days of geothermal

Archaeological evidence shows that the first use of geothermal heating occurred more than 10,000 years ago with the settlement of Native Americans using hot springs. A source of warmth and cleansing, the spring minerals were known as a source for healing.

The modern use of geothermal dates back to 1864 at the Hot Lake Hotel near La Grande, Oregon. By 1930, the first commercial use of geothermal energy was produced using a 1,000-foot well in Boise, Idaho.

Wood

Wood-burning fireplaces have long been a sentimental vision of home. The sounds of the crackling fire and the warmth of the hearth are comforting and romantic notions. But in recent years, local building codes have banned their use, in favor of cleaner-burning gas fireplaces.

According to the U.S. Department of Energy, wood-burning fireplaces emit nitrogen oxides, carbon monoxide, organic gases, and particulate matter. These pollutants can cause serious health problems for children, pregnant women, and people with respiratory problems. Some of these are even known carcinogens.

If you have an existing wood-burning fireplace, an EPA-certified clean-burning fireplace insert and a glass screen will protect your family from the gases entering the room. Instead of using petroleum-based premanufactured logs, look for eco-friendly versions, like a fire log made from recycled, dried coffee grounds (www.java-log.com).

Gas

Gas fireplaces are cleaner burning, and do not require cleaning up ash from the bottom of the fireplace. The burners can be set into sand, stones, or glass for a modern, high-tech look. Most models are even available with remote controls. However, gas fireplaces still use a fossil fuel as their energy source, making them less than ideal.

Pellet stoves

The most efficient fireplace available is a pellet stove, which uses small cylinders of compressed sawdust as a fuel. The combustion chamber is sealed, so instead of a crackling fire, you see a flame behind glass. Though not as romantic as a wood fireplace, pellet stoves provide the most heat with the least amount of fuel.

Open fireplaces

If you don't like the sterile flame or fake wood inserts of gas fireplaces, Eco-Smart Fire (www.ecosmartfire.com) has introduced an environmentally friendly open fireplace. Fueled by renewable methylated spirits (fermented sugar cane), the EcoSmart burns and does not require a flue. Imagine having a fireplace in the center of your dining room table.

Cooling systems

On a hot day, nothing beats walking into a nice, cool, air-conditioned home. Unfortunately, running your air conditioner is expensive and eats up energy. Fortunately, some simple decisions can help you reduce the amount of energy you use to cool your home, even on the hottest days.

Air conditioners

Central air conditioning is the biggest single user of energy in your home, and the most wasted one as well. Most people set the thermostat lower than necessary, because they think it'll make the cold come out faster (it won't). Compare your utility bills from March with those in August and you can see firsthand how much air conditioning is costing you.

Ironically, air conditioning produces more heat outside than it relieves inside. During the summer, it's estimated that air conditioning is responsible for nearly half the electricity used in the United States.

Although you may think you can't live without your air conditioner, in truth, a home can be built to never need air conditioning. If you're still considering a central air-conditioning system, purchase an Energy Star–rated unit, with a Seasonal Energy Efficiency Ratio (SEER) of 12 or higher. Also, look for units with a fan-only option and a replaceable filter.

In the following sections, I fill you in on your air-conditioning options.

Individual window units

Instead of installing central air (see "Forced-air systems: Heating and cooling," earlier in this chapter), consider individual window units. They cost less to operate and they cool only the areas you need.

Be sure to properly size the unit for the room; people tend to buy the biggest air conditioner they can find, wasting money and energy. Place the unit in a window away from direct sunlight, or plant a tree outside to shade that window.

Ductless units

A more attractive and less noisy option, ductless air conditioners use a simple outdoor condenser unit to run power and refrigerant to small, wall-mounted fans. Instead of filling a window, the ductless unit can go anywhere on the wall. Because the refrigeration takes place outside, ductless units are much quieter than a central or window unit system. But expect to pay double the cost of a simple window unit for a ductless unit.

Ice energy

Ice energy is an innovative and cost-effective system for cooling a building. A large box in your yard produces a block of ice at night, when the temperature is cool and electricity costs are lower. During the day, a fan blows air over the ice, creating air conditioning. By time-shifting most of the energy use to night, an ice energy system can save you hundreds off your utility bills. Commercial units have been around for some time, and smaller residential units are now finally available as well from companies like Ice Energy (www.ice-energy.com).

Ceiling fans

When it's warm, most people really just need to feel comfortable. Air conditioners blow cold air, taking a long time to cool the entire home. A ceiling fan offers the same level of comfort, but costs must less to operate. It circulates the air, generating a feeling of comfort and carrying cooling breezes through the home. Save the air conditioner for the really hot days, and use the ceiling fan instead.

Because warm air rises and collects around the ceiling, ceiling fans have two settings: winter and summer. That little switch on the side of the fan controls the setting. The default summer setting pulls air upward, sucking in breezes from open windows and cooling things down. The winter setting pushes the warm air gathered at the ceiling down onto you below. Make sure you have your fan set on the correct setting.

Whole-house fans

A whole-house fan is installed in the ceiling of the top floor of your home. When it's switched on, the fan sucks air into the attic, drawing in cool air from the outside. In order to work effectively, open the windows of the rooms you want to cool, and close the doors of unused rooms. Highly effective and much less expensive than central air conditioning, a whole house fan can keep you cool through the summer.

Solar attic fans

If your home has an attic space, install a solar-powered attic fan. These inexpensive fans turn on automatically when it gets too hot, siphoning the hot air out of the attic. Use of an attic fan will lower the temperature of the attic, reducing the strain on your air conditioner and saving you money.

Natural Methods

Believe it or not, nature provides its own methods of maintaining a regular temperature. For thousands of years, human beings used the systems of nature to stay comfortable. But in traditional modern homes, if it's too hot or cold, people just pump in energy. Before consuming energy to heat or cool your home, consider the following methods.

Insulation

A well-insulated home will hold in temperature, lowering your heating and cooling bills. Insulation keeps your heat from leaking out through the walls. The more you have, the better it works, and the lower your heating and cooling bills will be.

Nothing else you can do will have as big an impact on your monthly utility bills as insulating your home sufficiently. When it comes to insulation, if some is good, more is definitely better. (Refer to Chapter 11 for more on insulation.)

Insulation doesn't just go in the walls. Be sure to insulate in the following places, too:

- ✔ **Attic:** Be sure to insulate the floor and roof of your attic.

- ✔ **Foundation:** More than half of the heat in the average home leaks out of the edges of the foundation slab. Insulate the edges prior to erecting the walls.

- ✔ **Crawl space:** An average of 80 percent of the air in a home's moldy, dank, cold crawl space will end up in the house. Insulate the floors to prevent this from happening.

- ✔ **Hot-water pipes:** Adding insulation wrap to the hot-water pipes is simple to do and especially important for pipes in crawl spaces. Try to avoid running ducts and pipes through unheated attics or crawl spaces.

Thermal mass

If insulation is the ability of a material to *hold in* temperature, thermal mass is the ability of a material to *absorb and store* temperature. Sometimes referred to as a *heat sink,* we can use this to keep a building cool in the summer and warm in the winter in one of the simplest methods to reduce heating and cooling costs.

If you've ever gone swimming at night, you've experienced thermal mass. The sun heats up the pool water all day, and the water stores that heat. At night, when the surrounding temperature drops and the water releases this heat, the pool feels like bathwater. You're feeling the stored heat being released in the water. This is thermal mass in action (water has a very high thermal mass).

Heavy, massive materials such as concrete, brick, and stone have a high thermal mass. This is why your basement is always so cool in the summer, and why your dog sleeps on the tiles. The mass of the concrete basement and tile floor store in the cold and release it when the air around it is warm.

An exposed concrete slab is a simple way to utilize thermal mass. In the winter, let the sun come through the windows and warm up the concrete. In the summer, use curtains or overhangs to block the sun from coming in, keeping the concrete cool. Just this simple method will ensure you maintain a consistent temperature year-round.

Thermal mass is ideal in a climate where it's warm during the day and cool at night. Build the south-facing walls of your home out of adobe, rammed earth, or concrete. The sun will warm the walls all day, and keep the house warm at night. (See Chapter 9 for more information on natural building methods.)

You can use thermal mass to maintain a consistent temperature in your home. Materials with a high thermal mass are not affected by sudden temperature swings; they take a long time to heat up and cool down. Using thermal mass in the winter requires positioning a mass wall such that the sun warms it all day (see Figure 12-4). At night, after the temperature drops, the wall will release heat and keep you warm.

Because thermal mass requires changes in temperature in order to work, it won't work in areas that are always hot or always cold. In fact, using thermal mass in these areas will work against you. For example, a concrete building in a hot desert, where it's hot all day and night, will never have the chance to release the heat. This building will be even hotter inside from the saturated thermal mass.

Figure 12-4:
Examples
of how
thermal
mass
regulates
the
temperature
in your
home.

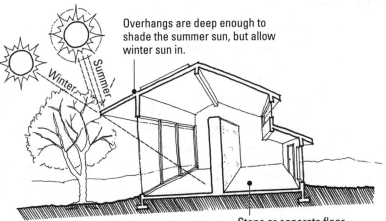

Overhangs are deep enough to shade the summer sun, but allow winter sun in.

Stone or concrete floor absorbs winter sun.

Passive cooling

Through the physics of convection, heat rises. Warm air is lighter than cool air, and as the warm air rises, cooler air rushes in to take its place. Passive cooling uses this principle to create ventilation.

You can use this idea to keep cool in the summer by funneling air through your home. Using something called a *thermal chimney* (a tall, vented space), this rising heat is directed up and out of the house. As wind passes over the building, it pulls more air through the chimney. Cool air from the outside is pulled into the lower part of the house.

A tall, open stairwell can function as a thermal chimney. Place operable skylights at the top of the stairwell to allow the heat to escape on warm days. You can create air movement even if there is no breeze.

Ventilation

The movement of air, even slightly warmer air, across your skin causes a cooling sensation. The air removes heat and evaporates perspiration, creating the illusion of feeling comfortable. By simply moving air through your home, you can reduce the need for air conditioning.

Here are three simple ways to do that:

- ✔ **Operable windows:** The easiest way to create natural ventilation is to install operable windows. Locate windows at different heights and on opposite walls to encourage cross-ventilation. Windows placed at the same height will only allow air to pass straight across the room.

- ✔ **Bathroom fans:** Bathroom fans exhaust the hot, steamy air from your bathroom to the outside. Not only does this lessen the need for air conditioning, but it reduces potential problems with moisture and mold.

- ✔ **Switch boxes for clothes dryers:** Install a switch box on the hose of your clothes dryer. In the summer, the hot air is pumped outside, as it normally would. In the winter, flip the switch box to redirect the heat back into the room. These inexpensive boxes are available at any hardware store.

Earth berms

Slope the earth up against the house to protect it from cold winters and hot summers. Called *berms,* these mounds use the high thermal mass of the earth to keep your building cool. Berms can be an attractive addition to your landscape.

Passive solar

Passive solar integrates insulation, thermal mass, and passive cooling into one cohesive approach. When used correctly, a passive solar home can use the sun to provide for the heating, cooling, and daylighting of most of your needs.

The process is simple: Passive solar design takes advantage of the fact that the summer sun is higher than the winter sun. Overhangs shade the building from the summer sun, keeping it cool. The same overhangs allow the lower winter sun to enter the building and heat an interior thermal mass wall.

Passive solar design works in most climates, but it works best in areas with seasonal changes in weather. When a sun-facing, thermal mass wall is placed behind some glass, this is called a *trombe wall.* The space between the glass and the wall will fill with hot air. Vents at the top and bottom of the wall control this hot air, allowing it to be used to heat the building. The thick wall shown in Figure 12-5 shows how a passive solar is used throughout the year.

The best approach to passive solar is to use the principles to influence and shape the design of your home. Although considering passive solar during the initial design of your home is best, even an existing building can benefit from these ideas. Passive solar systems don't add to the cost of the building, and you'll see an immediate improvement in your energy use.

Active solar

Active solar is a strategy for designing high-performance, ultra-energy-efficient buildings. Active solar incorporates all the elements of a passive solar design (see the preceding section), but with additional mechanical equipment, such as pumps or fans, to take advantage of the heat from the sun. This equipment can include some elaborate technologies such as:

- **Motorized shades:** Timers and sensors control when window shades are raised and lowered, which controls heat gain from the sun.

- **Solar trackers:** Solar panels are turned throughout the day to follow the path of the sun. This increases the output of the solar panels.

- **Vents:** Thermostats and sensors control vents, which open to allow warm air into the house.

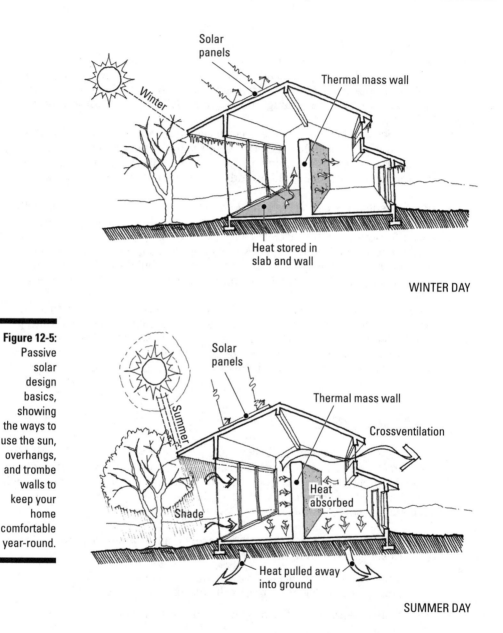

Solar panels

Thermal mass wall

Winter

Heat stored in slab and wall

WINTER DAY

Figure 12-5: Passive solar design basics, showing the ways to use the sun, overhangs, and trombe walls to keep your home comfortable year-round.

Solar panels

Thermal mass wall

Crossventilation

Summer

Heat absorbed

Shade

Heat pulled away into ground

SUMMER DAY

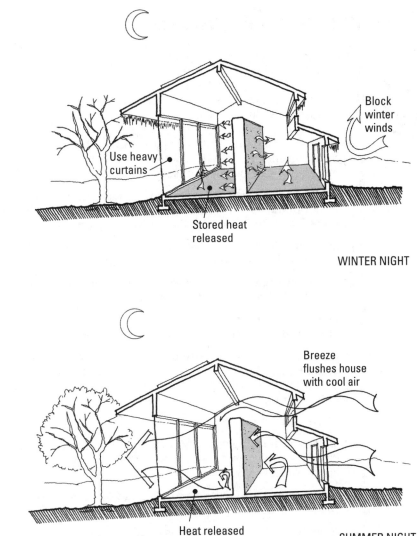

Block
winter
winds

Use heavy
curtains

Stored heat
released

WINTER NIGHT

Breeze
flushes house
with cool air

Heat released

SUMMER NIGHT

Conservation Techniques

Conserving energy in the first place is even more important than which type of heating or cooling system you install.

Here are some ways to conserve energy in your home, to reduce your reliance on heating and cooling systems:

- **Orient the building with the sun in mind.** The greatest heat will come from the sunlight from the south and west exposures, so keep this in mind when placing your house on the land.

- **Use trees to shade the house on the south and west sides.** The bare winter branches will allow the sunlight to come through and warm your home. (Turn to Chapter 14 for more on using trees.)

- **Minimize the size of windows on the west and south sides.** Control the amount of hot sun you receive with smaller windows.

- **Use double-paned, low-e glass in your windows.** This will allow the light, but not the heat, into your home.

- **Keep the flue of the fireplace closed when not in use.** Install thermal fireplace doors. Keep your expensive cooled air from escaping.

- **If you're hot, open the windows at night instead of running the air conditioner.** Most of the time, a cool breeze is all you need to stay comfortable. Set your programmable thermostat to turn off the air conditioner at night.

- **Close vents in unoccupied rooms.** Don't heat empty space.

- **Shade south-facing windows with overhangs, trellises, or awnings.** Remember the summer sun is higher than the winter sun, so these overhangs will keep you cool.

- **Use window treatments on south-facing windows.** Thick curtains can shade your home and keep the hot sun from baking the room.

- **Insulate your walls as much as possible.** The more insulation you have, the better.

- **Install a radiant barrier in your attic.** For just 25¢ a square foot, this reflective film will lower your attic temperature by 10 to 20 degrees. This will keep your home much cooler in the summer.

- ✔ **Choose a light-colored roof to reflect heat.** Dark colors absorb heat and can get as hot as 190 degrees in the summer.

- ✔ **Ventilate your attic and roof.** Allow the hot air to escape.

- ✔ **Caulk and seal all openings on the exterior walls.** Prevent your precious cooled air from leaking through the walls.

- ✔ **Keep windows and doors closed during hot, humid weather.** Higher humidity will make you feel warmer.

- ✔ **Use ceiling fans properly (summer and winter settings).** Save the air conditioner for only the hottest days.

- ✔ **Use fluorescent bulbs.** They give off much less heat than traditional bulbs. Go to Chapter 11 for more energy-saving techniques.

- ✔ **Insulate air-conditioning ducts.** This simple measure can reduce your cooling bills by 20 percent.

- ✔ **Insulate your hot water heater and pipes.** It takes minutes to do.

- ✔ **Have your heating system checked annually to ensure it runs at optimum efficiency.** Just keeping things running smoothly can increase effectiveness by 10 percent.

I cover additional conservation techniques in greater detail in the following sections.

Avoiding heat gain

The sun brings light, but also heat. In hot climates and during the summer months, you can block this heat gain using:

- ✔ **Curtains:** Heavy curtains block the hot summer sun.

- ✔ **Window films:** Put tinted window films on the south and west windows to block the heat gain from the summer sun.

- ✔ **Overhangs:** Awnings and overhangs over south-facing windows will block the heat gain from the high summer sun but allow the lower winter sun inside.

- ✔ **Trees:** A deciduous tree will shade your house in the summer. In the winter, its bare branches allow the light through to warm the home.

Heat islands

On warm days, the temperature in urban areas can rise by as much as 10°F when compared to the surrounding areas. These *heat islands* increase the need for air conditioning for everyone in the city. Reducing this heat island effect saves energy, reduces pollution, and makes cities more livable.

If you've walked barefoot on the sidewalk during a hot summer day, you've felt this heat island in action. All homes can benefit from reducing their heat island. Consider the following methods to cool the area around your home.

Cool roofs

There's a reason you don't wear black on a hot day: Dark colors absorb heat. The surface of a dark roof can get up to 190°F, greatly increasing the cooling load on a building. The simplest method to reduce heat islands is to choose a light-colored roof. This effortless change can save you as much as 20 percent to 70 percent in cooling costs. A planted green roof is an excellent type of cool roof. (Read more about green roofs in Chapter 13.)

Cool paving

Parking lots and driveways are notorious sources of heat islands. Typically made of asphalt, the black material absorbs so much heat your shoes can stick to the surface, increasing the air temperature by up to 15°F. Choose a light-color paving, such as concrete, for your driveway instead.

Porous pavers are perforated bricks made of concrete or stone that allow rainwater to sink into the ground. Grass sprouts up in the holes of the bricks, lowering the temperature. They're the greener — and more attractive — choice.

Stopping air leakage

One-third of your expensive heat is leaking out of your ducts. Save your money by sealing the joints in your ductwork with low-toxic mastic duct compound. Ironically, duct tape is actually not good for ducts, so avoid using it.

Caulk around windows and doors to keep more heat from escaping. If you were to add up the area of the cracks in a typical home, they add up to the equivalent of leaving a window open in the winter. Imagine all the heat that would escape if you left a window open!

Managing internal sources of heat

Sometimes the greatest source of heat gain in a building is the people within it. Lights, computers, ovens, and other equipment add additional unwanted heat. Turn off equipment you're not using to cool things off.

Incandescent light bulbs are only 10 percent light and 90 percent heat. Switching to fluorescent bulbs will greatly reduce the amount of heat inside your home — not to mention conserving energy.

Ninety-five percent of the energy in a clothes dryer is used for heating the clothes, not drying. Save your clothes from shrinkage by using a lower heat setting. Run the dryer at night when it's cooler. Or, for $5, buy a clothesline and make your own solar-powered clothes dryer.

Controls and sensors

A thermostat is a large hole in your wall that allows air to leak out. Put a foam gasket behind your thermostat so it reads the actual room temperature instead of the colder temperature inside the wall.

A programmable thermostat is inexpensive and ensures you run the heater or air conditioner only during specific times. Instead of running the heater all night, a programmable thermostat can turn on the heat a couple of hours before you get up. This can save you 30 percent off your heating bills.

Consider using zones to better control where the heat is located. For instance, the living areas can be one zone, and the sleeping areas another. You can have as many of these zones as desired, but each zone adds an additional manifold controller and thermostat.

Air filters

Install high-efficiency particulate arresting (HEPA) filters to your forced-air system. If you don't have a system with ductwork, purchase a portable HEPA filtration system for your bedroom and nursery.

Clean or replace furnace filters every month of use. Although it takes some effort, this alone will save you 5 percent to 10 percent on heating costs and remove dust and allergens from your home.

Chapter 13

Water and Waste Systems

*W*ater, water everywhere. . . . Water is one of the most abundant resources on earth. With water covering 70 percent of the planet, you might think our supply is endless. But we don't just need *water* — we need *drinkable* water.

A whopping 97 percent of the world's water supply is undrinkable seawater, with another 2 percent locked frozen in the polar ice caps. That leaves only 1 percent that's usable — and more than half of that water is polluted.

In this chapter, I explain how we use water in our homes, and the steps you can take to reduce the amount of water you use. From a flush down the toilet to a heavy rainfall, after reading this chapter you may never think about water the same way again.

Conserving Water

When it comes to water, Americans are extremely spoiled. If you live in the United States, you expect that, when you turn on your faucet, clean drinking water will always stream out. The typical U.S. household uses 293 gallons of water a day. When you compare that to the 5 gallons used by the typical home in Africa, you realize how Americans take water for granted.

In reality, most of the water Americans use is wasted. Here are some of the obvious activities that waste water:

- ✔ Running the faucet while you shave or brush your teeth
- ✔ Running the faucet or shower until the water becomes hot
- ✔ Taking long showers

 The most important and easiest way to lower water use is through conservation. And conservation begins with finding ways to use less water. Some simple changes to your behavior can add up to an immense saving in the amount of water you use. Look at how much water you can save just by doing these simple things:

- ✔ Turning off the water while brushing your teeth: 4 to 6 gallons
- ✔ Not letting the faucet run until the water is hot: 2 to 4 gallons
- ✔ Taking a 10-minute shower instead of a 20-minute shower: 25 to 50 gallons

A leaky faucet that loses one drop of water per second adds up to 16 bathtubs of water a month.

In the following sections, I fill you in on specific building and remodeling choices you can make when it comes to toilets, showers, and water heaters that will help you conserve water in your home.

Toilets

Toilets consume 40 percent of the water in the average home, making them the largest user of water. If your toilets were manufactured before 1980, they probably use nearly 6 gallons for every flush. Imagine, 6 gallons of clean drinking water wasted in a bowl that doesn't need to have drinkable water in the first place — despite what your dog thinks!

Most new toilets in the United States now use about 3.5 gallons per flush. Although this is an improvement over the pre-1980 figures, each flush still wastes a significant amount of fresh water.

In the following sections, I show you some alternatives to traditional toilets.

Low-flow and high-efficiency toilets

Low-flow toilets use only 1.6 gallons per flush and are just as effective at getting rid of waste as their traditional counterparts. Several states — including California and New Jersey — require all toilets to be this low-flow type. Choosing low-flow toilets is the least expensive and most effective way to conserve water in your home.

Some local municipalities now offer cash incentives for using water-efficient fixtures. And some of these incentives are generous enough to pay for your new toilet. If you're remodeling your existing home, be sure to check with your city's building department to see what incentives are available to you.

High-efficiency toilets use a minimum of 20 percent less water than standard low-flow toilets, typically a tiny 1.28 gallons per flush. They're surprisingly good at removing waste with such a small amount of water.

Nearly all toilet manufacturers (including Toto, American Standard, and Kohler) offer low-flow and high-efficiency toilets with a pressure-assist option. A special valve uses less water to create more force to better clear the bowl.

Dual-flush toilets

Dual-flush toilets conserve water by offering two types of flush options:

- **Liquid waste:** An ultralow flush of only 0.8 to 1.1 gallons of water is used.
- **Solid waste:** The standard low flush of 1.6 gallons is used.

Dual-flush toilets either use a two-way handle or have two separate buttons (the button you push depends on what you need to flush).

Saving thousands of gallons of water and dollars in sewer costs, dual-flush toilets are a no-brainer. Every toilet you buy should be a dual-flush type. All major toilet manufacturers offer dual-flush models.

An added bonus: If you have a septic system, dual-flush toilets will significantly reduce the overall load on it.

Composting toilets

Instead of using drinkable water to flush toilets, composting toilets use natural chemicals to flush and convert your waste into fertilizer. Similar to a plane or boat toilet, modern-day composting toilets have virtually no odor and avoid the expense of plumbing, piping, and sewer lines. They're an ideal solution in areas without a sewer or where a large septic system would be expensive. You can install a composting toilet anywhere you'd normally place a regular toilet.

A large composting tank sits hidden below the floor of the composting toilet. Although difficult to install into an existing home, composting toilets don't require any special tools or skills to install. The toilet looks a lot like a regular toilet, except there's no water sitting in the bottom of the bowl.

Simply clean out the compost once a year and use it to fertilize your nonfood plants in your garden. You'd be amazed at how little compost is generated; a year of normal use produces only about a gallon of compost. You can even have a service technician come and clean it for you.

Showers and faucets

People love long, hot showers. And why not? For most people, the shower is the place to relax, think, or even practice for *American Idol.*

Showers account for 22 percent of the water use in North America. Depending on the type of showerhead you have, you could be using anywhere from 2.5 to 5 gallons every *minute* you're in the shower.

Your faucets consume another 15 percent of your water just to provide for washing your hands, brushing your teeth, or shaving your face. The good news is, you can do some simple things to save water without sacrificing how you do all these everyday tasks.

Low-flow fixtures

Water-efficient showerheads can save you around $100 per year on your water and energy bills. Inexpensive and simple to install, low-flow showerheads and faucet aerators can reduce your home water consumption by half.

Because most of the water you use in the bathroom is hot water, this water is even more expensive and more important to conserve. Low-flow fixtures install in minutes. They don't lower the water *pressure* — just the *amount* of water used.

Foot pedals

Imagine how much water is wasted in between activities: while rubbing your hands with soap, while scrubbing dishes, or while brushing your teeth.

A fun and clever way to save water is to use foot-pedal controls at the sink. You set the temperature by hand, but the water only flows when you step on the pedal. You only use the water you need, because the water doesn't run when your foot is off the pedal.

You'll need a plumber to install the foot pedal, but it pays for itself in water savings in less than three years. Pedals can be installed to work with any faucet and in any sink cabinet.

Water heaters

If your home is like most, hot water is produced in a water heater. This large tank sits in your garage or basement, where it runs all day and night to keep 60, 80, or 100 gallons of water always hot and ready for use. When you turn on the hot water at a faucet, this hot water must run through a network of pipes in the walls where it could take several minutes to reach you. The farther away the faucet is from the hot water heater, the longer you have to wait for the hot water to emerge. Meanwhile, all the cool water pouring out of your faucet is wasted.

In the typical American home, 10,000 gallons of water are wasted each year as people wait for the hot water to arrive at the tap. In the following sections, I give you some options that can cut down on this waste.

Tankless water heaters

A typical water heater maintains a large tank of water, but a tankless water heater only heats the water you use. Also called an on-demand water heater, this small box mounts to the wall near your bathroom and only switches on when hot water is needed.

As you can see in Figure 13-1, cold water enters at the bottom where an efficient gas heater rapidly and instantly brings the water to a near boil. When you turn off the hot water, the tankless heater shuts off, so only the water you need is heated.

Although a tankless water heater doesn't directly save water, you aren't waiting for the water to heat up, and you're saving that cold water that would have gone down the drain. Because you only heat the water you use, a great deal of energy is saved as well.

If you're keeping your old water heater

If you're remodeling an existing home and you don't want to replace the existing water heater, or you just *want* to use a traditional water heater, be sure to insulate it with a water heater wrap. For less than $20, you can cut your water-heating bills by 10 percent by wrapping the water heater correctly.

Also, opt for a natural gas water heater instead of an electric one (unless you have solar panels on your roof). It will cost less to operate than an electric model. For more information on saving energy, check out Chapter 11.

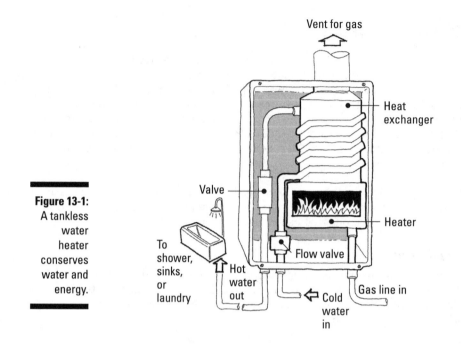

Figure 13-1:
A tankless
water
heater
conserves
water and
energy.

Tankless water heaters are typically warranted for 20 years, while a standard water heater usually only lasts about 7 to 10 years.

Tankless water heaters cost about twice as much as standard water heaters, but you see an immediate cost savings in the installation. Tankless systems don't require all the piping of a traditional heater because they're placed near the bathroom.

The energy and water savings will pay for the cost of the tankless heater within one to five years.

Hot water recirculation

Instead of waiting for the water to get hot, a hot water recirculation system quickly delivers hot water to your faucet. For less that $400, it uses a pump to rush the hot water where needed, saving you money on your energy and water bills.

Hot water recirculation systems can be activated by the push of a button, or by a thermostat, timer, or motion sensor. Hot water is always available at the faucet without any waiting. When activated, the pump starts recirculating cooled water that's been sitting in the *hot* water line and sends it back to the water heater through the *cold* water line. Instead of allowing the cold water to go down the drain, it's simply sent back to the water heater.

Another alternative is to install what is called a home-run plumbing system. Instead of pipes, small, flexible tubing is run directly to each fixture. Because each fixture has a direct line to the water heater, there is no waiting for the hot water to arrive.

Heat recovery systems

Hot water is expensive and requires energy. Don't let that valuable heat go down the drain. A drain-water heat recovery system is a $300 fixture a plumber installs under the drain in your tub or shower. As used hot water goes down the drain, the heat recovery system "steals" the heat out of the water and circulates it back to the showerhead or water heater.

A copper coil wraps around your drain, capturing the heat before it's gone (see Figure 13-2). The heat recovery system doesn't reuse the soapy shower water, just the heat.

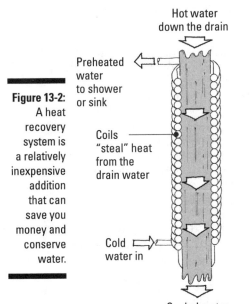

Figure 13-2: A heat recovery system is a relatively inexpensive addition that can save you money and conserve water.

Hot water down the drain

Preheated water to shower or sink

Coils "steal" heat from the drain water

Cold water in

Cooled water continues down drain

Reusing Water: The Controversy over Graywater

One of the major tenets of sustainability is to reuse whenever possible. Why not reuse your water? In fact, the concept of water reuse has been around for a long time.

In 17th-century Germany, the man of the house had the privilege of being the first to use the hot bath. After him, the other sons had dibs, followed by the women, then the children, and, last of all, the babies. After so many uses, the water was so dirty you could actually lose someone in it. Hence the expression, "Don't throw the baby out with the bath water."

Today, this wastewater is referred to as *graywater*. Graywater is all the wastewater generated in your home, excluding water going down the toilet. Instead of just using fresh water once, all the soapy water could potentially be used for something else.

Black water is the dirty water from a toilet. Due to its high level of toxins, it's not used in a graywater system and must be treated in a sewer or septic system.

In the hot and dry regions of the United States, the use of graywater has a long history in watering farmland and crops. Though graywater use has been common in rural areas for decades, recycling graywater is a very controversial subject because of concerns about public health.

The hair, chemicals, and bacteria in graywater are a minor, but potential, health threat. If someone in your family develops a communicable disease, such as the flu, measles, or chicken pox, stop using your graywater system until the person has recovered. A valve is typically installed to allow you to divert the graywater back to the sewer.

In the United States, no national regulations exist governing its use, but several states offer partial regulations to allow the use of graywater under restricted circumstances. The more proactive states are, not surprisingly, the ones where a shortage of fresh water is of greatest concern:

- ✔ **Arizona:** Arizona has perhaps the most open-minded stance on graywater use, though the regulations are still very restrictive. Given the dry climate, the use of graywater makes good sense. Because of this, many people install graywater systems without a permit to avoid dealing with the regulations.

  I do not recommend installing a graywater system without a permit — particularly because of the associated health concerns.

- ✔ **California:** California's Graywater Standards are now part of the State Plumbing Code, making it legal to use graywater everywhere in California. Despite the issues surrounding water shortages, the laws only permit graywater use in your yard. Only a handful of individual and prototypical cases using graywater in toilets have been permitted.

- ✔ **Colorado:** Graywater use is permitted, but only in below-ground irrigation systems.

- ✔ **Connecticut:** A pilot program permits graywater use if approved by the local water district.

- ✔ **New Mexico:** In New Mexico, graywater is only permitted for use in irrigating your yard, though several instances of builders using it for toilets have been allowed. For graywater toilet use, the rules vary from county to county within the state, so check with your local building department.

- ✔ **New York:** New York offers a green building tax credit that includes provisions for graywater use.

- ✔ **Texas:** Texas only permits the use of washing machine water in graywater systems.

- ✔ **Washington:** A recent bill allowing use of graywater in toilets did not pass, but that may change soon.

For more information on graywater use, visit `www.oasisdesign.net`.

If you've determined that a graywater system is allowed in your area, and you have the necessary permits to install such a system in your home, read on for more information on how these systems work.

Whole-house graywater systems

An extensive graywater system consists of dedicated pipes collecting drainwater from bathtubs, showers, sinks, and washing machines. This water is stored and treated in a large tank.

Because of the food waste, the wastewater from kitchen sinks and dishwashers is considered to be heavily contaminated and isn't included in a graywater system. Like the water from the toilet, this waste is instead sent to the sewer or septic system.

Because of the amount of extra plumbing required to make this system work, installing one into an existing home is not usually feasible or cost effective.

So what do you do with all this graywater now that you've collected it? The ideal place to use graywater is in your toilet. You don't need to flush your toilets with clean, drinking water; graywater does the trick just fine.

Most of the permitted uses of graywater are for irrigating your yard (see Figure 13-3). Graywater is directed to a tank buried below ground, where tiny microorganisms in the soil purify it as they water the plants. Because all this happens below ground, there is little risk of people coming into contact with the graywater directly.

Be aware of what you can put down the drain when you're using a graywater system. If you plan to reuse graywater in the garden, pay attention to the following:

- **Clothes washers:** Avoid using phosphate-based detergents and high amounts of bleach.

- **Bathtubs and showers:** Avoid petroleum-based lotions, soaps, shampoos, and fragrances. Natural and herbal products are best.

- **Sinks:** Oil, grease, dish detergent, and phosphate-based soaps can kill your plants.

Figure 13-3:
A diagram of a graywater system showing how the soapy water is collected from a variety of places and directed to the yard.

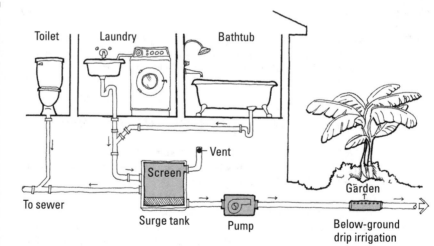

Individual graywater systems

Because of the complicated permitting and installation issues surrounding whole-house graywater systems, some clever individual graywater systems are now available.

Collecting the graywater from just one sink and diverting it to just one toilet, products such as the Aqus from Watersaver Technologies (www.water savertech.com) are a simple, cost-effective way to bring graywater into your home. Priced at under $200, such systems can be added to an existing bathroom by a plumber in about an hour without requiring a special building permit.

Pushing this idea even further, all-in-one units, such as the one from Envirolet (www.envirolet.com), combine a sink on top of a toilet. The soapy water from the sink is stored in the toilet tank just below it. Not only do these systems save water (because they're a sink and toilet in one), but they also save space.

Harvesting Rainwater

Nature provides a source of clean water that does not require any energy or effort. Your home can collect rainwater and put it to use. A typical home allows the rainwater to flow into gutters and drains, where it's sent into the storm sewer.

Just an inch of rainfall on an average-sized, 1,000-square-foot roof will produce 623 gallons of water. For example, San Francisco averages 20.5 inches of rainfall per year, potentially generating nearly 13,000 gallons of water from a typical roof.

Collecting this abundance of water is known as *rainwater harvesting*. As rain falls on the roof, it's channeled into tanks (see Figure 13-4). From there, it can be used throughout the home.

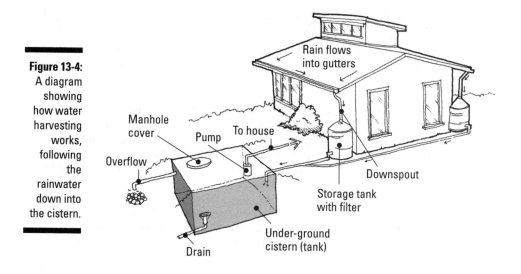

Figure 13-4:
A diagram showing how water harvesting works, following the rainwater down into the cistern.

If you live in a cold climate, the tanks must be placed below ground to avoid freezing. In warm climates, simple measures must be taken to keep mosquitoes from breeding in the water tanks. Mosquito Dunks (www.summit chemical.com) will kill off any mosquito eggs, but goldfish are a fun and natural way to control mosquitoes.

You can avoid the health and permitting issues of graywater (see the preceding section) by using rainwater harvesting instead. Companies such as Wonder Water (www.wonderwater.net) offer complete systems to store and filter rainwater for use in your toilets. Installing such systems into a new home is relatively simple; adding them to an existing home is difficult.

If you're interested in collecting water for use in your yard, rainwater catchment is simple to add even to an existing home. In dry areas, you'll want to purchase a tank large enough to provide enough water through the arid months. In wet areas, a small system is simple to install in an afternoon.

For a simple catchment system, you can put the pieces together yourself. There are several creative options to consider when installing a rainwater collection system:

✔ **Rain chains:** On a typical roof, water flows into a gutter and into a downspout, where it is dumped into your yard. Replace those ugly downspouts with a rain chain. When it rains, water trickles down the links of chain. The metal rings create a sound similar to a wind chime and are a more attractive option to a downspout. You can use rain chains with or without catchment systems.

✔ **Water barrels:** Several companies offer salvaged wine barrels as an attractive method of storing water for your yard. For small yards, these are an inexpensive do-it-yourself option. Place the barrels outside near one of the roof downspouts. Rainwater from the roof is fed directly into the barrels. A hose is attached to the barrel for your use to water the yard.

✔ **Roofing materials:** When considering a rainwater catchment system, you must also choose the right roofing material. An asphalt shingle or tar roof will contaminate the rainwater and make it undrinkable. If you want to use the water in your yard or toilets, you have to select an impervious roofing material, such as:

- Metal

- Terra cotta clay tiles

- Fiber cement shingles

- Poly-iso (spray-on foam)

- Slate

- Recycled plastic

- Wood shingles

Sizing the collection area and *cistern* (storage tank) is important. Start by calculating your water needs, including toilets, bathtubs, faucets, washing machine, dishwasher, and outdoor watering. Even people in a green home use about 55 to 75 gallons per day. Next figure out the amount of rainwater in your area. Go to www.weather.com/common/home/climatology.html, enter your city or zip code, and you can find this information. (Be sure to add the monthly averages to get the yearly average.) When in doubt, the cistern manufacturer can help you calculate the system you'll need.

Residential rainwater harvesting systems aren't cheap. The current low cost of water means you'll be waiting a long time for the savings to pay for the installation costs for a home. But as the demand for water increases, prices will increase. Installing a rainwater system now will make sense in the long run. As a general rule, comprehensive systems cost about $1 for each gallon of storage; simple barrel systems can be done at almost no cost.

Cleaning Your Water

People can't survive more than a few days without clean water. Over 70 percent of the world's water supply is considered polluted, and the demand for drinking water continues to rise. Because all the water you use will ultimately end up back in the ground, it's important to clean the water you use. In the following sections, I fill you in on some methods of cleaning your water, from using filters to using plants.

Water filters

According to the American Water Works Association, the United States has one of the better water systems in the world. Strict regulations and required testing protect the water systems throughout the country. Although the water may be safe, the pipes that carry the water often leech contaminants into what comes out of the tap. Some 20 percent of Americans' lead exposure comes from the drinking water. Tap water has thousands of possible contaminants.

Every year in the United States, Americans drink about 23 gallons of bottled water per person. If you're concerned about your water's safety, you can install water filters to clean your water instead of relying solely on bottled water.

You have two main options when it comes to water filtration:

- ✔ **Single-source water filters:** You may already have water filters in your home. Water pitchers with refillable cartridges are now commonplace in most kitchens. You may even have a filter attached to your kitchen faucet.

  These systems use sophisticated activated-carbon filters. Most of these filters remove chlorine, lead, and a range of other contaminants. Along with the potential health benefits, the primary motivation of these filters is to improve the taste of water. Most of these filters don't remove microorganisms (such as bacteria) or dissolved minerals (such as salt or fluoride). Because these systems are only used in one place, they only treat the water used for drinking or cooking; the other water in the home goes unfiltered.

- ✔ **Whole-house water filters:** Instead of only filtering one pitcher or one sink, a whole-house filter removes the contaminants from all the water entering the home. Shower water, laundry water, and bathroom sink water are all filtered. Because the water you consume comes from all these sources, a whole house filter is a wise investment. For around only $600, you can filter every drop of water in your home. The filter is installed near your water meter, so you can easily install it in an existing home as well.

Although the cost of any of the water filtration systems is relatively low, in some cases, the replacements for the filters cost more than the initial setup cost. Depending upon the amount of use, the filters need to be changed every one to four months. Be sure to factor this cost into your decision to install a water filtration system.

Septic tanks

If you live in a city, you probably don't need to worry about your wastewater. It simply goes into the city sewer where it's treated in a central plant.

Is bottled water better?

Bottled water requires a great deal of energy and produces even more waste. From the plastic bottles, to the refrigerated trucks used for shipping, to the storage of those bottles in your refrigerator, bottled water requires a lot of energy.

Most people assume that bottled water is safer and purer than tap water. The labels on the water bottles evoke thoughts of purity, with images of mountains, glaciers, and babbling brooks. In reality, as much as 40 percent of bottled water is merely bottled tap water. And in most cases, tap water is at least as safe as bottled water.

In rural areas, you may not have a city sewer available. In this case, you'll need a septic tank system. Imagine, you can treat all the sewage you produce with the plants in your backyard instead of paying to pump it miles away to a sewage treatment plant. In a septic tank system, wastewater is fed into a septic storage tank stored below the ground. A thin, perforated pipe is fed throughout your yard where the waste slowly "leeches" into the soil through what is called a *leech field*. Microorganisms in the soil naturally absorb and clean the waste. The size of your home, number of bathrooms, and number of people determine the size of septic system you need.

Green roofs

A green roof is not a roof with green-colored shingles — it's a supplemental roofing system made up of plant material that's applied over a conventional roof. Think of the green roof as an extension of the existing roof.

Understanding what goes into a green roof

A green roof is really just an assembly of materials. From top to bottom, the basic parts are as follows (check out Figure 13-5 for an illustration):

✔ **Plants:** It would not be a green roof without plants. The key to understanding a green roof is to think of it as a natural habitat. Select plants appropriate to your climate by choosing native, noninvasive, drought-tolerant plants. Your landscape architect or green roof manufacturer can help.

WARNING!

Fire is a serious concern with green roofs, so you want to select plants that can withstand the hot, dry environment on a rooftop.

✔ **Wind erosion blanket:** To prevent the wind from blowing the dirt away, a thin wind erosion blanket is placed on top of the dirt. The blanket is typically made of a material that dissolves after the plants take root (such as burlap).

✔ **Planting media:** To support the plants, your green roof needs to have some sort of soil. A green roof typically includes anywhere from 2 to 6 inches of soil for a basic roof, up to several feet of soil for tall plants, shrubs, and trees. The soil type and mixture will vary based on the types of plants you select.

✔ **Filter fabric:** A biodegradable fabric (such as jute or burlap) is used to filter the water running down to the roof.

✔ **Drainage/retention layer:** In order to prevent the water from sitting on the roof membrane, a drainage layer is used to allow the free flow of water to a drain. This is usually some type of egg-crate or filter fabric.

✔ **Insulation:** Although insulation is not really a required part of a green roof, it makes sense to add insulation to improve the energy efficiency of the building. Rigid insulation boards are typically used. In combination with the soil, a green roof provides an incredibly high amount of insulation.

✔ **Root barrier:** Because plant roots can penetrate this roof membrane, a green roof should have a separate root barrier for protection. Typically made of some sort of plastic or foil, the root barrier must be correctly installed to avoid leaks.

✔ **Roof membrane:** The most important component of any roof system is the waterproof membrane that keeps water out of the building. Several different types of roof membranes can be used with green roofs, including a typical liquid-applied asphalt roof or sheet membrane types of roofing. Select a membrane with a 20-year life and warranty.

✔ **Prepared roof surface:** The green roof should be installed on a clean, dry, and even roof surface.

✔ **Roof deck:** Almost any type of roof deck — steel, concrete, wood — can be used for a green roof, as long as it can support the weight. Low-slope roofs are most appropriate for green roofs, though there needs to be some slope (about ¼ inch per foot) to allow water to drain.

In this section, I discuss full green roof systems. Less expensive modular and tray systems are available from companies such as GreenGrid (www.green gridroofs.com). The trays snap together to quickly form a green roof appearance at half the cost. These modular systems don't provide the same amount of insulation, roof protection, or flexibility in planting as a full green roof system, however.

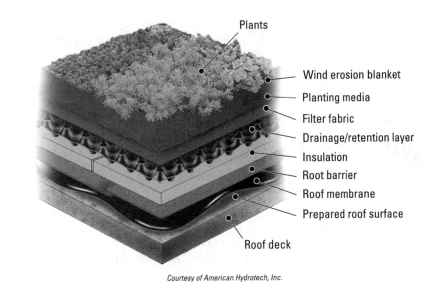

Plants

Wind erosion blanket
Planting media
Filter fabric
Drainage/retention layer
Insulation
Root barrier
Roof membrane
Prepared roof surface

Roof deck

Figure 13-5:
The individual layers of a green roof.

Courtesy of American Hydrotech, Inc.

The pros and cons of green roofs

Green roofs offer numerous benefits, including the following:

- **Insulation:** Because of their earthen mass, a green roof adds a lot of insulation to the roof, which saves you money on your energy bills.

- **Environmental factors:** The plants on the roof can be used to filter and clean water, while automatically absorbing pollution and giving off oxygen for you to breathe.

- **Protection:** Because a green roof sits *over* your roof membrane, it protects the roof from damage.

- **Appearance:** A roof is typically the least attractive part of any building, but a green roof is a beautiful replacement.

- **Cool temperatures:** Plants keep your roof cool, reducing the ambient temperature around a building (called a *heat island*).

- **Value:** The preceding benefits add to the value of your home.

Potential concerns and drawbacks including the following:

- **Uncertainty about long-term performance:** Green roofs are still considered a new technology in North America — too new to have a track record. Even in Europe, where green roofs have been around for over 25 years, experts are only beginning to gather information on long-term performance. The biggest concern with any roof is leaking. Because a green roof adds an additional layer of protection, you can at least expect a longer life from the conventional roof.

✔ **Cost:** Because a green roof is used in addition to, not instead of, a conventional roof, it costs more. As a general rule, you can expect an installed extensive green roof with waterproof membranes and irrigation to cost about $12 to $24 per square foot. This may sound expensive, but keep in mind that a green roof extends the life of the roof membrane and will reduce the heating and cooling costs of your home.

Although an extensive green roof may cost $12 to $24 per square foot, less expensive alternatives are available. Green grid systems consist of plastic trays that snap together into a grid. Priced at around $8 per square foot, these systems are a great alternative for existing buildings where an extensive green roof is not possible.

✔ **Difficulty of repairs:** Although a green roof covers and protects the conventional roof below, finding leaks and fixing repairs is much more difficult. You have to remove the vegetation, soil, and drainage in order to inspect the roof for leaks. Modular grid systems make this process much easier because they can be removed in pieces.

✔ **Competition with other green functions of a roof:** In a green building, roof space is valuable. A green roof competes for space with solar panels (see Chapter 11) and rainwater harvesting (see earlier in this chapter). By limiting the green roof to areas that are much more visible (because they're so beautiful), and locating the solar panels in areas more hidden (because they aren't as attractive), you can keep your roof attractive *and* functional.

Most new ideas in the building industry face significant hurdles, and that's certainly the case with green roofs. You may have some initial concerns about a green roof in terms of leaking, weight, or maintenance, but the benefits far outweigh these, especially when you consider the money saved in heating and cooling costs over the life of the building.

Determining whether a green roof is right for you

A green roof is a wonderfully simple and effective way to add value, beauty, and green features to a building. But when you're thinking about adding a green roof to an existing house, be sure to ask yourself the following questions:

✔ **Is the roof slope too steep for plants?** Flat and low-slope roofs are easier for the plants to fix into the soil.

A low-slope roof is any roof you could walk up without leaning forward.

✔ **Are the roof beams strong enough to support the weight of the green roof?** The roof plants sit in dirt, and dirt is heaviest when it's wet. To make sure the roof can support the weight of a green roof, assume that the roof weighs the same as water: about 60 pounds per cubic foot. Check with your architect or structural engineer to confirm that the roof can support this weight.

✔ **How will the roof drain?** A drainage layer allows water to filter down through the plants and drain into the roof drains.

✔ **Is there a way to access the roof to maintain it easily?** A modular grid system may be the best choice if roof access is important.

✔ **Does sunlight hit the roof?** Plants require at least some light.

✔ **Is the wind too strong for plants?** Plants are fragile, and you don't want to have your beautiful green plants simply blow away. A high wind area may require different types of plants, or may prevent you from using a green roof at all.

✔ **What kinds of plants can I grow on my roof?** The plants selected for the roof depend on a variety of factors, including climate, type and depth of roof soil, loading capacity, height and slope of the roof, and type of irrigation system. Consult a landscape architect for plants suitable for your climate.

Bioremediation ponds

Nature already has systems in place to treat dirty water. *Bioremediation* is the natural process of using plants, algae, enzymes, and microorganisms to filter water. You can clean water naturally through bioremediation and make it drinkable.

The concept of bioremediation has been around for centuries, but it fell out of popularity with the introduction of modern, synthetic chemicals to treat water. In reality, bioremediation offers a healthier and more natural method to restore water back to its pristine state.

A green roof can be used to clean (or bioremediate) water by running graywater through the soil. The filtered water is collected into drains where it can safely be used in your yard.

For larger amounts of wastewater, a *living machine* can be created. Living machines act as a man-made wetland to cleanse the water using only specific plants, algae, and fish. It functions the same way a natural wetland does to clean water. Living machines range in size from small ponds to large marshlands, adding natural beauty to the site. For homes with sewer or septic tank issues, such bioremediation systems offer a natural and healthier alternative.

Companies such as Worrell Water Technologies (www.worrellwater.com) can design and install a living machine for you, but you can build your own simple bioremediation pond. In order for a bioremediation pond to work, you need either a hot climate or an enclosed greenhouse to allow the cleansing bacteria to grow.

Wastewater from your home is collected into a storage tank and slowly flows into a variety of ponds. Each pond is a different stage of cleaning, with a combination of plants, algae, snails, and bacteria to slowly digest the waste. Although the water coming out at the end of this process is technically drinkable, it's not allowed to be used for drinking water, but it can be used for an assortment of uses around the home, including in the garden. Bioremediation is the pretty way to clean water, leaving only a lovely marshland around the building.

Chapter 14

Landscaping and Site Planning: Going Green in the Great Outdoors

In This Chapter

▶ Figuring out where to locate your home on a piece of property

▶ Analyzing your property to improve the environmental impact of your home

▶ Discovering how to locate the sun any time of any day

▶ Finding alternatives to lawns, mowing, and watering — and all that work

▶ Putting rainwater to work for you

*A*s you begin to plan building a new home or remodeling your existing one, keep in mind that the space surrounding your home is as important as the house itself. In this chapter, you discover that how a building sits on a property and its landscape can drastically improve energy, water, and resource use. You also discover new ways to care for your yard and save money at the same time. If the space outside your home is what you're interested in, this is the chapter for you.

Placing Your Home on a Site

Nothing has as big of an impact on your home as how it's placed on the property. From the heat the sun brings, to protection offered by trees, *site planning* (the analysis of the arrangement of the natural and built elements on a property) has an incredible impact on how comfortable your home will be for you, your family, and your friends.

Good site planning is both a technical skill and an art. If you want to build an environmentally friendly home, a site analysis is an important tool to help you do that. The more time you spend on a site or property, the better you can understand how light moves around, how the wind moves, and all the other natural patterns of the site.

Site selection and analysis

A site analysis consists of taking a drawing of your property (called a *site plan*) and mapping out the issues.

In order to create an analysis of your site, you need to start by mapping the good things (amenities) and the things to avoid (irritants). This exercise helps you figure out how to orient the house and where to locate rooms.

A typical site analysis includes

- Attractive views to maximize
- Unattractive views to minimize or views to block for privacy
- Noises to block
- Wind to allow in for cooling
- Wind to block
- Placement of activities oriented around the sun (breakfast room to the east; dining to the west)
- Possible patio and deck locations
- Existing trees to protect
- The path of the sun

Figure 14-1 shows a typical sketch of a site analysis, showing the source of noise, location of views, and areas to keep private. Consider the following items in looking at any property:

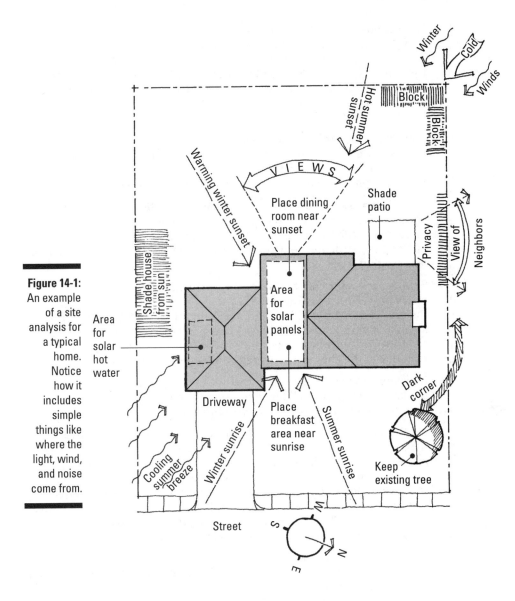

Figure 14-1:
An example of a site analysis for a typical home. Notice how it includes simple things like where the light, wind, and noise come from.

✔ **Use windows to frame the perfect view.** Imagine sitting in a bay window that perfectly frames the view of the nearby lake, but blocks the view of your neighbor's lawnmower or garage. The position of the views affects the placement of windows and doors and location of rooms. Instead of putting closets on the wall with the potential view, reserve that prime spot for a master bedroom, terrace, or dining room where the view will be appreciated.

✔ **Turn the house to face the sun and views.** Most people assume a house must sit oriented to the street. But you can set the building on an angle if you want to turn the walls toward the sun or toward the best views. Don't just plunk the house down in the first place you think of.

✔ **Provide access for construction vehicles.** The site should allow only enough access for trucks and equipment to build your home. Too much driving over the landscape will destroy plants, soil, and tree roots. Limiting construction vehicles to one area will save you money on future landscaping costs.

✔ **Supply access for cars and driveways.** Most urban and suburban properties provide an easy way for a car to get to the house: You just park in the garage or driveway. For more rural sites, this isn't so simple. Too steep a driveway, and it becomes impossible to drive during bad weather. Too shallow a slope, and you have to put in longer driveways, resulting in the site being covered with large areas of paving.

How you and your guests enter the house is important. Make it one of the first things you consider when laying out a house on a site. Make sure you can do it before you buy a remote property.

✔ **Let the sun shine in.** Natural light makes people more productive and happier in their environment. The sun always rises in the east and sets in the west, coming from the south (in the Northern Hemisphere — in the Southern Hemisphere the sun still rises in the east and sets in the west, but it comes from the north). Consider placing rooms where the sun will be. For example, put the breakfast room on the east side of the house so it gets the morning light. A dining room on the west side of the house will allow you to watch the sunset during dinner.

If you plan on adding solar panels to your home, place the house in a spot that will get adequate sunlight. *Remember:* The winter sun is lower than the summer sun (see Figure 14-2). Also remember that solar panels can be located anywhere on the site; they don't have to be on the roof of a building. You may want to place them in another sunny location on the property if the roof is covered in shade.

✔ **Capture the breezes on the site.** Typically, every property will have wind coming from a primary direction, known as *prevailing wind*. Wind carries with it sound, smells, and pollution. Depending on your climate, you want to either welcome in this wind, or block it.

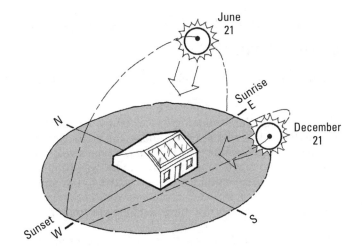

Figure 14-2:
A diagram
of the path
of the sun.
Notice how
the summer
sun is much
higher, and
the winter
sun is much
lower.

In hot areas, the prevailing wind can be directed to open windows using walls and hedges. Using these breezes will keep your house cool and prevent the need for air conditioning. Desirable breezes (that is, a cool breeze from the ocean) can be allowed into the house.

In cold climates, the prevailing wind will bring more unwanted cold air. Save energy by blocking this wind using evergreen trees (like pine trees — their leaves don't shed in winter) or walls from the house itself.

✔ **Build on a brownfield.** A *brownfield* is a polite name for a chemically polluted site. With a growing shortage of available clean sites, brownfields are fast becoming a common choice for building sites. Cleaning up a polluted brownfield is better than building on a pristine lot. Government subsidies are often available for the cleanup costs involved in building on a brownfield; check with your local building department for more information.

✔ **Choose a site near public transit.** If you have a choice between one site or another, consider the one closest to public transportation. This is especially important for urban properties. If public transit is nearby, you may use it more.

✔ **Find out the location of water lines, gas lines, and electrical wiring below ground.** Hand-dig the ground in these areas to avoid damaging these hidden utilities.

While thinking about utility lines, don't forget about telephone and electrical wires *above* your home. Trees planted today may grow and damage these wires years down the road.

Planning your site to incorporate outdoor rooms

If nothing moves in your backyard except the lawn mower, then it's time to rethink your yard.

Think about the landscaped areas around your home as outdoor rooms. Just as you decorate a room in your house, the landscape deserves the same treatment. From furniture, to finish materials, a well-done landscape is an opportunity to create a beautiful outdoor living room. Look beyond landscape materials selection to create a landscape worthy of the term green.

You want your backyard to have the following features:

- ✔ **Health and safety:** You want a safe place for your children to play unattended.

- ✔ **Durability:** Long-lasting materials will save you time and money for years to come.

- ✔ **Reduced maintenance:** Avoid extra maintenance and work for yourself with a yard that's easy to care for.

- ✔ **Functionality:** Your landscaping should be more than pretty to look at — it should be a useful place to relax and entertain.

- ✔ **Accessibility:** People and gardening equipment must be able to access the landscape.

- ✔ **Beauty:** Your landscape is an obvious way to capture the beauty of nature.

- ✔ **Ecological benefit:** Plants clean the air and water naturally, making your home healthier.

Keep these issues in mind when choosing your lot and planning your landscape.

Using the Natural Environment to Bring Beauty to Your Home

The natural landscape is a potential source of beauty for your home — it's a source of a lot of work, too. Many homeowners lose every weekend just trying to keep their yards looking good. If designed correctly, the maintenance can be kept to a minimum so you can spend more time enjoying your yard. Your landscape can provide beauty, recreation, and positive environmental effects. Trees, for example, shade your home, reduce energy consumption, create oxygen, filter the air, and even add to the value of your property. Figure 14-3 shows a typical house and provides examples of green landscaping considerations.

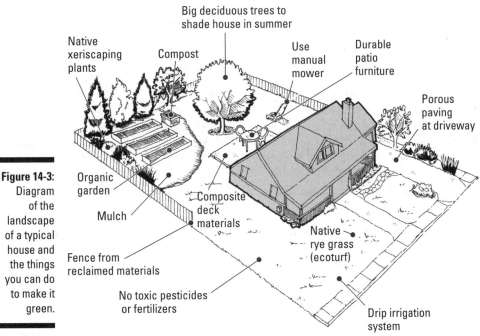

Big deciduous trees to shade house in summer

Native xeriscaping plants

Compost

Use manual mower

Durable patio furniture

Porous paving at driveway

Organic garden

Composite deck materials

Mulch

Native rye grass (ecoturf)

Fence from reclaimed materials

No toxic pesticides or fertilizers

Drip irrigation system

Figure 14-3: Diagram of the landscape of a typical house and the things you can do to make it green.

Feng shui

Feng shui (pronounced fung shway) is the ancient Chinese art of placement and arrangement of space to achieve harmony with the environment. The words literally translate to mean "wind and water."

The ancient Chinese believed that, in the features of the natural landscape, you can glimpse the mathematically precise order of the universe and all the beneficial and harmful forces that were harmoniously connected according to the principle known as the Tao (the Way).

Feng shui dates from the Han Dynasty (202 B.C.–A.D. 220) but wasn't established as a scientific practice until the Sung Dynasty (A.D. 960–A.D. 1126). Initially used to locate grave sites, it eventually came to be used to locate the homes of the living.

The underlying principal of feng shui is controlling the spiritual energy of Nature, known as *chi.* Trees and shrubs can be planted to cover undesirable views; streams can be rerouted; mounds built up or cut down. The greatest of all Chinese arts, gardening, grew out of this practice of placement. The picturesque villages of China with their elements of bamboo groves and front-facing ponds are not just landscape embellishments, but intentionally designed devices to fend off evil.

Whether you believe in the mystical nature of feng shui or not, the good common sense it offers provides lessons for use in planning modern homes. For example:

- In your office, face your desk to greet people as they walk into your office.

- In your bedroom, don't orient the bed so people enter the room facing your feet. Turn the bed to welcome in the chi.

- Avoid straight lines and sharp corners. Where they do exist, they should not point to where people sit, stand, or sleep.

For more on feng shui, check out *Feng Shui For Dummies,* by David Daniel Kennedy, and *Feng Shui Your Garden For Dummies,* by Jennifer Lawler and Holly Ziegler (Wiley).

Landscaping can cause damage to the environment, too. Landscaping consumes fossil fuels; contributes to air, soil, and water pollution; and fills landfills with yard waste.

In the following sections, I fill you in on measures you can take that will help save you time, save you money, and save our resources.

For more information on green landscaping ideas, check out the following:

- **GreenScapes (www.epa.gov/greenscapes):** This site by the U.S. Environmental Protection Agency (EPA) offers suggestions for green landscaping for homeowners.

- **California Integrated Waste Management Board (www.ciwmb.ca.gov/ Organics/Landscaping):** Although this is a California site, the free downloads and guides are useful for homeowners anywhere.

✔ **Integrated Pest Management (`www.askaboutipm.info`):** This site offers information on using natural methods to control insects.

✔ **Native Plant Database (`www.wildflower.org/plants`):** This extensive list of plants will help you find native plants local to your area, which are able to grow without as much watering.

✔ **Forest Stewardship Council (FSC; `www.fscus.org`):** Here you can find sources for sustainably harvested wood for your deck, fence, or trellis.

Grading

In order to drain rainwater, everything is slightly tilted. Decks, patios, roads, even flat roofs are all sloped to drain the rain. The same is true for the ground. If your property is too flat, the water won't drain and you'll have a muddy mess. Sloping the ground so it drains water is called *grading*.

In this section, I discuss two main ways of grading: excavating and using berms. Both of these methods reduce the amount of paving you'll need to control the water falling on the property. (Typically, concrete is used to control rainwater on a site.)

Every building needs to have a foundation to help support it in the ground. Even the smallest house requires the foundation to be excavated into the ground. A steeply sloping site requires more excavation — and more money. You can save money and disturbance of the soil using a cut-and-fill technique, which balances the *cut* (the dirt dug out of the ground) and the *fill* (the dirt brought in to backfill against the house). This technique (shown in Figure 14-4) reduces the cost of your foundation by using less earth and making less waste. Instead of setting your home on stilts above the ground, or burying it into the earth, this balance saves you money and fits the home into the site.

Figure 14-4:
The cut-and-fill technique balances the amount of dirt excavated.

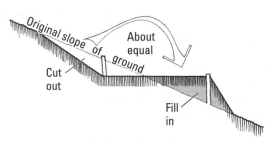

In addition to excavation, earth berms provide another way to control the slope of the ground. A *berm* is a mound of dirt piled up against an exterior wall. Berms provide wind protection and thermal insulation to your home, while adding natural beauty and blending the home into the landscape. Berms are an inexpensive method of insulating a building, working especially well in colder climates. When building a berm, be sure to waterproof the wall the same way you would waterproof a foundation.

Lawns

Each weekend, 54 million Americans get up early on their day off and roll the trusty, old mower out of the garage to mow some 20 million acres of lawn. From mowing to watering to fertilizing, lawns consume an immense amount of resources and are responsible for an equally offensive amount of pollution.

Lawn care is a big business, totaling some $25 billion each year in the United States alone. But beyond the cost of the materials and equipment, you can't talk about lawns without mentioning their environmental cost.

Anyone who has ever used a lawn mower will attest to the fact that lawn-mower engines are not very efficient. They emit high levels of carbon monoxide, producing up to 5 percent of the nation's air pollution. A conventional lawn mower pollutes as much in an hour as driving your car for 100 miles. In an effort to keep the lawn looking good, Americans use 800 million gallons of gas per year, producing tons of air pollutants.

Switching to a push-type mower instead of a power mower will help reduce carbon dioxide in the atmosphere by 80 pounds per lawn per year.

Perhaps more surprising than the gas used, is the gas misused. According to the EPA, 17 million gallons of gasoline are spilled each year while refueling lawn equipment. To put that into perspective, that's more than all the oil spilled by the Exxon *Valdez* in Alaska in 1989. The lawn clippings generate over 160 million tons of solid waste annually. The second largest component of Americans' solid waste is yard waste.

Ironically, most grass is not supposed to be cut as short as most people cut it. A short, well-manicured lawn doesn't shade the soil and increases the need for water. Tall grass can have a much deeper root system than short grass, resulting in less need for watering.

Grasscycling is leaving the clippings on the lawn after mowing, so they decompose and release their nutrients into the soil. Not only is grasscycling less work for you, but if you do it, you'll see a positive difference in the growth of the lawn, too.

Although a hand-powered mower reduces pollution, and grasscycling cuts down on yard waste, you may be asking, "Why plant something that needs cutting at all?" *Ecoturf* (or eco-lawn or native meadow) is a variety of meadow grasses selected to reduce these typical needs of mowing, watering, and fertilizing. A dense mix of English daisy, yarrow, strawberry clover, or perennial ryegrass, Ecoturf only grows to a certain height and will not need frequent mowing. The addition of clover in this mix provides valuable soil-fixing nitrogen, helping eliminate the need for fertilizer. Because it's so hardy, Ecoturf only requires regular watering during the hot summer months. Ecoturf needs to be seeded and will take a year or two to fully take root. During this initial period, just water it regularly, as you would a regular lawn.

Be sure to consult a landscape architect to select species appropriate and native to your area.

Plants and trees

Lawns are the only plants in some people's yards. Adding plants and trees to the outside of your home is a simple way to improve its appearance.

Protect the plants you do have by limiting traffic from construction vehicles and equipment. You can wrap planted areas with burlap or hemp fabric to protect them. Tell your contractor about your desire to protect the plants.

Typically, a construction site is cleared of any topsoil or vegetation before construction begins. Skip this practice and coordinate the location of the home to only remove the soil required. Set aside any soil you excavated during construction for reuse. Preserving these native soils reduces the need for additional watering or chemical fertilizers.

Using native plants to save water and work

Nature understands the needs of each plant species and adapts each for their unique climate. Unfortunately, most people plant anything they like without considering whether those new plants will harm the other plants. They plant Kentucky Bluegrass on the lawns of their Arizona homes and wonder why it needs to be watered day and night. By using *native plants* (plants native to your specific geographic area), you'll save water, minimize the need for landscape maintenance, and eliminate the danger of introducing a foreign species into the plant ecosystem.

Xeriscaping is landscaping with drought-tolerant plants in ways that don't require additional water or fertilizer. The word *xeriscaping* (from the Green *xeros,* meaning "dry") encourages the use of native and indigenous plants already suited for their specific climate. A rich, native landscape provides more visual interest and requires much less effort to maintain than a lawn does. Often, attractive succulents, such as agave and cactus, are used.

Permaculture principles

Permaculture means "permanent agriculture," but also refers to an edible landscape. It's a relatively new concept in gardening and farming. Instead of compartmentalizing a garden into groups of single plants, Permaculture recognizes the connections between plants and shows you to plant strawberries under your corn. The leaves of the corn shade the strawberries, and the strawberries provide valuable nutrients to the corn. Permaculture teaches you to look at a garden as an interconnected system of inputs and outputs of resources.

> Permaculture philosophy is one of working with, rather than against, nature; of protracted and thoughtful observation, rather than protracted and thoughtless action; of looking at systems in all their functions rather than asking only one yield of them; of allowing systems to demonstrate their own evolution.

—Bill Mollison, Founder of Permaculture

The term *Permaculture* was coined in the 1970s by Australians Bill Mollison and David Holmgren. It was initially designed as a way to turn the Australian deserts back into usable farmland.

Although it initially focused on food production and land use, today Permaculture is considered both a philosophy and a lifestyle. It is a design approach using whole-systems thinking to create sustainable human habitats by analyzing and duplicating nature's patterns. Permaculture seeks productive and sustainable ways of living by integrating ecology, landscape, organic gardening, architecture, agroforestry, green or ecological economics, and social systems.

Whether you're talking about designing a backyard or an entire forest, the core values of Permaculture are

✔ **Earthcare:** Recognizing that the Earth is the source of all life; that we are a part of the Earth, not apart from it

✔ **Peoplecare:** Supporting and helping each other to change ways of living

✔ **Fairshare:** Placing limits on consumption; protecting Earth's resources

David Holmgren developed a list of 12 design principles to develop a simple design process to follow when using the ideas of Permaculture. The design principles are as follows:

✔ **Observe and interact.** Nature is a complex and beautiful example of how to live in balance. Study nature to learn the proper way to build.

✔ **Catch and store energy.** Nature provides abundant sources of energy from the sun and wind. Use these to your advantage.

✔ **Obtain a yield.** Use your land to create an abundance of food. Grow food you can eat, not just pretty plants.

✔ **Apply self-regulation and accept feedback.** Think of nature as a system of positive and negative feedback. Change your design based on the feedback you receive.

✔ **Use and value renewable resources and services.** Choose natural resources over man-made ones. Put the services from plants and animals to work for you.

✔ **Produce no waste.** Natural has no such thing as waste. Everything is food for something else.

✔ **Design from patterns to details.** Step back to see the big picture. Look for the larger patterns and how the smallest details connect together.

✔ **Integrate rather than segregate.** Don't separate plants or animals. Allow them to work together to make complex interconnections.

✔ **Use small and slow solutions.** Learn patience so you can use the natural systems of nature, which are often slow. Industrial thinking looks for fast, forceful solutions. Instead, look for natural and slow ones.

✔ **Use and value diversity.** The more diverse a natural system is, the stronger it is. Include diversity and variation into your design.

✔ **Use edges and value the marginal.** The edge between two things is where the most interest and activity occurs. Maximize these edges by increasing the places where different things meet.

✔ **Creatively use and respond to change.** Permaculture is about the durability of natural systems, but this durability depends on being flexible and open to change.

For more information on Permaculture, check out the following:

✔ **Permaculture Wiki (http://perma culture.wikia.com):** This free Permaculture designers manual is open to anyone to contribute or discuss ideas.

✔ **Holmgren Design (www.holmgren. com.au):** The site from one of the founders of Permaculture, Holmgren's site offers articles and information on using Permaculture principles.

✔ **Permaculture Institute of Santa Fe (www. permaculture.org):** Here you can find information on books, workshops, and events on Permaculture.

✔ **Permaculture Institute of Northern California (part of the Regenerative Design Institute) (www.regnerativedesign. org):** This site offers case studies, classes, and workshops on Permaculture.

Controlling insects and pests

In the United States, 67 million pounds of synthetic pesticides are used each year. Although pesticides are effective at killing weeds and insects, they're also killing people.

 If possible, avoid the use of these dangerous chemicals. Natural alternatives such as garlic, hot pepper, and used dishwater are all healthy and effective methods to deal with insects. Simply spray a watery mixture of one of these over the plants you want to protect from bugs.

Integrated pest management (IPM) is an effective and environmentally friendly way to deal with insects, rodents, and other pests without using chemical pesticides.

To rid your garden of pests, IPM uses natural predators (insects eating other insects) of the pest you're trying to remove. By using this healthy method, insects, rodents, and weeds can be controlled.

Knowing what to plant in your yard

Annual flowers are beautiful, but they require a great deal of water, fertilizers, and work in order to grow. Save yourself the trouble and plant perennials instead.

Native annual plants will reseed themselves year after year.

While you're out in the yard, consider planting some of your favorite herbs and vegetables. Not only will you save money on your grocery bill, but the energy used to transport vegetables to the store and from the store back to your house will be saved. Plus, you get fresh food to eat!

Trees are an important part of any green building. Trees:

- Shade your home to keep it cool
- Stabilize the soil
- Regulate moisture in the air
- Create oxygen
- Absorb carbon dioxide and other pollutants
- Soak up rainwater
- Provide a habitat for birds and animals
- Increase the value of your property

Protect your existing trees during construction and keep as many as possible. Tie a colored ribbon around the trees you want to keep to alert the contractor of their importance.

Be careful of digging near trees, too. If you're digging under the tree, you're probably damaging some of the roots. As a general rule, the tree *drip line* (the overhang of the branches) and *canopy* (the top of the tree) are about the same size as the roots below the ground.

Deciduous trees (trees with falling leaves) are perfect for controlling the temperature in a building. In the summer, the full leaves shade the building and keep it cool, but in the winter, the bare branches allow sunlight to pass through and warm the building.

Mulching

Mulch is a protective cover used in gardening. Because it covers the ground, it blocks the sun, keeps the soil moist, prevents erosion, and prevents weeds from growing. Some environmentally friendly mulch alternatives include

✔ **Compost:** Collect the food scraps from your kitchen and place them into a large pile in your backyard. Over time, the food breaks down into a rich soil, called *compost*.

✔ **Leaves:** Rake up the fallen leaves and spread them around the base of your plants to feed and protect the soil.

✔ **Wood chips:** Place wood chips around the base of your plants to create an attractive mulch. You can find these at any lumber yard, but ask for reclaimed wood.

✔ **Nutshells:** Used nutshells are a natural, alternative mulch. Find some at your local farmers' market, grocery store, or garden shop.

Irrigation systems

Most yards require some water, even if you plant only native plants and you don't have a lawn. If you're thinking, "So what? I'll just turn on a sprinkler and call it a day," think again. Sprinklers are incredibly wasteful. In fact, 30 percent to 60 percent of the average home's fresh water is used for watering the yard.

The good news: Several alternatives to sprinkling can save water. I cover these alternatives in the following sections.

Most people water their lawns during the day, when the sun is the hottest. But more than half the water evaporates and is wasted. If you want to water the yard, run the water at night to allow it to soak into the ground.

Drip irrigation systems

Traditional watering and sprinklers spray water at the top of the grass, wasting more than half the water. A drip irrigation system sits *under* the soil and applies water slowly to the plants' roots. By using less water and providing the water exactly where it's needed, drip irrigation pays for itself in water savings in one to three years.

The cost of a drip irrigation system is around $600 to $1,200 per acre to install. Because it's placed below ground, you have to dig up your yard to install one. If you're planning on regrading your yard, that would be a great time to install a drip irrigation system.

Weather-tracking systems

A weather-tracking system, such as one made by HydroPoint (www.hydro point.com), is a small box that checks the weather and turns off your watering system if rain is forecast. Priced starting at $400, a weather-tracking device will save enough water to pay for itself within a year or two. It's the perfect complement for your new drip irrigation system.

Up your nose with a rubber hose

Most garden hoses are made of polyvinyl chloride (PVC). Vinyl has a terrible impact on human health and environmental safety. If you have to use a hose, choose a reinforced rubber hose — they're more durable and healthier to use than PVC.

Remember: No matter what material your hose is made of, don't drink from a garden hose. Bacteria breeds in the standing water of a warm hose, and they can make you very ill.

Stormwater management

When it rains, water collects from the roof, parking lots, driveways, and other impervious surfaces. Instead of soaking back into the ground, this rainwater, called *stormwater,* gets funneled to a storm sewer drain. The sudden flash flood from the rain creates an incredible strain on the local water system.

Stormwater runoff is a large source of pollution. Rain falling on an acre of parking lot collects up to 4 gallons of oil and gas each year. Other pollutants include pesticides, fertilizers, and trash. When the rainwater runs off the parking lot, these toxic compounds end up in your groundwater (and the lakes, rivers, and oceans). Many cities and towns now require some form of stormwater management to treat and slow the rainwater before it floods into the storm sewer.

Plus, every time it rains, the water runs downhill and slowly erodes your landscape. To keep the water from leaking into your home, it must be directed around and away from your house. Although this is typically done with concrete or asphalt paving, in this section I fill you in on some natural options.

Gabions: Natural erosion control

A *gabion* is a large wire basket filled with stones. You place them along the edges of areas where water will flow, to prevent erosion. The wire baskets hold the stones in place. Instead of building concrete walls to control erosion, a gabion serves as a more natural and inexpensive method. Over time, sediments will get trapped between the stones, and plants will grow over the basket.

Swales: Carving the land to move water

A *swale* is a ledge or depression in the landscape terrain to encourage water to flow in a specific direction. Using swales, you can manage the flow and direction of the stormwater around your site.

If too *much* water is sent in a specific direction, the water may cause erosion along the landscape.

Retention ponds

A method to slow stormwater is to use retention ponds. Simply direct the rainwater to a depression in the ground. The plants and soils filter the water, slowing the rate the water soaks into the ground. For a house, a small retention pond can work well.

Be sure to keep children away from retention ponds, not only because they collect trash but because they can be drowning hazards after a rain.

Rainwater harvesting and catchment

Why pay for water when nature provides it for free? Instead of directing rainwater to the sewer, you can save it and put it to good use watering the yard. The idea of collecting rainwater is not new. In fact, people have done it for centuries. Based on your climate, a vast amount of valuable water may be available for your use. By using this water, you'll save valuable resources and money at the same time.

The term *stormwater* refers to all the water running off your roof, driveway, or landscape, but *rainwater catchment* only refers to collecting rainwater from your roof.

Adding rainwater catchment to an existing home is simple. If your home already has gutters and downspouts, purchase a *rain barrel* or *cistern* (a small tank for holding water). Place the barrel below the downspout to capture water for your yard.

Several companies — including Green Culture (www.composters.com) and Oak Barrel Winecraft (www.oakbarrel.com) — offer attractive barrels made from recycled wine barrels.

Bioremediation

Bioremediation uses algae, plants, and bacteria to naturally clean polluted water to make it (nearly) drinkable. Often called *living machines,* they mimic the same cleansing function as a natural wetland. Think of it as a small man-made wetland on your property. Not only can a living machine clean stormwater, but it can be designed to filter the soapy water from a sink (called graywater).

Your landscape architect can help you design such a system. You can also find useful information on living machines at www.worrell water.com.

Patios, walkways, and driveways

Paved areas give you access to the outdoors. Typically, a large paved area (such as a parking lot or driveway) is covered with an impervious surface, like asphalt, forcing rainwater into storm sewers instead of back into the ground (not a good thing). But green alternatives do exist:

✔ **Porous pavers:** *Porous pavers* are made of brick or stone and have holes in them to allow water to sink into the ground below instead of having the water sheet down an impervious surface. If the water is allowed to soak naturally into the ground, the water table will remain constant.

✔ **Poured concrete with fly ash:** Fly-ash-based concrete is an environmentally friendly alternative to traditional concrete (see Chapter 5). More durable than asphalt, the light color of concrete will also reduce the heat issues caused by asphalt (see the "What's wrong with asphalt" sidebar).

✔ **Recycled (broken) concrete:** Broken-up concrete from sidewalk demolition can be found, often for free, from concrete contractors. Lay it down like large pieces of flagstone.

✔ **Salvaged stone:** Pavers salvaged from demolition make an attractive walkway.

✔ **Decomposed granite:** Decomposed granite is a gravel stone. It makes a wonderful sound when you walk or drive on it.

✔ **Reclaimed brick:** Salvaged bricks from a demolished building can be placed in a wide variety of patterns. However, saving these bricks is very labor intensive.

✔ **Crushed stone:** Crushed stone is perfect for a driveway and makes a great sound as people drive up to your house. Instead of gravel, use locally sourced quarry stones.

✔ **Wood chips:** Low-cost or free wood chips are available from your local tree services. You'll need to replenish the chips after heavy use.

✔ **Nutshells:** Nut growers generate tons of empty shells. See if local sources exist by looking to your local farmers market or grocery store. The shells biodegrade over time and will need to be replenished.

✔ **Tumbled glass:** Local glass recyclers can provide raw recycled glass. Have the pieces tumbled to soften the edges. It makes for an attractive walk or driveway.

Every paved area should slope a tiny bit to drain rainwater. Driveways should not slope more that 15 percent, or they'll be undrivable. A walkway should not slope more than 5 percent, especially if someone in a wheelchair may use it.

Slope is calculated as the rise of the slope over the run of the distance. For example, a 15 percent slope would go up 15 feet over 100 feet of distance.

A light-colored patio will reflect light. The reflected light from the ground can bounce illumination into your home. Keep this in mind when locating windows over a light colored patio. If you have a dark room, a light patio may bring more light indoors. Dark-colored materials will absorb heat from the sun, increasing the ambient temperature around it. If you live in a hot climate, choose light colors instead.

Decks

The right deck is great for entertaining, but it can also be a maintenance headache. Encourage outdoor living with these durable, low-maintenance decking alternatives to wood:

✔ **Pressure-treated wood:** Wood framing used outside is typically pressure treated with chromated copper arsenate (CCA), which is a form of arsenic and bad for your health. The EPA has now banned CCA wood, but it's still in use, especially in children's playgrounds. Look for wood treated with the healthier ammoniacal copper quaternary (ACQ).

Choose wood certified by the Forest Stewardship Council (FSC); the FSC stamp ensures that the wood has been *sustainably harvested* (collected from well-managed forests to guarantee the forest wasn't clear-cut). Although FSC-certified wood is the best choice, plan on paying 20 percent more for this certification.

✔ **Composite lumber:** Combining recycled plastic and sawdust, composite lumbers are much healthier and environmentally friendly. Look for brands with 100 percent recycled content.

✔ **Reclaimed beams (railroad ties):** Salvaged ties from old railroad tracks are attractive and did not require any new trees to be made. Coat them with two coats of a water-based sealer to seal in the CCA.

If you're concerned that your existing deck or playground may contain CCA-treated wood, you can purchase CCA test kits, such as the one available from Safe2Play (www.safe2play.org).

No matter what material you choose for your deck, consider the following:

✔ **Size your deck to match the size of the material you're using.** If you're using boards that come in 8-foot lengths, design with that size in mind to reduce waste.

✔ **Locate the deck in a sunny area to avoid dry rot and moss growth.**

✔ **Avoid handrails.** If your deck is less than 18 inches off the ground, the local building code probably doesn't require a handrail. Not using handrails saves you money and keeps the view open. It also reduces the amount of wood you need to use. Check your local building code for the exact handrail requirements.

✔ **Create interesting shapes to turn the deck toward the view or the sunshine.** Be creative!

Fences, trellises, and arbors

Fences define space while protecting your pets and kids. Instead of a fence, consider using a simple row of upright plants or stalks of bamboo to create a hedge. You'll get all the privacy of a fence, plus natural beauty. Adding a trellis or arbor can provide shade for your home on south- or west-facing sides of the house.

Consider the following materials for fences, trellises, and arbors:

✔ **Wood:** When using wood, choose rot-resistant species like cypress and ipe. The best choice is FSC-certified wood.

✔ **Composite recycled plastic lumber:** Combining recycled plastic and sawdust, composite lumbers are more environmentally friendly than wood. Look for brands with the highest recycled content.

✔ **Salvaged metal:** Found or salvaged metal railings, pipes, or fencing make a great trellis or arbor. Your local salvage yards carry a wide selection.

✔ **Fiber cement:** These durable panels are made from cement, sand, and wood fiber. Often used as a siding, it can also be used for fencing.

Because the winter sun is lower than the summer sun, you can design a trellis to block the hot summer sun but still allow the winter sun into the home. The boards of the trellis can be arranged as shown in Figure 14-5. This layout will block the summer sun but still allow the winter sun in to warm your house.

Swimming pools and hot tubs

Having a swimming pool in your backyard can make yours the most popular house on the block on a hot summer day. Unfortunately, the chemicals, maintenance, and safety issues make pool care a headache. The water and energy needed to maintain your pool has an impact on the environment as well.

Consider these ways to improve the efficiency of your pool:

- ✔ **Choose the smallest pump and the largest filter suitable for your pool.** This will save energy and the installation cost of your pool system.

- ✔ **Circulate the water in the pump for the shortest time needed to clean it (usually less than three hours).** Pool pumps often run much longer than needed, using up more electricity than necessary.

- ✔ **Install a timer on the pump and set it to run for several short cycles throughout the day.** Doing this will drastically reduce your energy costs for your pool.

- ✔ **Use a pool cover to keep heat (and water) in your pool.** A cover reduces evaporation of water from the pool when it's not in use. In fact, a cover can reduce water loss by 30 percent to 50 percent.

- ✔ **Significantly reduce pool heating costs by installing a solar pool heater on your roof.** Solar pool heating is the most cost-effective use of solar energy in many climates.

- ✔ **Skip the chlorinated water.** A natural pool, saltwater pool, or ozone pool is a healthier and easier-to-maintain option than the standard chlorine variety.

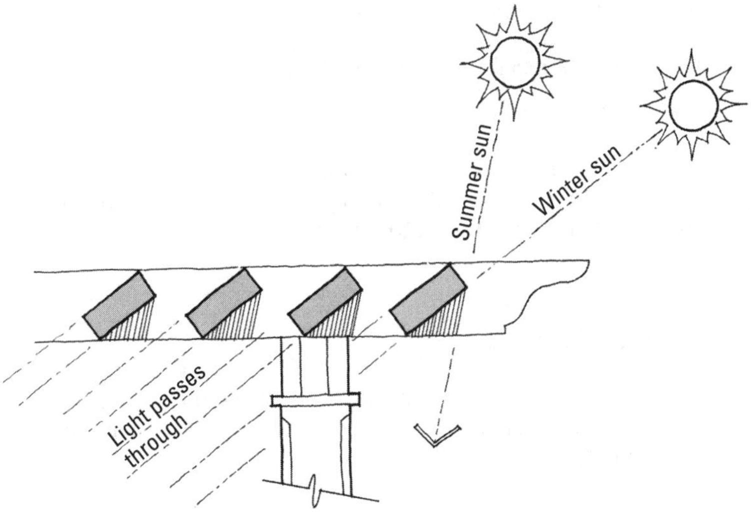

Figure 14-5:
A trellis like this one blocks the hot summer sun but lets in the winter sun.

Summer sun

Winter sun

Light passes through

What's wrong with asphalt?

Asphalt, also called blacktop, is a sticky mixture of petroleum and *bitumen* (a product of crude oil). Asphalt is the most common material for creating driveways, parking lots, and roads, but it poses the following problems:

✔ Asphalt is made of a nonrenewable resource.

✔ On a hot day, an asphalt parking lot can increase the temperature around a building by up to 15°F.

✔ As rainwater hits the asphalt, toxic chemicals soak into the water, polluting it.

For all these reasons, you should avoid asphalt whenever possible.

Sheds

You need a place for your tools and garden equipment, and a nice garden shed can be an attractive addition to your yard. Store-bought shed kits are simple to build, but they're usually made of the cheapest and least environmentally friendly materials.

You can construct your own small, uninsulated shed using salvaged materials. Also, consider these green alternatives:

✔ **Used sheds:** Your local classified ads may have the perfect shed.

✔ **FSC-certified wood:** If you're building a new shed, use FSC-certified wood.

In most places, accessory buildings less than 100 or 150 square feet in size don't even need a permit. Of course, as always, be sure to check with your local building department to be sure.

Accessories

Such accessories as outdoor furniture, pots and planters, and lighting will put the finishing touches on your yard. You can find green alternatives for nearly everything you need.

Furniture

Lawn and patio furniture comes in a variety of types. For wood furniture, choose naturally rot-resistant woods like ipe and cypress, or FSC-certified wood. Avoid tropical rain forest hardwoods such as teak.

Plastic furniture is typically made of harmful PVC. Skip the PVC and look for high-content recycled plastic.

Extend the life of your furniture by storing it in the garage for the winter.

Pots and planters

Add a dash of color and flexibility with a variety of planters around the deck and patio. Recycled-content pots are readily available at most garden stores.

If you choose the right plants, you won't need to water as often. Clay and terra-cotta pots hold in the water and help the plants survive the hot days.

Lighting

Accent lighting can add safety and drama to your yard. But too much lighting is a waste of energy, so include just enough so guests can safely find their way around.

Pointing lights upward can create *light pollution,* which disrupts your neighbors and reduces your ability to see the stars. Avoid light fixtures that shine upward.

Although low-voltage lighting uses only a small amount of energy, you still need to run wires to make them work. Instead, purchase solar-powered landscape lights. They store power all day from a small solar panel and light up at night. They aren't very bright, however, so use more of them to safely light walkways.

Turn off landscape lights when you don't need them, or use motion sensors to operate lights only when you do need them.

Part V
The Part of Tens

The 5th Wave   By Rich Tennant

"Dual-flush toilets, recycled-content tile, flow-reduced faucets...Where's it all end, Stan?"

In this part . . .

This would not be a *For Dummies* book without these handy chapters of tens. Because green building is so misunderstood, I dispel ten myths about green building and remodeling in Chapter 15. Chapter 16 explains the things you should do for every green building project. You may start drooling when you read Chapter 17 and the ten materials you can't live without. Finally, plan your weekend projects with this list of ten things you should do right now in your own home, in Chapter 18.

Chapter 15

Ten Common Myths about Green Building and Remodeling

In This Chapter

▶ Arguing in favor of green building and remodeling

▶ Dispelling myths about going green

▶ Changing the minds of people who are against green building

Green building and remodeling are mysteries to most people. And like any good mystery, this one is rife with rumors, myths, and misconceptions. When you start telling people about your green building or remodeling project, you'll hear a wide range of odd and funny comments about going green. Most of them will be wrong. In this chapter, I fill you in on ten of the most common myths and replace the rumors with reality.

Green Buildings Always Cost More Than Traditional Buildings

Not true. Good architects and contractors know how to save their clients money. With a clear budget, there is no reason you can't build a green building for the same price or *less than* the cost of a traditional building.

The U.S. Green Building Council (USGBC) provides, among other things, data on the costs of green buildings. In 1995, it estimated that a green building added only 7 percent to the upfront cost of construction. For that small amount, you got energy efficiency, lower water bills, and happier occupants.

But that was a long time ago.

Today, the USGBC estimates that green buildings add 0 percent to 1 percent to the upfront cost of the building. In other words, there is *no difference* in cost.

Green Materials Are More Expensive

Although some green materials cost more than their traditional counterparts, many more green materials cost far less than the standard. As green materials have grown in popularity, their cost has come down. At the same time, because most traditional materials involve oil in their production, and because oil is now so expensive, the cost of those traditional materials has gone up.

Advances in recycling, new materials, and better designs have allowed for a new generation of environmentally friendly products that are less costly to produce. Some of the most innovative, beautiful, and unique finishes available today are coming from green manufacturers.

Green Buildings Take Longer to Build

This myth is a myth for a reason: It's completely false. Most green buildings simply substitute one material for another, more sustainable one. These substitutions have no effect on the construction time.

The type of *construction* determines the construction time. For example, the walls of a straw-bale house can be built in a day or so, while a traditional wood-frame building takes much longer. As another example, a home built with structural insulated panels can be erected in half the time of a wood-frame house.

Because some green buildings are designed to reduce construction waste, they may even *speed up* the construction process.

Green Buildings Look Like Mud Huts or Rice Cakes

Most green buildings look like just like their traditional, non-green counterparts. In fact, you've probably been in an environmentally friendly building and not known it. Some green buildings *are* made out of mud or straw — and, understandably, they get lots of attention because of their unusual appearance. But the truth is, green buildings come in all shapes and forms. Design anything you like — you can make it a green building.

Green Buildings Offer No Economic Advantage

The amount of money you can save on energy costs in a green building could pay for the green improvements within one to five years. A 2005 study by Capital E and the University of California, Berkeley, found that any money spent on a green building feature will pay for itself *ten times* over the life of the building. Can you think of any other investment that pays so well?

One Building Doesn't Make a Difference to the Environment

Each snowflake in the avalanche pleads "not guilty."

Of course, each building makes a difference! Today, buildings are designed to last for 50 to 100 years. Most of the environmental impact comes from the operation of the building, not the construction. A green home uses less water, energy, and materials during its day-to-day operations than a traditional house.

Look at these facts:

- For every incandescent bulb you replace with a compact fluorescent bulb, you'll save $30 per year on energy costs.
- Unplugging your TV, microwave, and DVD player when not in use will save you $50 a year.
- Installing a programmable thermostat can save you 30 percent off your heating bills in the winter.

And one house plus another house plus another house adds up:

- If every home in the United States was insulated, we could completely remove our need for oil from the Middle East.
- If every home in the United States used an Energy Star refrigerator, we could close ten aging power plants.

Nobody Cares Whether a Building Is Green

New market studies are released each month showing that a majority of people would be willing to pay more for green building features — and even *more* for healthy features. The surging media interest in green building, the rise of new green-themed magazines, and the increasing number of new green materials all show how much in demand green building has become.

In the future, all buildings will be green. Until that time, people are demanding it from their builders, architects, and employers. Which means that home *buyers* are demanding it, too — if your home is green, it'll be more appealing to buyers. And if you're the first green building on your block, you'll have a leg up on your neighbors when it comes time to sell.

Green Buildings Are Just Buildings with Recycled Materials

Although recycled materials are commonly used in green building, recycled stuff alone is not enough. A green building is made up of much more than just recycled materials — it involves water use, energy use, and the indoor air quality.

What you recycle is as important as the *act* of recycling itself. A countertop made from recycled toxic waste is still toxic waste. As manufacturers race to release new products made out of recycled materials, you need to check whether these materials are healthy. For example, natural rubber comes from a rubber tree and is a natural product. Tire rubber, on the other hand, is actually *vulcanized rubber* (rubber treated with sulfur) and is a toxic material. When a product claims to use recycled rubber, be sure to ask which rubber was used: natural or tire. (The answer you want to hear is natural, of course.)

Don't be fooled by claims from manufacturers offering recycled content. A material containing just 1 percent recycled content can still call itself "recycled." Ask the manufacturer for a Material Safety and Data Sheet (MSDS) to know for sure how much of the material is recycled.

Green Buildings Are Fragile and Require More Maintenance

Durability is an important part of green building. If you build something that'll last, you'll save materials, save energy, and save natural resources — and those are some of the core goals of a green building.

Some people assume that natural materials, because they're soft, aren't durable. Not only are many natural materials durable, but they wear *better* than most synthetic materials. Think of the old wooden floor in your grandparents' house, worn with age. This natural wear adds character to buildings and shows the life inside. Other materials, such as natural linoleum, actually become stronger over time.

The exteriors of green buildings often use natural materials in an exposed and unfinished way. Natural materials have a *patina* (natural aging) to them. This is the reason that copper turns green and cedar shingles turn gray. This natural aging adds to the character of buildings, while also saving money on maintenance.

If you paint something outside, you'll have to repaint it every few years. But if you finish natural materials with a light stain or natural oils, you can let them age naturally with little maintenance.

You Can't Have High-End Design in a Green Building

In the future, all buildings will be green buildings. Whether by necessity, regulation, or choice, every building will be environmentally responsible. But this does not mean the end of well-designed buildings! You can design anything you like, and make it green. Green buildings cut down on energy use, increase water efficiency, improve indoor air, and use materials wisely. None of these things get in the way of designing something beautiful. So go crazy, and design anything you can imagine!

For example, the Gap corporate headquarters in San Bruno, California, offers a green roof with local plants, fresh air, and ultrahigh energy efficiency. But this building has won just as many design awards as it has won green awards. Completed in 1997 by William McDonough, the Gap headquarters exceeds the minimum energy requirements by over 30 percent.

Want another example? The LivingHomes Z6 house in Santa Monica, California, generates its own electricity and recycles its water. Plus, the design is a modern masterpiece. Nothing was sacrificed for the sake of being green.

Chapter 16

Ten Green Things to Do on Every New-Home Project

In This Chapter

▶ Identifying items for your home that conserve energy, water, or materials

▶ Developing new standards for any new home project

*I*f your head is swimming with new ideas for your green home project, you may not know where to start. In this chapter, I fill you in on ten things you should do *automatically* on every new home. Aside from their just being the green things to do, I've chosen all these measures because they cost the same as their traditional counterparts, have a short payback of less than a few years, or just make sense. Think of them as "best practices" for building your green home.

Turn toward the Sun

When you're building a new home, put some thought into where you position your home on your property and where the windows are located. If possible, orient your home to take advantage of the unchanging path of the sun. In the morning, the light will be coming from the east; in the afternoon, more light and heat will come from the west. Providing light and warmth, the sun can drastically change the comfort of your home. Don't ignore it. A well-positioned home can reduce heating, cooling, lighting, and maintenance costs.

Most of the light and heat from the sun will come from the south. If you're in a hot climate, reduce the size and number of windows and provide overhangs and shading for the remaining windows. In cold climates, place large windows on the side of your house that faces the south. Use the thermal mass of a concrete floor or a thick concrete wall to soak up the heat coming through these south-facing windows. These simple things will keep your home comfortable year-round. (Turn to Chapter 12 for more on using thermal mass.)

Because the sun rises in the east, position rooms that have lots of morning activities — such as the breakfast room — on the east side of the house. The sun sets in the west, so consider placing the dining room on that side so you can watch the sunset as you have dinner. Not only do these ideas make good design sense, they save you from having to turn on the lights during the day.

Use Recycled-Content Drywall

Drywall, also known as gypsum wallboard, is one of the most common materials used in construction today. All the walls in your new home are likely to be covered with drywall. Drywall accounts for more than a quarter of all construction waste, and its chief ingredient, gypsum, has to be mined out of the earth and requires an immense amount of energy to produce. All this effort gives off carbon dioxide and other greenhouse gases.

Drywall made from recycled and synthetic gypsum is now readily available — you just have to ask for it. The backing is made from 100 percent recycled, unbleached paper that is bonded without adhesives onto a gypsum core. Keep in mind the boards come in standard heights of 8 feet, 9 feet, and 10 feet, so if you design to those ceiling heights (or have your architect design to those ceiling heights), you'll reduce cutting and waste.

Here are some recycled-content drywall manufacturers you may want to try:

- ✔ **Georgia-Pacific Building Products,** 55 Park Place, Atlanta, GA 30303 (phone: 800-225-6119 or 404-652-4000; Web: www.gp.com/gypsum)

- ✔ **National Gypsum Company,** 2001 Rexford Rd., Charlotte, NC 28211 (phone: 800-628-4662 or 704-365-7300; e-mail: ng@nationalgypsum.com; Web: www.national-gypsum.com)

- ✔ **Temple-Inland,** P.O. Drawer N, Diboll, TX 75941 (phone: 800-231-6060; e-mail: mktgcomm@templeinland.com; Web: www.temple.com/gypsum)

- ✔ **USG,** c/o Corporate Secretary, 550 W. Adams St., Chicago, IL 60661-3676 (phone: 800-874-4968; e-mail: usg4you@usg.com; Web: www.usg.com)

Stuff the Walls with the Right Kind of Insulation

The inside of your walls should be filled with insulation — and when it comes to insulation, the more the better. Although insulation lowers your energy bills, most traditional fiberglass insulation contains a phenol-formaldehyde binder, which releases harmful chemicals. In addition, the airborne fibers are a health hazard.

 As an alternative to fiberglass, consider using a natural insulation made from recycled cotton. Unlike fiberglass, recycled cotton insulation has no microfibers that cause health problems. Another option is cellulose insulation, which is made from recycled newspaper and blows in easily.

Use only formaldehyde-free or recycled-content insulation. Most fiberglass insulation already has at least 30 percent recycled content, but ask for insulation with the highest amount of recycled content available. Be sure to insulate your attic and the edges of the concrete floor slab — most people forget them. Use as much insulation as will fit into your walls — but don't stuff or pack it in: Insulation needs to be fluffy in order to work.

 While you're up in the attic, install a radiant barrier on your roof. It'll save even more off your energy bill. (You can find more energy-saving tips in Chapters 11 and 12.)

Some healthy insulation manufacturers include the following:

- ✔ Formaldehyde-free insulation:
  - **CertainTeed,** P.O. Box 860, 750 E. Swedesford Rd., Valley Forge, PA 19482 (phone: 800-782-8777; Web: www.certainteed.com)
  - **Johns Manville,** P.O. Box 5108, Denver, CO 80217-5108 (phone: 800-654-3103; Web: www.jm.com)
- ✔ Natural cotton insulation:
  - **Bonded Logic,** 411 E. Ray Rd., Chandler, AZ 85225 (phone: 480-812-9114; Web: www.bondedlogic.com)
  - **Insulcot Insulation,** 411 S. Fox St., Post, TX 79356 (phone: 806-777-2811; Web: www.insulcot.com)
- ✔ Cellulose insulation:
  - **Clayville Insulation,** P.O. Box 713, Burley, ID 83318 (phone: 800-584-9022; Web: www.safelink.net/clayinsu/index.html)

- **Energy Control, Inc.,** 804 W. Mill St., Ossian, IN 46777 (phone: 800-451-6429)

- **Igloo Cellulose,** 195 Brunswick, Pointe-Claire, Québec, Canada H9R 4Z1 (phone: 800-363-7876; Web: www.cellulose.com)

- **International Cellulose,** P.O. Box 450006, 12315 Robin Blvd., Houston, TX 77245-0006 (phone: 800-444-1252; Web: www.spray-on.com)

Choose Healthy Paints

People spend 80 percent to 90 percent of their time indoors, so the quality of the indoor air is important to our health. Common paints, adhesives, and floor finishes contain *volatile organic compounds* (VOCs), which are known carcinogens that are directly related to asthma in children.

Most major manufacturers now offer low-VOC products, but *low* only means "lower than normal." Look for *very*-low-VOC or preferably *zero*-VOC paints and adhesives.

Healthy paint manufacturers include

- **AFM (makers of Safecoat),** 3251 Third Ave., San Diego, CA 92103 (phone: 800-239-0321 or 619-239-0321; e-mail: info@afmsafecoat.com; Web: www.afmsafecoat.com)

- **Antique Drapery Rod Company (makers of Healthy Paint),** 2263 Valdina St., Dallas, TX 75207 (phone: 214-653-1733; Web: www.antiquedraperyrod.com)

- **Benjamin Moore (makers of Eco Spec),** 101 Paragon Dr., Montvale, NJ 07645 (phone: 800-344-0400; e-mail: info@benjaminmoore.com; Web: www.benjaminmoore.com)

- **Best Paint,** 1728 Fourth Ave. S., Seattle, WA 98134 (phone: 206-783-9938; e-mail: paint@bestpaintco.com; Web: www.bestpaintco.com)

- **BioShield Paint,** 3215 Rufina St., Santa Fe, NM 87507 (phone: 800-621-2591; Web: www.bioshieldpaint.com)

- **Chem-Safe Products Company (makers of Enviro-Safe Paint),** HC32 Box 122, Uvalde, TX 78801 (phone: 888-281-6467; Web: www.envirosafepaint.com)

- **Duron Paints & Wallcoverings (makers of Genesis Odor-Free),** 10406 Tucker St., Beltsville, MD 20705 (phone: 800-723-8766; e-mail: paintinfo@duron.com; Web: www.duron.com)

- **Kelly-Moore Paints (makers of Enviro-Cote),** 987 Commercial St., San Carlos, CA 94070 (phone: 888-677-2468; Web: www.kellymoore.com)

Change Your Concrete Mix

Every construction project uses concrete in one way or another. Concrete is a mixture of sand, water, stone, and Portland cement. The cement is the key ingredient in concrete — acting as the binding agent — but it requires a great deal of energy from mining, grinding up, and heating. Cement production alone is responsible for 5 percent to 10 percent of all greenhouse gas emissions.

Replace up to 50 percent of the Portland cement in your concrete with fly ash. *Fly ash* is the fine powder residue by-product from coal-fired, electric-generating plants. Because the burning of coal provides up to 85 percent of your electricity (depending on where you live), a great deal of fly ash is produced.

Currently, the fly ash is released into the air, buried in a landfill, or illegally dumped into the ocean. All this leaks mercury into the food supply. But you can take this waste product and use it to substitute for 20 percent to 50 percent of the Portland cement in the concrete mix, which not only reduces the amount of fly ash released into the environment, but reduces the expenditure of energy on mining, grinding up, and heating Portland cement.

Pick the Right Toilet

Toilets use 40 percent of the water in the average home. You'd never think of flushing gasoline down the toilet, yet clean drinking water costs more per gallon. The average toilet uses 3½ gallons of fresh drinking water for every flush, and the average household in the United States consumes nearly 300 gallons of clean drinking water a day, most of which goes down the toilet.

Choose dual-flush toilets for your home. Here's how it works: For liquids, lift the handle and only ⅚ gallon goes down the drain; for solids, push the handle down and the full 1⅔ gallons is used. Every major toilet manufacturer now offers dual-flush models at the same cost. At the very least, choose low-flow toilets using only 1⅔ gallons per flush.

If you keep your existing toilets, kits are available to retrofit them into dual-flush or low-flow models for as little as $5 (see www.twoflush.com or www.niagaraconservation.com).

Heat Your Water with the Sun

Making sure you have instant hot water available any time is expensive. It costs you 17 percent of your heating bill. A typical water heater runs all day, even when you don't need hot water, making it more wasteful.

A solar water heater sits on the south-facing side of your roof, has no moving parts, and has virtually no maintenance. The sun preheats the water and sends it to a conventional water heater for storage, reducing the need for using any energy.

Solar water heater manufacturers include

- ✔ **Dawn Solar Systems,** 183 Rte. 125, Suite A-7, Brentwood, NH 03833 (phone: 866-338-2018 or 603-642-7897; Web: www.dawnsolar.com)

- ✔ **Heliodyne,** 4910 Seaport Ave., Richmond, CA 94804 (phone: 510-237-9614, e-mail: sales@heliodyne.com; Web: www.heliodyne.com)

- ✔ **Rheem Water Heating,** 1100 Abernathy Rd., Suite 1400, Atlanta, GA 30328 (phone: 334-260-1586; Web: http://waterheating.rheem.com)

- ✔ **SunEarth,** 8425 Almeria Ave., Fontana, CA 92335 (phone: 909-434-3100; Web: www.sunearthinc.com)

If a solar water heater sounds out of reach, consider an on-demand hot water system. In a typical home in the United States, up to 10,000 gallons of water are wasted each year waiting for hot water to reach the tap. The on-demand system is tankless, and it only heats the water you need. It runs only when you use the hot water faucet, saving you hundreds of dollars a year.

Recycle Construction Waste

Construction waste takes up a large portion of valuable landfill space. Nearly all this could be recycled if handled properly. The high cost of disposal is finally forcing builders to rethink their approach to construction waste.

Organize construction waste into piles for possible reuse during construction or simple salvage after. Contact local salvage yards to take away any old appliances, fixtures, doors, and windows you don't reuse or useful scraps of building materials. Any remaining waste should be sorted for recycling at the dump. Many cities are now requiring recycling of construction waste.

Choose Your Carpet Carefully

Carpet is an environmental problem. Typically made from synthetic, oil-based materials, carpets release harmful chemicals. They're usually backed with vinyl, making them unhealthy and nearly impossible to recycle. Wall-to-wall carpet creates a place for mold, pests, and allergens to reside. With their short life span, carpets are responsible for sending 4 billion pounds of waste to the landfill each year.

Use natural fiber carpets from companies with recycling take-back programs. Avoid any carpet with a vinyl backing. Try using carpet tile instead of wall-to-wall carpeting; you can replace damaged tiles individually without having to replace an entire floor. (Of course, avoiding carpet altogether would be best.) Select a natural padding below the carpet to avoid using toxic and difficult-to-remove adhesives.

Healthy carpet manufacturers include

- ✔ **Bentley Prince Street,** 14641 E. Don Julian Rd., City of Industry, CA 91746 (phone: 800-423-4709; Web: www.bentleyprincestreet.com)

- ✔ **InterfaceFLOR,** 1503 Orchard Hill Rd., LaGrange, GA 30240 (phone: 866-281-3567; Web: www.interfaceflooring.com)

- ✔ **J&J/Invision,** 818 J&J Dr., P.O. Box 1287, Dalton, GA 30722 (phone: 800-241-4585; Web: www.jj-invision.com)

- ✔ **Milliken Carpet,** P.O. Box 1926, Spartanburg, SC 29304 (phone: 800-241-4826; Web: www.milliken.com)

- ✔ **Mohawk Industries,** P.O. Box 12069, Calhoun, GA 30703 (phone: 800-266-4295; Web: www.mohawkind.com)

- ✔ **Shaw Contract Group,** 380 S. Industrial Blvd., Calhoun, GA 30701 (phone: 800-257-7429; Web: www.shawcontract.com)

Watch Your Plywood

Used for siding, flooring underlayment, and cabinetry, plywood is a versatile and popular material. Plywood consists of wood cut into thin layers that are alternately glued together. Typically, the wood comes from newly cut trees. The adhesives are typically toxic and contain formaldehyde, which releases unhealthy chemicals.

All plywood used should carry the FSC label (meaning that it's certified by the Forest Stewardship Council) to ensure that sustainable practices were used in the extraction of the wood.

Oriented-strand board (OSB) is an efficient alternative use of wood because it is produced from small pieces and low-grade species of wood. The same concerns about using nontoxic adhesives still apply, however.

For any wood you choose, select nontoxic glue and formaldehyde-free boards.

Chapter 17

Ten Green Materials You Can't Live Without

In This Chapter

▶ Discovering unique and beautiful green products

▶ Locating green alternatives for standard construction materials

*I*f you're like most homeowners, you probably don't have strong feelings about toilets, roofing, or siding . . . but your eyes always light up when the subject of finishes comes up. If that sounds familiar, you've come to the right chapter. Here, I fill you in on ten gorgeous materials you should consider for every construction project. Order samples of each — when you see these in person, you'll fall in love with them.

As I often tell my clients, being green is not a black-and-white issue. Nearly every product has some good green characteristics and some not-so-green characteristics. There is no perfect material with zero impact on the planet. As you look through the list, try to figure out which material works best for *your* needs.

Recycled-Paper Countertops

Made from recycled paper and a resin binder, these composite countertops have a warm, neutral look that fits well with most decorating styles. This material looks similar to other popular solid-surface countertops like Corian, but because they're only about one-third plastic, they have a more natural look and feel. Many people compare these green alternatives to soapstone.

You can have special features incorporated into the countertops, such as a drain board next to an under-mount sink, or casting metal rods near the stove, creating a built-in trivet.

Manufacturers of recycled-paper countertops include

- ✔ **Paneltech International,** 2999 John Stevens Way, Hoquiam, WA 98550 (phone: 360-538-9815; Web: www.kliptech.com/index.shtml; e-mail: info@kliptech.com)

- ✔ **Richlite Company,** 624 E. 15th St., Tacoma, WA 98421 (phone: 888-383-5533; Web: www.richlite.com; e-mail: info@richlite.com)

Recycled Glass Terrazzo

Terrazzo typically consists of small pieces of marble set into cement, which is then highly polished. Instead of marble, several manufacturers have discovered using recycled glass instead. The result is an ethereal surface so beautiful that you won't notice that this particular glass happens to be made from recycled soda bottles. You can choose the colors of both the glass and the cement binder, giving you an endless list of possibilities. The surface is durable, heatproof, and easy to maintain.

Manufacturers of recycled-glass terrazzo include

- ✔ **Vetrazzo,** Ford Point, Suite 1400, 1414 Harbour Way S., Richmond, CA 94804 (phone: 510-234-5550; Web: www.vetrazzo.com; e-mail: info@vetrazzo.com)

- ✔ **IceStone,** Brooklyn Navy Yard, 63 Flushing Ave., Unit 283, Building 12, Brooklyn, NY 11205 (phone: 718-624-4900; Web: www.icestone.biz; e-mail: info@icestone.biz)

- ✔ **EnviroGLAS,** 5048 Tennyson Pkwy., Suite 202, Plano, TX 75024 (phone: 888-523-7894 or 972-473-3725; Web: www.enviroglasproducts.com; e-mail: communications@enviroglasproducts.com)

Recycled-Glass Tiles

These gemlike tiles are so gorgeous that you'd want them even if they *weren't* made from recycled glass. The glass is from broken, discarded windows, which is then crushed to a sandlike texture and mixed with other ingredients, including minerals that add color. The process uses far less energy than fired ceramic tile. Although the surface is smooth, a slight pebbly texture appears to be embedded in the interior of the tiles. Perfect for a tiled wall or counter backsplash, these tiles add color and texture to any room.

Manufacturers of recycled-glass tiles include

- **Bedrock Industries,** 1401 W. Garfield St., Seattle, WA 98119 (phone: 877-283-7625 or 206-283-7625; Web: www.bedrockindustries.com; e-mail: info@bedrockindustries.com)

- **Oceanside Glasstile,** 2293 Cosmos Court, Carlsbad, CA 92011 (phone: 760-929-4000; Web: www.glasstile.com; e-mail: info@glasstile.com)

Eco Resin Panels

These recycled and recyclable plastic panels are available in an endless variety of thicknesses, sizes, textures, and colors. You can embed anything you want inside the panel — from bamboo stalks to rose petals to your favorite cartoons — giving you an infinite number of home-décor possibilities. Instead of a wall, consider these panels for a clever room divider. Hide your clutter by using them in cabinet doors. Create a unique shower enclosure with these beautiful panels.

Manufacturers of eco resin panels include

- **3form,** 2300 S. 2300 W., Suite B, Salt Lake City, UT 84119 (phone: 800-726-0126 or 801-649-2500; Web: www.3-form.com; e-mail: info@3-form.com)

- **Veritas,** 6200 49th St. N., Pinellas Park, FL 33781 (phone: 877-411-8008 or 727-521-2393 ext. 227; Web: www.veritasideas.com)

Kirei Board

With a look similar to exotic plywood, Kirei Board is not made of wood at all. Formed from pressed stalks of rice sorghum, *kirei* is cellulose from an agricultural waste material, the by-product of rice farming. You can use the boards for everything from furniture to cabinetry, and because no glues are needed in their manufacture, they're healthy for you and your family as well.

The manufacturer of Kirei Board is Kirei, 1805 Newton Ave., San Diego, CA 92113 (phone: 619-236-9924; Web: www.kireiusa.com; e-mail: info@kireiusa.com).

Earthen-Clay Plaster

White walls are boring, show dirt, and need to be repainted every few years. Cover your walls in this natural plaster finish to add color and depth to your home. This all-natural material doesn't give off any harmful chemicals, and adds style and beauty to your walls.

Manufacturers of earthen-clay plaster include

- **American Clay Enterprises,** 2601 Karsten Court SE, Albuquerque, NM 87102 (phone: 866-404-1634; Web: www.americanclay.com; e-mail: sales@americanclay.com)

- **TransMineral USA,** 501 Lakeville St., Suite F, Petaluma, CA 94952 (phone: 707-769-0661; Web: www.limes.us; e-mail: transmin@sonic.net)

Bamboo Flooring

Bamboo is a rapidly growing grass harvested by cutting the stalks. Unlike with trees, the bamboo is not killed in the process, making it sustainable. Although it looks very similar to a traditional wood floor, bamboo has a distinctive knuckle in the grain. It's available in solid and engineered flooring options from dozens of different manufacturers.

Be sure to choose a floor made completely of solid bamboo, with nontoxic glues and sealers.

Manufacturers of bamboo flooring include

- **EcoTimber,** 1611 Fourth St., San Rafael, CA 94901 (phone: 415-258-8454; Web: www.ecotimber.com)

- **Smith & Fong,** 375 Oyster Point Blvd. #3, South San Francisco, CA 94080 (phone: 866-835-9859 or 650-872-1184; Web: www.plyboo.com; e-mail: sales@plyboo.com)

Linoleum Flooring

Made from sawdust and linseed oil, linoleum is a safe and natural product. Vinyl floors are cheap, but they only last a few years and are toxic in their production. Natural linoleum, however, is durable, easier to clean than vinyl, and naturally antistatic. Because it hardens with age, some homeowners have reported over 50 years of use from their linoleum floors.

One manufacturer of natural linoleum flooring is Forbo Linoleum, Humboldt Industrial Park, P.O. Box 667, Hazleton, PA 18201 (phone: 570-459-0771; Web: www.forbo-flooring.com or www.forbolinoleumna.com; e-mail: info@fl.na.com)

Cork Flooring

Traditionally, cork flooring is made from the bark of a cork tree. Because harvesting the bark doesn't hurt the tree, and the bark grows back quickly, cork is considered a sustainable material. Several manufacturers now offer cork flooring made from recycled wine bottle corks in a wide variety of patterns.

Manufacturers of cork flooring include

- **Expanko Cork,** 1129 W. Lincoln Hwy., Coatesville, PA 19320 (phone: 800-345-6202; Web: www.expanko.com; e-mail: sales@expanko.com)

- **Natural Cork,** 1710 N. Leg Court, Augusta, GA 30909 (phone: 800-404-2675 or 706-733-6120; Web: www.naturalcork.com)

Recycled Denim Cotton Insulation

Although it lives hidden inside your walls, insulation is an important part of any green home. In addition to lowering your heating bills, natural cotton insulation is healthier for your family. This formaldehyde-free product is made from recycled blue jeans, giving it its blue color.

Manufacturers of recycled denim cotton insulation include

- **Bonded Logic,** 411 E. Ray Rd., Chandler, AZ 85225 (phone: 480-812-9114; Web: www.bondedlogic.com)

- **Inno-Therm,** 1633 Shea Rd., Newton, NC 28658 (phone: 877-466-0612; Web: www.inno-therm.com)

Chapter 18

Ten Green Things You Can Do in Your Home Right Now

*I*f you're building a brand-new home, you could easily do all the things I discuss in this book to make your new home green. But what if you're not building a new house? What if the house you live in isn't exactly green? If your home isn't green, it's losing money. Most people think that their current homes can't be greened. But there are many simple things you can do to reduce energy use, conserve water, and save money in your current home.

Each of the items in this chapter is a weekend project you can do with the entire family.

Replace Your Old Appliances with New Energy-Efficient Ones

If your appliances were purchased before 1990, you're spending a lot more on energy than you need to, and it's time to upgrade them.

A new Energy Star refrigerator consumes 75 percent less energy than one from the 1970s, saving you more than $100 a year. Because you're getting a new one anyway, locate the refrigerator away from direct sunlight and the oven. In the winter, turn up the refrigerator temperature and save yourself even more money.

While you're shopping, keep in mind that bigger is not better — at least where refrigerators are concerned. Size your new refrigerator for what you actually *need*. A model with an upper or lower freezer uses 10 percent to 15 percent less energy than a side-by-side model.

Energy Star dishwashers are designed to use less water than hand washing. To take full advantage of this feature, only run your new Energy Star dishwasher when it's full.

An Energy Star washing machine uses half the energy of a model made before 1990, saving you about $110 a year. Also, front-loading washers use less water than top-loaders.

Some states and local utility companies offer rebates for buying new Energy Star appliances. You can save hundreds off the purchase of that new appliance! Find your local rebates at `www.energystar.gov/index.cfm?fuse action=rebate.rebate_locator`.

Buy a Water Filter instead of Bottled Water

The average American consumes about 23 gallons of bottled water every year. The plastic bottle and the energy required to ship it all take their toll on the planet. Instead of buying bottled water, save your money — and the environment — and purchase a water filter for your kitchen.

A freestanding pitcher with a built-in filter will cost you about $12 to $15; one that attaches directly to your kitchen faucet will run you about $20 to $30. If you're feeling more ambitious, a whole-house water filter will clean all the water in your home, including the water for the shower and laundry.

Install Water-Saving Devices in Your Bathroom and Kitchen

The typical four-person household uses about 260 gallons of water every day. Most of this water is used in the bathroom. You can take some steps to save an incredible amount of water. Here's a list of simple things you and your family can do today:

✔ **Be sure to turn off the faucet while you're brushing your teeth or shaving.**

✔ **Take quick showers instead of baths, and switch to a low-flow showerhead.** An efficient showerhead can cost less than $15 and cuts annual water consumption by half. You can install one in minutes, and it'll save you an estimated $10 per person every year from the water-heating savings alone.

✔ **Install an aerator on every bathroom faucet.** An aerator is a small screen that attaches to the end of a faucet. It will cost you about $2 and you can install it in one minute.

✔ **If you're handy, consider replacing your old 5-gallon-per-flush toilet with a new 1.6-gallon-per-flush toilet or a dual-flush toilet.** That can save 22,000 gallons of water per year for a family of four.

Until you replace the toilet, fill a 2-liter plastic soda bottle with water and set it inside the toilet tank. It will save that amount of water with every flush.

Install a Solar-Powered Clothes Dryer (a.k.a., a Clothesline)

Instead of running your clothes dryer every time you do a load of laundry, invest $5 in a clothesline. A clothesline is free to operate and will leave your clothes smelling fresh. Save the dryer for rainy days — and when you do use your clothes dryer, keep the lint traps clear to save energy.

While you're doing the laundry, run only full loads, using warm water instead of hot.

Insulate in Normally Forgotten Locations: Pipes, Water Heater, and Attic

Water heaters consume nearly 20 percent of all the energy used in your home. They run all day, even if you don't need any hot water. To cut that water-heating bill in half, turn down your water heater to 120°F and insulate it with a wrap blanket, available at any hardware store. Just be careful not to cover the air vents.

If your gas water heater is more than ten years old, it's inefficient and should be replaced. When shopping for a new water heater, choose one with a timer so it only heats water when your family needs it.

While you're down in the basement, add insulation wrap to the hot water pipes, especially if they run in a crawl space. It takes minutes to do, but will save you noticeably on your water-heating bill.

If your home was built before 1981, chances are you have inadequate insulation in your attic. Place insulation between both the floor joists and roof joists in the attic. Although any insulation will do, spray-in natural cellulose made from recycled newsprint is the best choice for the attic floor; formaldehyde-free or recycled cotton batt insulation is best for the roof. Be sure to install the insulation with the foil side facing the sun.

While you're up there, install a solar attic fan. For around $300, this exhaust fan operates from a small solar cell that sits hidden on your roof. When it gets too hot and stuffy in the attic, the fan kicks on automatically to vent the hot air from your attic.

Go Green with Your Yard

From mowing, to watering, to fertilizing, lawns consume an immense amount of resources and are responsible for an equally offensive amount of pollution. Lawn mowers create 5 percent of the nation's air pollution. Don't forget about the gas, toxic pesticides, and grass clippings that are also part of caring for your lawn.

Switch to an old-fashioned hand-powered mower. The exercise is good for you and it will save you money on gas.

Watering your lawn consumes 30 percent to 60 percent of all your summer water use. If you want to use the sprinkler, use it at night. The sun evaporates most of the water you spray on the lawn anyway. Better yet, install a drip irrigation system. It uses less water, and brings the water to the roots, where it's needed.

If all this information is starting to make you rethink your lawn, you aren't alone. People are giving up their lawn to plant native species turf, nicknamed *ecoturf*. Because these plants are local to your area, they can grow without needing to be cut or watered. A landscape architect can talk to you about the options in your area.

Convert Your Wood-Burning Fireplace to a Gas Fireplace

Wood-burning fireplaces have long been a sentimental vision of home. But in recent years, local building codes have banned their use, preferring the cleaner-burning gas fireplace. Convert your old, dirty wood-burning fireplace to an energy-efficient gas model. Be sure to install glass fireplace doors, they keep gases from entering the room and block heat from escaping up through an open flue.

Attach a small metal hanger in your fireplace to indicate when the flue is open. In most homes, the flue is left open, which results in a huge energy loss. So be sure to keep the flue closed when the fireplace is not in use.

If you keep your old wood-burning fireplace, instead of using petroleum-based premanufactured logs, look for eco-friendly versions, like the Java-Log made from recycled, dried coffee grounds. (For information on the Java-Log and to find stores in your area that carry them, check out www.java-log.com.)

Weatherize Your Windows and Doors

Windows provide views, sunlight, ventilation, and solar heating, but they also let 10 percent to 25 percent of your heating leak outside. Because the glass in the window doesn't hold in temperatures as well as your walls, consider caulking and sealing around them to fill any air leaks.

If you live in a warm climate, install tinted window films on south- and west-facing windows that get the most heat gain. For better performance, consider installing an awning or overhang on really hot windows.

Planting a tree in front of the window provides shade and makes your home more attractive.

If you live in a colder climate, install plastic sheeting to cover the window and keep out any drafts. For even better performance, have storm windows installed. It costs more, but you'll be much more comfortable in the winter.

Make Your Heating and Cooling Work Better

If you added up all the cracks in a typical house, it would be equivalent in size to leaving an entire window wide open all winter long. The good news: You can fill these cracks with caulk, sealants, and weather-stripping. This job is one of the easiest and quickest things you can do to improve the energy use in your home.

One-third of the heat in your home is leaking out of your ducts. Seal the joints in your ductwork with low-toxic mastic compound. Avoid using duct tape — ironically, duct tape is not good for ducts.

 Also, be sure to clean the air-conditioner filter regularly.

If you shade the air-conditioner, it won't have to work as hard.

Use ceiling fans instead of air-conditioners when possible. Look for a ceiling fan with two settings: winter and summer (to pull air up or push it down).

Clean or replace furnace filters each month of use. This simple measure will easily save you 5 percent to 10 percent on heating and remove allergens from your home.

The thermostat is another large hole in your wall that allows air to leak out. Put a foam gasket behind your thermostat so it reads the actual room temperature instead of the colder temperature inside the wall.

A programmable thermostat is inexpensive and ensures that the heater or air-conditioner runs only during specific times. For example, instead of running the heater all night, a programmable thermostat can turn on the heat a couple of hours before you get up, which can save you 30 percent off your heating bills.

Switch to Compact Fluorescent Light Bulbs and Install Occupancy Sensors

Switch your incandescent bulbs to compact fluorescent (CFL) bulbs. CFL bulbs use a fraction of the energy of their incandescent counterparts, produce 70 percent less heat, and last ten times longer than traditional bulbs. All this saves you $30 or more over the life of *each* bulb.

Prices of CFL bulbs have dropped. They now cost nearly the same as their less-efficient incandescent bulbs. Where a CFL will cost you $10 in electricity during its lifetime, an incandescent will use up $40 in the same time period. If every American home replaced just one light bulb with a CFL bulb, the Untied States would save enough energy to light more than 2.5 million homes for a year.

Kids have a habit of leaving lights on. Teach them not to. Better yet, install occupancy sensor switches to automatically shut off the lights when people leave the room. They're ideal for mud rooms, powder rooms, playrooms, garages, basements, and anywhere else your kids — or you! — may forget to turn off the lights.

Dimmer switches can save energy and extend bulb life. The energy saved is not quite proportional to the amount you dim. A light dimmed down to one quarter of its input still uses half the energy.

Appendix

Resources

· ·

*B*uilding or remodeling your green home requires countless decisions for everything from tile to flooring to faucets. In order to help make this design process easier for you, I've assembled places to find green materials and the various green certifications you can trust, all in this handy appendix. I also provide sources of rebates and incentives for your green home.

Locating Green Materials

When it comes to green materials, the primary complaint people make is that they can't find them. Given the popularity of green building, finding green materials has never been easier — and in the future, it'll be even more so. Here are several places to start your research:

✔ **BuildingGreen.com:** The publishers of the *Environmental Building News* and *GreenSpec* have put all their unbiased and perfectly presented information together in a wonderfully straightforward site. Pay a reasonable fee (one-week subscriptions start at $12.95) and you get access to their wealth of research reports and product findings. Organized by construction and homeowner categories, BuildingGreen.com has emerged as the *Consumer Reports* of green building.

✔ **GreenHomeGuide.com:** Although targeted at homeowners, GreenHome Guide.com provides reviews and descriptions of green products by the real professionals using them. Their know-how sections provide all the information you need for greening a kitchen or a bathroom.

✔ **Sales reps:** When visiting product showrooms and talking to the salesperson, be sure to communicate your desire for green products. Start the conversation and you'll be surprised by the suggestions they provide. Today, many traditional manufacturers are offering greener versions of their products.

✓ **American Institute of Architects (AIA):** For years, the AIA's Committee on the Environment (COTE) has been a place where architects could discuss how to green their buildings. Today the AIA provides resources and case studies for homeowners to use to green their homes. Contact your local chapter of the AIA (you can find it in the phone book or at `www.aia.org`) and ask about their green resources. Through your local AIA chapter, you'll also be able to find a local architect familiar with green building.

✓ **United States Green Building Council (USGBC):** The USGBC is a valuable source for data on green building, great for making the argument to skeptical developers and city officials. One of the reasons for the creation of the USGBC was to provide a credible authority on green building, so use them as such. You can point to their combined experience and knowledge to find hundreds of reports and case studies. Visit the USGBC online at `www.usgbc.org`.

✓ **Local showrooms:** Each month, new showrooms open up around the United States offering green materials. Although these showrooms initially opened around the green-building hubs (San Francisco, California; Austin, Texas; Portland, Oregon), new stores are open in Santa Monica, California; Chicago, Illinois; and even Fairfield, Iowa. Your architect or contractor will be able to help you find a local showroom, but the green product manufacturers you find online can also point you to local distributors.

✓ **City offices:** Dozens of cities have a Department of the Environment or an equivalent office, concerning themselves with green building, environmental justice, and toxics disposal. If you can't locate one in your city, look at the county and state level. Your local recycling collection company can also point you to a waste management authority or commission. Such departments are invaluable resources and will be able to provide you with information you never knew existed. Chances are, they'll also have a directory of local green resources and showrooms.

Finding Rebates and Incentives

Numerous financial opportunities and incentives exist for greening your buildings. These incentives tend to center around energy (efficiency or production), but sources exist for educational programs, community building, and renovating your home.

Most of these programs exist at the local level, so contact your local public utility commission, building department, and energy sources. In the meantime, Table A-1 lists general national sources for various building types and uses to get you started.

Table A-1		Rebates and Incentives for Green Building and Remodeling			
Source	**Name of Program**	**Eligibility**	**Use of Funds**	**Amount**	**Resource**
Home Depot	The Home Depot Foundation	Nonprofit organizations	Environmental grants encourage green building and sustainable design in affordable housing.	Grants typically range from $5,000 to $25,000.	www.homedepot foundation. org
Federal	Solar and Geothermal Business Energy Tax Credit	Commercial/ industrial sectors	Solar water heat, active solar space heat, solar thermal process heat, photovoltaics, geothermal electric	$25,000 per year plus 25 percent of the total remaining after the credit is taken.	www.mdvseia. org/federal_ incentives. htm

(continued)

Table A-1 (continued)

Source	Name of Program	Eligibility	Use of Funds	Amount	Resource
U.S. Department of Energy (DOE)	Renewable Energy Research And Development Grants	For-profit organizations, private nonprofit institutions, intrastate, interstate, and local agencies and universities	Research and development of solar buildings, solar electricity, solar thermal, biomass, alcohol fuels, wind, hydropower, hydrogen, and geothermal technologies.	$10,000 to 100,000	www.cfda.gov/ static/ 81087.htm
U.S. Department of Energy (DOE)	Small Business Innovation Research (SBIR) and Small Business Technology Transfer (STTR) Programs	Small businesses	STTR grants must involve a substantial cooperative research collaboration between a small business and a nonprofit research institution. Energy efficiency and renewable energy; zero net energy buildings; low-cost power electronics and sensors for distributed energy resources; bioproducts and bioenergy research; heat transfer research; recovery; recycle and reuse of energy intensive materials; reactive separations.	SBIR Ph I: Up to $100,000 SBIR Ph II: Up to $750,000 STTR Ph I: Up to $100,000 STTR Ph II: Up to $500,000	http://sbir. er.doe.gov/ sbir

Source	Name of Program	Eligibility	Use of Funds	Amount	Resource
Kresge Foundation	Green Building Initiative	Nonprofit organizations	Grants to fund the planning/design of green buildings; educational materials and green building workshops also available to nonprofits.	Varies	www.kresge. org/initia tives/

Source	Name of Program	Eligibility	Use of Funds	Amount	Resource
Enterprise Foundation	Green Communities	Anyone	Grants to fund community building projects	Varies	www.enter prisefounda tion.org/ resources/ green/index. asp

Identifying Green Product Certifications

Several green certification systems have developed over the years, but only a handful have become accepted and recognized. Although some of the following certifications apply to only one product, you can consider this a comprehensive list of the various certifications available:

- ✔ **Carpet and Rug Institute's Green Label Plus:** Green Label Plus is an independent testing program that identifies carpets with very low emissions of volatile organic compounds (VOCs). *For more information:* www.carpet-rug.org.

- ✔ **Cradle to Cradle Certification (C2C):** Cradle to Cradle Certification is a rigorous evaluation of the sustainability and health of specific building products. The seal certifies the use of environmentally safe materials; design for reuse; the use of renewable energy; and reduction of pollution caused by the manufacturing process. *For more information:* www.mbdc.com.

- ✔ **Energy Star:** Energy Star energy efficiency guidelines are set by the U.S. Environmental Protection Agency (EPA) and the U.S. Department of Energy (DOE). Energy Star guidelines exist for many residential building products, including appliances, heating and cooling systems, lighting, roof products, and windows and doors. *For more information:* www.energystar.gov.

- ✔ **Forest Stewardship Council (FSC):** The FSC is an independent, not-for-profit, nongovernment organization. It sets standards that reflect agreed-upon principles for responsible forest management, and accredits organizations that certify the achievement of those standards by specific forests or woodlands. *For more information:* www.fsc.org.

- ✔ **GREENGUARD:** The GREENGUARD Certification Program is an independent, third-party testing program for low-emitting products and materials. GREENGUARD has developed standards for adhesives, appliances, ceiling, flooring, insulation, paint, and wall-covering products. *For more information:* www.greenguard.org.

- ✔ **Green Seal:** Green Seal is an independent, nonprofit organization that sets standards for environmentally preferable products, conducts product evaluations, and certifies products meeting those standards. Green Seal meets the environmental standards for ecolabeling set by the International Organization for Standardization (ISO). Green Seal's environmental standards for paints, household cleaners, and window products date to the mid-1990s, but they're still useful baselines. *For more information:* www.greenseal.org.

- ✔ **Organic Trade Association (OTA):** The OTA has developed standards for the processing of organic fibers. Its organic fiber processing standards, approved in January 2004, address all stages of textile processing, from post-harvest handling to wet processing (including bleaching, dyeing, and printing), fabrication, product assembly, storage and transportation, pest management, and labeling of finished products. They also include an extensive list of materials permitted for, or prohibited from, use in organic fiber processing under the standards. *For more information:* www.ota.com.

✔ **Scientific Certification Systems (SCS) Environmentally Preferable Product (EPP):** SCS has developed a certification program for Environmentally Preferable Products and Services such as adhesives and sealants, cabinetry and casework, carpet, doors, flooring, paints, and wall coverings. This program complies with internationally recognized ISO standards, the U.S. EPA guidelines for environmentally preferable products, and U.S. Federal Trade Commission (FTC) guidelines for responsible environmental labeling. *For more information:* www.scs certified.com/manufacturing/manufacture_epp.html.

✔ **Unified Sustainable Textile Standard:** Unified Sustainable Textile Standard is an emerging standard. The purpose of the standard is to provide a market-based definition for a *sustainable textile,* establish performance requirements for public health and environment, and address the triple bottom line (economic-environmental-social) throughout the supply chain. The standard is inclusive, is based on lifecycle assessment (LCA) principles, and provides benchmarks for continuous improvement and innovation. *For more information:* www.sustainableproducts.com.

✔ **U.S. Green Building Council:** The LEED green building rating system certifies the greenness of entire buildings, not individual materials. Four levels of certification exist: Certified, Silver, Gold, and Platinum. *For more information:* www.usgbc.org.

The certification process varies based on the organization, but essentially all require:

1. **Authorization:** The applicant provides information to help the organization determine whether certification is even possible. Fees are involved to pay for this process.

2. **Data review:** The applicant submits a detailed and confidential disclosure form of the materials and processes involved.

3. **Claim verification:** An independent verifying engineer conducts an audit, including an inspection of facilities and suppliers as necessary.

4. **Certification:** If all the product claims are substantiated, the organization issues the certification.

5. **Monitoring:** The certified company submits updated data on a regular basis to the organization to ensure that the certification remains valid.

Index

Notes

BUSINESS, CAREERS & PERSONAL FINANCE

0-7645-9847-3

0-7645-2431-3

Also available:
- Business Plans Kit For Dummies
  0-7645-9794-9
- Economics For Dummies
  0-7645-5726-2
- Grant Writing For Dummies
  0-7645-8416-2
- Home Buying For Dummies
  0-7645-5331-3
- Managing For Dummies
  0-7645-1771-6
- Marketing For Dummies
  0-7645-5600-2

- Personal Finance For Dummies
  0-7645-2590-5*
- Resumes For Dummies
  0-7645-5471-9
- Selling For Dummies
  0-7645-5363-1
- Six Sigma For Dummies
  0-7645-6798-5
- Small Business Kit For Dummies
  0-7645-5984-2
- Starting an eBay Business For Dummies
  0-7645-6924-4
- Your Dream Career For Dummies
  0-7645-9795-7

HOME & BUSINESS COMPUTER BASICS

0-470-05432-8

0-471-75421-8

Also available:
- Cleaning Windows Vista For Dummies
  0-471-78293-9
- Excel 2007 For Dummies
  0-470-03737-7
- Mac OS X Tiger For Dummies
  0-7645-7675-5
- MacBook For Dummies
  0-470-04859-X
- Macs For Dummies
  0-470-04849-2
- Office 2007 For Dummies
  0-470-00923-3

- Outlook 2007 For Dummies
  0-470-03830-6
- PCs For Dummies
  0-7645-8958-X
- Salesforce.com For Dummies
  0-470-04893-X
- Upgrading & Fixing Laptops For Dummies
  0-7645-8959-8
- Word 2007 For Dummies
  0-470-03658-3
- Quicken 2007 For Dummies
  0-470-04600-7

FOOD, HOME, GARDEN, HOBBIES, MUSIC & PETS

0-7645-8404-9

0-7645-9904-6

Also available:
- Candy Making For Dummies
  0-7645-9734-5
- Card Games For Dummies
  0-7645-9910-0
- Crocheting For Dummies
  0-7645-4151-X
- Dog Training For Dummies
  0-7645-8418-9
- Healthy Carb Cookbook For Dummies
  0-7645-8476-6
- Home Maintenance For Dummies
  0-7645-5215-5

- Horses For Dummies
  0-7645-9797-3
- Jewelry Making & Beading For Dummies
  0-7645-2571-9
- Orchids For Dummies
  0-7645-6759-4
- Puppies For Dummies
  0-7645-5255-4
- Rock Guitar For Dummies
  0-7645-5356-9
- Sewing For Dummies
  0-7645-6847-7
- Singing For Dummies
  0-7645-2475-5

INTERNET & DIGITAL MEDIA

0-470-04529-9

0-470-04894-8

Also available:
- Blogging For Dummies
  0-471-77084-1
- Digital Photography For Dummies
  0-7645-9802-3
- Digital Photography All-in-One Desk Reference For Dummies
  0-470-03743-1
- Digital SLR Cameras and Photography For Dummies
  0-7645-9803-1
- eBay Business All-in-One Desk Reference For Dummies
  0-7645-8438-3
- HDTV For Dummies
  0-470-09673-X

- Home Entertainment PCs For Dummies
  0-470-05523-5
- MySpace For Dummies
  0-470-09529-6
- Search Engine Optimization For Dummies
  0-471-97998-8
- Skype For Dummies
  0-470-04891-3
- The Internet For Dummies
  0-7645-8996-2
- Wiring Your Digital Home For Dummies
  0-471-91830-X

* Separate Canadian edition also available
† Separate U.K. edition also available

Available wherever books are sold. For more information or to order direct: U.S. customers visit www.dummies.com or call 1-877-762-2974.
U.K. customers visit www.wileyeurope.com or call 0800 243407. Canadian customers visit www.wiley.ca or call 1-800-567-4797.

WILEY

SPORTS, FITNESS, PARENTING, RELIGION & SPIRITUALITY

0-471-76871-5   0-7645-7841-3

Also available:
- Catholicism For Dummies
  0-7645-5391-7
- Exercise Balls For Dummies
  0-7645-5623-1
- Fitness For Dummies
  0-7645-7851-0
- Football For Dummies
  0-7645-3936-1
- Judaism For Dummies
  0-7645-5299-6
- Potty Training For Dummies
  0-7645-5417-4
- Buddhism For Dummies
  0-7645-5359-3

- Pregnancy For Dummies
  0-7645-4483-7 †
- Ten Minute Tone-Ups For Dummies
  0-7645-7207-5
- NASCAR For Dummies
  0-7645-7681-X
- Religion For Dummies
  0-7645-5264-3
- Soccer For Dummies
  0-7645-5229-5
- Women in the Bible For Dummies
  0-7645-8475-8

TRAVEL

0-7645-7749-2   0-7645-6945-7

Also available:
- Alaska For Dummies
  0-7645-7746-8
- Cruise Vacations For Dummies
  0-7645-6941-4
- England For Dummies
  0-7645-4276-1
- Europe For Dummies
  0-7645-7529-5
- Germany For Dummies
  0-7645-7823-5
- Hawaii For Dummies
  0-7645-7402-7

- Italy For Dummies
  0-7645-7386-1
- Las Vegas For Dummies
  0-7645-7382-9
- London For Dummies
  0-7645-4277-X
- Paris For Dummies
  0-7645-7630-5
- RV Vacations For Dummies
  0-7645-4442-X
- Walt Disney World & Orlando
  For Dummies
  0-7645-9660-8

GRAPHICS, DESIGN & WEB DEVELOPMENT

0-7645-8815-X   0-7645-9571-7

Also available:
- 3D Game Animation For Dummies
  0-7645-8789-7
- AutoCAD 2006 For Dummies
  0-7645-8925-3
- Building a Web Site For Dummies
  0-7645-7144-3
- Creating Web Pages For Dummies
  0-470-08030-2
- Creating Web Pages All-in-One Desk
  Reference For Dummies
  0-7645-4345-8
- Dreamweaver 8 For Dummies
  0-7645-9649-7

- InDesign CS2 For Dummies
  0-7645-9572-5
- Macromedia Flash 8 For Dummies
  0-7645-9691-8
- Photoshop CS2 and Digital
  Photography For Dummies
  0-7645-9580-6
- Photoshop Elements 4 For Dummies
  0-471-77483-9
- Syndicating Web Sites with RSS Feeds
  For Dummies
  0-7645-8848-6
- Yahoo! SiteBuilder For Dummies
  0-7645-9800-7

NETWORKING, SECURITY, PROGRAMMING & DATABASES

0-7645-7728-X   0-471-74940-0

Also available:
- Access 2007 For Dummies
  0-470-04612-0
- ASP.NET 2 For Dummies
  0-7645-7907-X
- C# 2005 For Dummies
  0-7645-9704-3
- Hacking For Dummies
  0-470-05235-X
- Hacking Wireless Networks
  For Dummies
  0-7645-9730-2
- Java For Dummies
  0-470-08716-1

- Microsoft SQL Server 2005 For Dummies
  0-7645-7755-7
- Networking All-in-One Desk Reference
  For Dummies
  0-7645-9939-9
- Preventing Identity Theft For Dummies
  0-7645-7336-5
- Telecom For Dummies
  0-471-77085-X
- Visual Studio 2005 All-in-One Desk
  Reference For Dummies
  0-7645-9775-2
- XML For Dummies
  0-7645-8845-1

HEALTH & SELF-HELP

0-7645-8450-2

0-7645-4149-8

Also available:

- Bipolar Disorder For Dummies
  0-7645-8451-0
- Chemotherapy and Radiation For Dummies
  0-7645-7832-4
- Controlling Cholesterol For Dummies
  0-7645-5440-9
- Diabetes For Dummies
  0-7645-6820-5* †
- Divorce For Dummies
  0-7645-8417-0 †

- Fibromyalgia For Dummies
  0-7645-5441-7
- Low-Calorie Dieting For Dummies
  0-7645-9905-4
- Meditation For Dummies
  0-471-77774-9
- Osteoporosis For Dummies
  0-7645-7621-6
- Overcoming Anxiety For Dummies
  0-7645-5447-6
- Reiki For Dummies
  0-7645-9907-0
- Stress Management For Dummies
  0-7645-5144-2

EDUCATION, HISTORY, REFERENCE & TEST PREPARATION

0-7645-8381-6

0-7645-9554-7

Also available:

- The ACT For Dummies
  0-7645-9652-7
- Algebra For Dummies
  0-7645-5325-9
- Algebra Workbook For Dummies
  0-7645-8467-7
- Astronomy For Dummies
  0-7645-8465-0
- Calculus For Dummies
  0-7645-2498-4
- Chemistry For Dummies
  0-7645-5430-1
- Forensics For Dummies
  0-7645-5580-4

- Freemasons For Dummies
  0-7645-9796-5
- French For Dummies
  0-7645-5193-0
- Geometry For Dummies
  0-7645-5324-0
- Organic Chemistry I For Dummies
  0-7645-6902-3
- The SAT I For Dummies
  0-7645-7193-1
- Spanish For Dummies
  0-7645-5194-9
- Statistics For Dummies
  0-7645-5423-9

Get smart @ dummies.com®

- **Find a full list of Dummies titles**
- **Look into loads of FREE on-site articles**
- **Sign up for FREE eTips e-mailed to you weekly**
- **See what other products carry the Dummies name**
- **Shop directly from the Dummies bookstore**
- **Enter to win new prizes every month!**

---

* Separate Canadian edition also available
† Separate U.K. edition also available

Available wherever books are sold. For more information or to order direct: U.S. customers visit www.dummies.com or call 1-877-762-2974.
U.K. customers visit www.wileyeurope.com or call 0800 243407. Canadian customers visit www.wiley.ca or call 1-800-567-4797.